Moral Epistemology Naturalized

Moral Epistemology Naturalized

edited by
Richmond Campbell
and Bruce Hunter

© 2000 Canadian Journal of Philosophy

University of Calgary Press
Calgary, Alberta, Canada

ISSN 0229-7051   ISBN 0-919491-26-X

University of Calgary Press
2500 University Drive NW
Calgary, Alberta
Canada T2N 1N4

National Library of Canada Cataloguing in Publication Data

Main entry under title:
Moral epistemology naturalized

(Canadian journal of philosophy.
Supplementary volume, ISSN 0229-7051 ; 26)
Includes bibliographical references and index.
ISBN 0-919491-26-X

1. Knowledge, Theory of. I. Campbell Richmond.
II. Hunter, Bruce, 1949- III. Series.

BD161.M77 2001   121   C00-911646-X

Printed and bound in Canada by AGMV Marquis.
Cover design: Doyle Buehler, Aces High Graphics.

∞ This book is printed on acid-free paper.

In memory of
Willard Van Orman Quine
1908-2000

Table of Contents

CANADIAN JOURNAL OF PHILOSOPHY
Supplementary Volume 26

Introduction

RICHMOND CAMPBELL AND BRUCE HUNTER

1. What is Naturalized Moral Epistemology?

A traditional task of epistemology is to establish and defend systematic standards, norms, or criteria that must be satisfied in order for us to have knowledge or simply to have beliefs that are justified or warranted. A naturalized epistemology tries to arrive at such standards through an empirical investigation into how we interact with our fellows and the world around us as we form our beliefs and evaluate them, what we seek in these activities, and the particular ways in which we can and can't succeed.[1] A naturalized *moral* epistemology is simply a naturalized epistemology that concerns itself with moral knowledge.

Since Quine introduced the concept of naturalized epistemology over three decades ago,[2] much has been written on this topic and identified as exemplifying this approach. Surprisingly, very little has been written specifically on naturalizing moral epistemology. Witness the bibliography in Hilary Kornblith's well-known anthology, which lists 856 articles and books on naturalized epistemology but nothing on a

---

1 Alvin Goldman, "Epistemic Folkways and Scientific Epistemology," in *Naturalizing Epistemology,* 2d ed., ed. Hilary Kornblith (Cambridge: MIT Press, 1994), 293; reprinted from Alvin Goldman, *Liaisons* (Cambridge: Bradford, 1992).

2 W. V. Quine, "Epistemology Naturalized," in Kornblith, *Naturalizing Epistemology* 2d ed.; reprinted from W.V. Quine, *Ontological Relativity and Other Essays* (New York: Columbia University Press, 1969).

naturalized approach to moral knowledge.[3] The paucity of literature that explicitly identifies itself in the latter category is puzzling, especially given the increasing interest in and discussion of moral naturalism. We think that a philosophical work that addresses directly the prospect of naturalizing moral epistemology is long overdue.

The present topic needs to be carefully distinguished from its more familiar cousin, naturalism in ethics. To naturalize morals is to appeal to an understanding of the natural world in order to explain the most important features of the institution of morality and the practice of moral judgment and evaluation. To naturalize moral epistemology is different and more specific. It is to explain how moral knowledge is possible (or why it is not) by appealing to an empirically based understanding of the natural world and our place within it. For example, one can hold that no epistemology of any kind should be naturalized yet be a moral naturalist who regards morality as a natural phenomenon that is best studied empirically. A moral naturalist might even consider moral properties to be nothing more than empirical properties of the natural world but still reject the project of naturalizing epistemology.

Hedonistic utilitarianism is perhaps the most familiar example that illustrates this last point. Just as one might think that the standards of empirical knowledge, e.g., the canons of inductive logic or statistical inference, must be established non-empirically, one *might* think that the standards of the empirically discoverable moral worth of an action, e.g., the principle of utility itself, must be established non-empirically. From this standpoint, the degree of pleasure or pain that an action causes, compared to alternative actions, would constitute its relative moral worth – an empirical matter – but knowledge that the standard of utility is a valid moral principle would be non-empirical. On the other hand, accepting the project of naturalizing epistemology does not mean that one must hold that moral knowledge is possible, much less that moral properties like rightness and wrongness can be identified with empirically discoverable properties of the natural world. Quine, for example, initiated the project of naturalizing epistemology

---

3 Kornblith, ed., *Naturalizing Epistemology*, 427-73.

but believes that it shows the opposite.[4] Naturalized moral epistemology, broadly conceived, is a naturalistic approach to learning about moral knowledge, including perhaps that it is not possible.

The distinction just drawn between moral naturalism and naturalized moral epistemology may help to explain why the latter seems to be so little in evidence, despite the enormous interest in naturalizing epistemology generally. Two main cases need to be considered. First, there are those philosophers who are strongly drawn to naturalism in philosophy, including epistemology, but who also believe that a scientific perspective on morals leads directly to denying possibility of moral knowledge. J. L. Mackie had this perspective on morals, arguing that intrinsically prescriptive moral properties would be "ontological queer" entities.[5] Michael Ruse is another example. Though he embraces an evolutionary approach to understanding morals and human cognition, he argues that no objective justification of moral beliefs exists and thus no moral knowledge exists of the kind traditionally thought to be possible.[6] Even Quine, as we noted, denies the existence of moral knowledge while urging a scientific perspective on morals and epistemology. Don't all such examples exemplify moral epistemology naturalized? Yes, but only in the very broad sense explained above. These philosophers aren't likely to identify themselves as engaged in a naturalized form of moral epistemology, since naturalized epistemology has come to be associated with a methodological strategy. This strategy, ironically Quine's own, is to assume tentatively that apparent scientific knowledge can be explained within science until it proves otherwise. If one applied a parallel strategy in the case of moral knowledge, one would tentatively assume this apparent knowledge too could be explained within science, allowing in the end that it might prove otherwise. Of course, the philosophers in question are not ready to make the latter assumption, since it appears evident to them from the start that moral knowledge is incompatible with the world that is already

---

4 W. V. Quine, "On the Nature of Moral Values," in *Theories and Things* (Cambridge: Harvard University Press, 1981). See sec. 3 below.

5 J. L. Mackie, *Inventing Right and Wrong* (New York: Penguin, 1977).

6 Michael Ruse, *Taking Darwin Seriously* (Oxford: Blackwell, 1986).

revealed by science. It is understandable, then, that the label "natural-ized moral epistemologist" isn't very often applied to them, since it suggests a methodological assumption about moral knowledge that they explicitly reject.

The second main case to be considered consists of those philoso-phers who think of morals as a natural phenomenon to be understood empirically but who also believe that moral knowledge does exist. Aren't they good candidates for the label? Not necessarily. As noted earlier, it is possible to see moral knowledge as empirical knowledge (as the hedonistic utilitarian does) but to hold in addition that the under-lying moral principle or principles that explain moral knowledge can be established only non-empirically. After all, how could one possibly establish a general moral principle except by reference to examples that exemplify the principle? Yet, as Kant argued, to identify any such example as having moral relevance, one must first, it seems, appeal at least implicitly to a moral principle and thus to reason in a circle.[7] One might, on the other hand, be a particularist about moral knowledge, holding that moral properties are perceived directly without recourse to general principles.[8] Those who take this position tend not, however, to endorse a thoroughgoing moral naturalism in which the mechanism underlying the perception can be explained within science. One reason for resistance here is that such a reduction of the moral to the natural would either be open to the Humean objection that it robs moral perception of its normative dimension or else be open to Mackie's objection that it builds a peculiar perscriptiveness into the natural world.

The two main cases have in common the perception that naturalized epistemology may not be compatible with the existence of moral knowl-edge. Those who endorse a naturalized approach to non-moral episte-mology tend not to think that this approach can be extended to moral epistemology in the sense of an epistemology that explains moral knowledge. Those who believe that moral knowledge is possible tend

---

7 Immanuel Kant, "Groundwork of the Metaphysics of Morals," Preface, in *Practical Philosophy*, ed. by Mary Gregor (Cambridge: Cambridge University Press, 1996), 63.

8 David McNaughton, *Moral Vision* (New York: Blackwell, 1988).

not to think that it can be explained within a naturalized moral epistemology, even if they regard moral knowledge as a kind of empirical knowledge. In short, the idea of a naturalized moral epistemology that explains the existence of moral knowledge appears to many if not most philosophers as far more difficult to accept than either a moral naturalism without a naturalized epistemology or a naturalized epistemology of non-moral knowledge alone. Whether this idea is acceptable when properly interpreted is a central issue addressed in the articles to follow.

2. Are the Standard Objections to Naturalized Epistemology Intensified?

Another important reason why the idea of a naturalized moral epistemology meets with resistance is that the standard objections that have been raised against a naturalized epistemology of non-moral knowledge appear to intensify when this naturalized approach is extended to moral epistemology. Perhaps the most familiar objection is that the subject of epistemology cannot be naturalized, since doing so would mean that it is no longer normative and thus remove a defining feature of epistemology. As remarked at the outset, we expect epistemology to establish and defend standards for determining when we have knowledge or when our beliefs are justified. This task is essential to our understanding of what epistemology is. If in naturalizing epistemology we thereby reduce it to the task of describing how we form our beliefs, how we reason, what claims to knowledge we make, we miss entirely the point of epistemology, namely, to evaluate our beliefs, methods of reasoning, and claims to knowledge. We would in effect not be doing epistemology, as the term has been traditionally understood. The proposal to naturalized it is therefore best interpreted as the suggestion to stop doing epistemology and to do something else that, however worthy, is fundamentally different.[9]

One strategy for meeting this objection is to argue that the naturalizing process need not undermine the normative status of

---

9   Jaegwon Kim, "What Is 'Naturalized Epistemology'?" in Kornblith, *Naturalizing Epistemology*, 2d ed. See also Kornblith's introduction.

epistemology. The mistake in thinking that it would, it could be argued, is based on the false supposition that an empirical investigation of how we come to have knowledge would be merely descriptive. On the contrary, a study of the social enterprise of knowledge acquisition may raise normative questions about our goals and means for pursuing them that would not arise except in the context of such an empirical investigation. Moreover, the empirical study would itself presuppose normative assumptions about the direction that the study should take in the first instance, and these assumptions can be the subject of intense deliberation and reflection. In short, it may be replied that the normative and the descriptive are inseparable facets of any empirical investigation and that self-conscious reflection about how and what we ought to think would not disappear in naturalized epistemology.

But we can press the same kind of objection at the moral level and then this mode of reply may seem less inviting. Perhaps we are prepared to admit that science, at least when practised well, has a legitimate normative dimension reflected in its deliberations about evidence and methodology. Perhaps we would also say that this dimension could be enhanced if science were to reflect on how knowledge is acquired from the standpoint of its own evolving knowledge of human and other cognition. Do we also want to say, though, that the normative dimension of morality enters into the naturalizing project in the same way? Notice an important asymmetry here. In the case of non-moral knowledge, both the reasoning involved in the acquisition of knowledge and reasoning used to study that reasoning are non-moral. When studying the reasoning needed for moral knowledge, however, the reasoning employed to investigate this knowledge empirically would be non-moral as well, unless (as seems unlikely) we are prepared to think of science itself as drawing on moral knowledge in its empirical inquiries. It would appear, then, that in naturalizing *moral* epistemology we would be using a purely non-moral means to achieve insight into standards appropriate for determining what should count as moral knowledge. If this is so, might we not worry that we are losing a normative dimension that is critical for moral epistemology, namely, the moral standards that we should use to explain when our moral claims reflect moral knowledge?

Another standard objection, probably as well known as the first, is that the new form of epistemology appears to reject a central problem in traditional epistemology: to explain how any knowledge is possible at all.[10] This problem is usually put as the problem of answering the Cartesian skeptic. So understood, the problem demands an answer that does not presuppose that we already know something. But, as we have seen, naturalizing epistemology is practised with the methodological assumption that we do know a great deal already and that we have reason to doubt this only if we eventually prove unable to explain how we know what we think we know. In the context of the traditional problem, this strategy can only seem question begging in the extreme. It will seem tantamount to rejecting outright the central problem of modern epistemology since Descartes.

Two main kinds of reply have been prominent. One is to concede the judgment that the old problem has been rejected but at the same time to defend its rejection. The rejection is defended on the ground that the old problem presupposed falsely that one could vindicate scientific and other empirical knowledge from a prior standpoint that presupposes no empirical knowledge and is knowable *a priori*. Quine gives systematic reasons for thinking this style of epistemology is not viable, and for this reason many have concluded that the old problem can be safely abandoned. Another reply does not reject the problem of global skepticism but rejects the charge of vicious circularity. While Quine rejected the possibility of answering the skeptic by appeal to *a priori* knowledge, he allowed that the skeptic might be vindicated if the naturalizing approach should be unable to explain how knowledge is possible from within science.[11] Thus, the problem of skepticism is not dismissed as uninteresting, but the means of dealing with it is entirely new and consistent with Quine's reasons for rejecting traditional epistemological answers.

If we find either of these strategies of reply appealing, we might be tempted to take the same line with the moral skeptic. We find, however,

---

10 Barry Stroud, "The Significance of Naturalized Epistemology," *Midwest Studies in Philosophy*, vol. 6, *The Foundations of Analytic Philosophy*, ed. P.A. French, T.E. Uehling and H.K. Wettstein (Minneapolis: University of Minnesota Press, 1981).

11 W. V. Quine, "Things and Their Place in Theories," in *Theories and Things*, 22.

that we are again facing an important difference in the moral case. We are convinced that we already know many things and are more convinced of this than of the soundness of any skeptical argument to the contrary. We are, therefore, apt not to be unhappy sticking with our conviction for the foreseeable future and in the interim trying to explain how we know these things. No sane person, we may remind ourselves, has ever been a global skeptic. The situation is entirely otherwise with moral skepticism. As is reflected in the articles to follow, serious doubts about the possibility of moral knowledge are not uncommon, and the arguments giving rise to these doubts are not insignificant. So to follow the same strategy in the moral case and assume that we already know many moral facts may indeed seem illegitimately question begging. Moreover, to take seriously the skeptic's question does even appear to presuppose that there is an external standpoint from which to evaluate all knowledge claims. Since the skepticism here is limited, the same form of response to the skeptical problem may not seem appropriate.

Consider another familiar objection. How will the naturalized epistemologist go about explaining and thereby justifying norms of reasoning without recourse to principles that are justified *a priori*? Apropos of Hume's problem of explaining why good inductive reasoning is so often reliable, Quine has famously noted "the pathetic but praiseworthy tendency of creatures inveterately wrong in their inductions to die out before reproducing their kind."[12] In his appeal to Darwin (as well as other empirical assumptions, e.g., that inductions are gene-linked), Quine obviously opens himself to the charge of circularity just discussed. But another problem comes quickly on its heels. We may expect that a strong correlation exists between creatures who tend to make reliable inductions, say about whether there is a predator lurking nearby, and creatures who survive to reproduce. Unfortunately, finding out the truth through inductions and being fit in the biological sense are two different things. What Quine's explanation shows, allowing for the moment that natural selection explains why we reason

---

12 W. V. Quine, "Natural Kinds," In *Naturalizing Epistemology*, 65-6, reprinted from *Ontological Relativity and Other Essays.*

as we do, is at best that good inductive reasoning enhances fitness. It does not show that such reasoning continues to be a reliable guide to discovering the truth in circumstances where discovery of the truth is no longer correlated with enhanced fitness. Thus, inferences to the existence of God may be fitness enhancing because they lower blood pressure whether or not God exists. But discovery of the truth is precisely the purpose of induction and why epistemology cares about good inductions. The Darwinian explanation of induction, however interesting in its own right, appears totally irrelevant to the question of justification posed by Hume, quite apart from its circular nature. Only if one conflates truth with fitness might one think otherwise.[13]

Several mutually supporting replies to this objection are possible. We can point out, first of all, that if natural selection explains why X has a function Y (so that X does Y today because past X's that did Y were more biologically fit than X's that didn't), it doesn't follow that the function Y is to increase X's fitness.[14] Let us assume that natural selection explains why hearts have the function of circulating blood. It follows that circulating blood gave past hearts a selective advantage, not that the function of hearts is to increase fitness. Similarly, Quine's Darwinian story (assuming again that it is true) invites the conclusion that the function of our native inferential tendencies is to reliably shape our expectations regarding our immediate environment. We are not forced to the conclusion that their function is to increase fitness. Second, the Darwinian explanation does not imply that such native inferential tendencies do not have a conservative bias or cannot be fooled, especially if the circumstances are different from those in which the tendencies evolved. But a deeper empirical understanding of how the tendencies function is apt to provide an analysis of their limitations (in non-standard environments) and advantages (when operating in real

---

13 For a version of this objection, see Stephen Stich, "Evolution and Rationality," in *The Fragmentation of Reason* (Cambridge: MIT Press, 1990).

14 Here we rely on a leading account of biological functions due originally to Larry Wright. See, for example, Philip Kitcher, "Function and Design," in *The Philosophy of Biology*, ed. M. Ruse and D. Hull (New York: Oxford University Press, 1998).

time) and thus to improve our standards and means of inductive reasoning.[15]

Whatever we might think of these rebuttals, an attempt to apply similar reasoning to the moral case raises additional problems. It is not hard to imagine native inductions leading to reliable expectations about our environment, say that a predator is nearby or that a companion will come to our aid. But what exactly would the corresponding moral expectations be like? It is easy, of course, to think of Darwinian stories about how certain native moral dispositions might have evolved, such as a disposition to aid someone in need or to do what's required in a cooperative undertaking. Notice, though, that these are cases at best of tendencies to moral action rather than moral knowledge. We can imagine attending moral feelings and moral talk involving moral approbation and censure, all of which could play a role in moral motivation and have an evolutionary origin.[16] But, once again, such evolutionary accounts would not thereby explain how moral beliefs could be justified or what standards would be appropriate for their justification. It must be stressed that the point here is not that such explanations cannot be given, but rather that providing them is an additional problem that remains to be solved even if we are able to meet the objection to naturalizing epistemology in the ways suggested.

3.   Drawing Some Lessons from Recent Epistemology

For a thoroughgoing empiricist like Quine, the problem of justifying moral beliefs is both easier and more difficult. On the easier side, the significance of our theories and non-observational beliefs for him ultimately lies in the consequences that their truth has for experience. The warrant for them is ultimately a matter of the warrant that experience

---

15   This line of reply is taken in Hilary Kornblith, "Our Native Inferential Tendencies," in *Inductive Inference and its Natural Ground* (Cambridge: MIT Press, 1993).

16   For example, an evolutionary account of moral action, feelings, and discourse without any commitment to the existence of moral knowledge is given in Allan Gibbard, *Wise Choices, Apt Feelings* (Cambridge: Harvard University Press, 1990).

provides for predicting these consequences. Thus, Quine identifies three main tasks for epistemology: a conceptual one of determining the empirical content of our observation reports and theories, a doctrinal one of showing when and how they may be true,[17] and later a normative one of establishing norms of inquiry and hypothesis formation concerned with the anticipation of sensory experience.[18] This last draws on the applied mathematics of statistics, anecdotal evidence from the history of science, and the psychological study of the various perceptual and linguistic processes that allow us to respond reliably to stimuli and underwrite our successful theorizing. Unlike most epistemologists, Quine concentrates on the first task. That is because the general problem of justifying beliefs and establishing norms for them is basically just the problem of induction, answered largely, Quine thought, by appeal to natural selection. Indeed it is no more a problem for moral knowledge than it is for empirical knowledge in general, *so long as the key problem of determining empirical content for moral beliefs is solved.* Here psychology, itself the product of inductive inference, is queen, taking over from introspective awareness and *a priori* conceptual analysis. It does so by determining, to the extent this can be done, the range of stimuli prompting our unreserved assent to observation reports and by investigating empirically how our verbal theorizing relates to the empirical evidence that prompts it and leads us to revise it or continue with it. The moral epistemologist would be thus freed from the shackles of Fregean and Moorean conceptual analysis that plagued naturalism in the first half of the twentieth century. For Quine, the fact that a person might, on reflection or when questioned, think it an open question whether something is good, knowing it makes people happy or elicits approval from sympathetic persons, won't show that the belief that it is good doesn't have one of these properties as its empirical content.

On the more difficult side, Quine thought even simple moral beliefs like "That's outrageous" won't count as observations, even affective ones rather than sensory ones, since they don't prompt our assent

---

17 "Epistemology Naturalized," in Kornblith, ed., *Naturalizing Epistemology,* 16, 18-9, 24-5, 29-30.

18 *Pursuit of Truth* (Cambridge: Harvard University Press, 1990), chap. 1.

without considerably more collateral information than is needed for genuine observation reports like "That's red" or "That's a rabbit."[19] At the same time, moral beliefs also won't count as theoretical beliefs unless the naturalizing epistemologist can find in the empirical investigation of moral belief clear patterns of sensory and affective expectation. Moreover, they must be strongly enough associated with expressions of moral beliefs to provide empirical content for the latter and thus to provide our moral beliefs with observational checkpoints.[20] Because of these difficulties, Quine is a skeptic about moral belief. Not only does variation exist within and between individuals and societies in their moral values and ends; more importantly, the values common to sociable creatures are vague and open-ended. Predicates like "makes happy," "is lovable," and "sympathizes with" don't support inductive inferences from case to case in the way that "green " or "conducts electricity" do.[21]

The narrow strictures of such empiricism thus may have to be loosened for naturalized moral epistemology to amount to much. However, this may not be too hard to do. Strictly stimulus-based empiricism is already out of favour as an account even of our non-moral beliefs. For example, many psychologists and philosophers have argued that living in a world of natural kinds that matter for us, we have some tendency, thanks to natural selection, to classify objects into natural kinds. We classify, moreover, with a degree of reliability that could not be inferentially supported just from reports of the stimulation received by the receptors of our five senses. With enough investigation and theorizing, further inquiry may tell us, at least tentatively, precisely which classifications correspond to genuine kinds. It may tell us, finally, in ways quite different from our initial and perhaps quite

---

19 Quine, "Reply to White," in *The Philosophy of W.V. Quine,* ed. L.E. Hahn and P.A. Schilpp (Lasalle, Ill.: Open Court, 1986).

20 As a holist, Quine thinks individual non-observational beliefs have empirical content and warrant only in conjunction with other beliefs.

21 Quine, "On the Nature of Moral Values," 65. Quine's point, though hardly his conclusion, is oddly reminiscent of one of Kant's critical remarks concerning happiness as a moral end. Cf. "Groundwork of the Metaphysics of Morals," in *Practical Philosophy,* 70.

varying conceptions of them, what their real nature is, as well as how to extend and modify our classification of kinds. The contributions to this volume by David Copp, Margaret Urban Walker, Louise Antony, Susan Babbitt, and Lorraine Code explore at length how a naturalist might develop an account of moral knowledge that diverges from a narrow, stimulus-based empiricism.

Nor, as Code and Walker argue below, need the inferentially warranted conclusions to which the moral epistemologist helps herself be restricted to the conclusions of psychology and natural science. History, common sense, literature – who knows, maybe even literary criticism – might aid the moral epistemologist. Familiarity with the variety and possibilities of human activity and moral experience that are represented in history may be essential for any well warranted moral epistemology and a useful antidote for the ahistorical scientific inquiries Quine appeals to. Further, as feminist epistemologists have emphasized, familiarity with the history of our own scientific practices and the historical contingencies, interests, and institutional structures that produced them may provide a useful corrective to an uncritical acceptance of their results. However, here a word of caution needs to be interjected and perhaps a small gesture made toward Quine's scientism. An empirically warranted conclusion is one whose degree of warrant reflects the quantity and quality of the evidence in its favour. The number and variety of instances and the representativeness of samples matter. However, the deliverances of historical studies, as historians themselves often recognize, may be much less warranted than the empirically warranted conclusions of the sciences, and carry less weight accordingly. Attempts to apply Mill's methods for assessing causes and effects to history, for example in comparative history, tend to be very crude.[22] Feminist epistemologists have warned us to be wary of appeals to "Science shows...." but we should be at least equally wary of appeals to "History shows...."

---

22 See especially Paul Veyne, *Writing History: Essay on Epistemology*, trans. Mina Moore-Rinvolucri (Middletown, Conn.: Wesleyan University Press, 1984), but also even C. Behan McCullough's much more optimistic *The Truth of History* (London: Routledge, 1998).

Naturalistic epistemology, Quine thinks, must drop its "scruples against circularity."[23] However, here perhaps is a potential limitation to Quine's naturalizing. Faced with the apparently incompatible triad of propositions

(1)   we know stuff

(2)   we are cognitively limited beings living in a world we did not make, and

(3)   knowledge requires 'Cartesian' validation, i.e., non-circular justification that, on reflection, is self-evident

the skeptic rejects (1), the claim to know, whereas Quine pragmatically decides to reject (3). As he says concerning the idea that knowledge requires certainty or infallibility, "we must hedge the perhaps too stringent requirements of the verb 'know'."[24] Quine's hedging presumably is buoyed by his rejection of *a priori* conceptual or analytic truths, as well as the skeptic's apparent reliance on the quasi-scientific assumption of our cognitive limitations. However, dropping the idea that knowledge requires 'Cartesian' validation, as well as the normative scruple against circularity that goes with it, doesn't seem so much an empirically warranted discovery about knowledge as a pragmatic decision, albeit empirically informed, about how to define or explicate the word 'know.'

Must naturalistic epistemology be as cavalier as Quine with our scruples about circularity? Alvin Goldman, its most prominent recent exponent, thinks not. The circularity/regress concerns that lead its critics to embrace *a priori* epistemology, and lead Quine to embrace circularity, rest on a common assumption about justified belief. In the absence of self-evidence we need good reasons for thinking our beliefs true that we ourselves can, on reflection, recognize to be good reasons. Otherwise, as Laurence BonJour, a noted critic of naturalistic epistemology, argues, from our subjective perspective it is an accident that our beliefs are true. Intuitively persons with ostensible clairvoyant

---

23 "Epistemology Naturalized," in Kornblith, *Naturalizing Epistemology,* 2d ed., 20.

24 "Reply to Stroud," in *Midwest Studies in Philosophy,* vol. 6, *The Foundations of Analytic Philosophy* (Minneapolis: University of Minnesota Press, 1981), 474.

powers who lack good reasons for thinking clairvoyance reliable aren't justified in their clairvoyant deliverances.[25] However, Goldman rejects this assumption and these intuitions. What matters for justification is whether the processes that produce our beliefs reliably yield true beliefs. So long as inductive inference is reliable and some causal story about us in relation to our environment explains why this is so, whether or not we now know it, it is no accident that inductive inferences from true premises have true conclusions in some significantly high number of cases. Such inductive conclusions are thereby justified. Nor, Goldman insists, does any circularity exist.[26] The reliability of induction isn't itself a premise in a piece of inductive reasoning. So naturalizing epistemologists can *scrupulously* use induction from their empirical knowledge of past inductive reasoning to investigate inductive inference itself. More generally, they can *scrupulously* establish norms for evaluating our various cognitive capacities and practices and the beliefs they produce. These norms would be justified based on an assessment both of their reliability and their feasibility for us in the light of our empirically discovered psychological limitations.

Nonetheless, Goldman originally still saw a limitation to naturalistic epistemology. He contrasts normative epistemology with descriptive

---

25 *The Structure of Empirical Knowledge* (Cambridge: Harvard University Press, 1985), 9-10, 19-20, 43-5, and "Against Naturalized Epistemology," in *Midwest Studies in Philosophy*, vol. 19, *Philosophical Naturalism*, ed. P.A. French, T.E. Uehling and H.K. Wettstein (Notre Dame: Notre Dame University Press, 1994). Somewhat analogously, before appealing to circularity/regress considerations to defend the *a priori* character of moral principles in section II of the "Groundwork," Kant famously argues in section I that an action has moral worth only if done from duty, from a recognition of the requirements of morality. He explains in the *Preface* that "in the case of what is to be morally good it is not enough that it *conform* to the moral law, it must be done *for the sake of the law:* without this, that conformity is only very contingent and precarious, since a ground that is not moral will indeed now and then produce actions in conformity with the law, but it will also often produce actions contrary to the law" (45).

26 A. Goldman, *Epistemology and Cognition* (Cambridge: Harvard University Press, 1986), 393-4, and approving reference to van Cleve, "Reliability, Induction, and Justification," in *Midwest Studies in Philosophy*, vol. 9, *Causation and Causal Theories*, ed. P.A. French, T.E. Uehling and H.K. Wettstein (Minneapolis: University of Minnesota Press, 1984).

epistemology. Normative epistemology seeks to make epistemic judgments concerning beliefs and practices and to formulate systematic norms for such judgments, departing from our ordinary epistemic judgments and norms when advisable. It may go on in turn to formulate norms to guide our inquiries themselves, not just our retrospective evaluations of it. In doing this, it may avail itself of relevant empirical information concerning the reliability and feasibility for us of various processes and practices in the light of our empirically discovered psychological limitations and possibilities. Descriptive epistemology, on the other hand, aims to describe and elucidate our commonsense epistemic concepts and the norms connected with them. Descriptive epistemology gives us the reliabilist norm, but it does so as a product of *non-empirical* philosophical analysis tested against our intuitions concerning the implications of reliabilism for various hypothetical cases.[27] Hypothetical clairvoyants may matter for assessing the adequacy of the hypothesis that justification is a matter of the reliability of our cognitive processes; hypothetical white crows don't much matter for the empirical confirmation of the hypothesis that all crows are black.[28]

---

27 Goldman, *Epistemology and Cognition*, 66 "Psychology and Philosophical Analysis," in *Liaisons*, 143; and "Naturalistic Epistemology and Reliabilism," in *Midwest Studies in Philosophy*, vol. 19, *Philosophical Naturalism*, 306.

28 The issue might seem different with accounts of evaluative concepts and standards whose acceptability depends on a *wide reflective equilibrium* of evaluative standards, intuitive or paradigmatic cases of actual empirical knowledge and good reasoning, pragmatic concerns with the point of evaluative concepts, and background theories and beliefs about the human situation and its possibilities, epistemic or moral. However this doesn't make the acceptability of the account straightforwardly empirical. First, there is the non-evidential dimension of what we want in an evaluative concept, which may lead us to consider the implications of an account for hypothetical cases so as to decide whether it is one we can accept. Second, what may matter more for a relevant background theory is widespread acceptance, not empirical warrant, especially if part of the point of having evaluative concepts is to facilitate human interaction and so be interpersonally acceptable. Thirdly, even if such intuitions are themselves instances of empirical knowledge, these paradigmatic cases of empirical knowledge that epistemologists may reflect on hardly exhausts the full range of empirical evidence and empirically warranted judgment. The connections between reflective equilibrium and naturalistic epistemology need careful exploration.

Of course, our intuitions won't always straightforwardly line up in favour of reliabilism. Besides appealing to our intuitions about hypothetical clairvoyants, BonJour, for example, defends the place of the thinker's own epistemic conception of his situation by appeal to intuitive links between justification and responsibility. Believing something in the absence of any good reason for thinking it true is irresponsible and epistemically unjustifiable. Similarly, from the moral standpoint it is irresponsible and unjustified to go ahead and do something in the absence of any reason for thinking it is consistent with the requirements of morality. Goldman implicitly grants the idea that part of the point of the concept of justification is to mark responsibility. However, he concedes only that it is irresponsible to believe when one has reason for thinking one's belief false, not that it is irresponsible to believe in the absence of reason for thinking one's belief true.[29] Still, however much force this retort may have in the case of our perceptual beliefs concerning trees and hands we putatively see, this merely negative conception of responsibility may seem quite inadequate for moral knowledge. Its inadequacy appears especially evident when one considers the consequences of moral error for others and our responsibilities as moral agents to and for others. A more active account of epistemic agency, such as Louise Antony's (below), may seem preferable.

Recently, Goldman has suggested a deeper role for naturalistic epistemology, arguing that psychological theories of how we represent concepts, moral and epistemological ones in particular, can support the plausibility or implausibility of philosophical analyses of evaluative concepts, and the significance of the counterexamples posed by philosophers to them.[30] According to Goldman, evaluators have a mentally stored list of virtues and vices. In evaluating actual or hypothetical cases of belief or action, we consider the processes or dispositions that produced them and match them against our list of virtues or vices.

---

29 L. BonJour, *The Structure of Empirical Knowledge* (Cambridge: Harvard University Press, 1985), 43-5, and A. Goldman, *Epistemology and Cognition*, 63.

30 Goldman, "Epistemic Folkways and Scientific Epistemology" and "Naturalistic Epistemology and Reliabilism." Also "Ethics and Cognitive Science," *Ethics* 103 (1993): 337-60.

This meshes, he thinks, with recent psychological literature on concepts. For example, according to the exemplar view, the concept of pants isn't represented by a definition or abstract characterization but by exemplary types of pants, e.g., blue jeans, suit pants, etc., with new cases judged by their similarity or dissimilarity from them or their foils. The basis for inclusion in the list of epistemic virtues, Goldman says, is ultimately an associated high ratio of true beliefs to false beliefs, whereas the basis for inclusion in the list of moral virtues, he suggests in Humean fashion, is chiefly utility. Of course, there is no reason why exemplary epistemic irresponsibility in the case of moral judgment should contain exactly the same features as it does in the case of perceptual judgment. Nor is there any reason why the epistemic virtues and vices of moral judgment should be exactly the same as those for other areas of knowledge. The point nonetheless is that ordinary moral cognition will be a matter of comparing contemplated actions to exemplars rather than formulating or applying general principles or rules to cases and acting on them.

Consider then some counterexamples: first, the hypothetical cases of reliable clairvoyants and, second, persons who trust and rely on their perception, memory, and powers of reasoning every bit as responsibly as we do but who are placed in an evil demon world where these intellectual capacities are quite unreliable. Our intuitions still tend to deem the former unjustified – because reliance on clairvoyance is on our list of vices – and tend to deem the latter justified – because perception, memory, and 'good' forms of reasoning are on our list of virtues. Evaluators apparently don't easily revise the types of things in terms of which they represent concepts, especially not in response to rare or hypothetical cases. Clearly, a similar story could be told about what goes on in stock counterexamples to utilitarianism, e.g., our hesitation in finding moral merit in the actions of explorers who kill one innocent person to save nine. So Goldman can explain why we have the intuitions we do concerning the counterexamples, but deny that they undermine the reliabilist account of the content of our epistemic categories. Likewise, a utilitarian could deny that stock counterexamples to utilitarianism serve to undermine a utilitarian account of the content of our moral categories.

Elsewhere, Goldman embeds his story in a frame-semantical account of how we represent concepts, according to which concepts are defined by prototypes but in the context of a simplified world view or idealized cognitive model.[31] The concepts of justified and unjustified belief are introduced against the background of an idealized cognitive model in which perception, memory, and 'good' reasoning are reliable, and wishful thinking, hasty generalization, etc. are not. However the attribute of being reliable may not hold outside the idealized cognitive model in which words get their original foothold, and intuitions outside this source aren't trustworthy indicators of the originating rationale. Reliabilism's "theoretical importance isn't diminished by its recessive role in semantic intuitions" (152). Of course, all this supposes that the reliabilist or the utilitarian has correctly identified the fundamental content of our evaluative categories. Goldman says his view is ultimately based on examining cases where beliefs that were formed by perception, memory, and good reasoning were all considered justified and where these processes apparently shared the property of reliability. He might defend the utilitarian basis of moral virtue similarly (151).

There may be a problem here, however. It seems anyone who thinks that these cognitive capacities are epistemic virtues will think that their products in their own case are ones they think they are 'normally' justified in thinking true, at least in the absence of anything they regard as defeating evidence. Hence, on a little reflection such a person will think that their cognitive capacities are 'normally' reliable. Indeed, even Kant, despite his penchant for examples of the miserably dutiful, thinks that we have a duty to make ourselves and others happy, albeit without being paternalistic, and so thinks that the dutiful at least *normally* have some tendency to be happy and surrounded with happiness. What then is the cart and what's the horse, so to speak of our epistemic and moral categories? At one level, all we have is a set of factors associated with each other. The traditional way to determine which factor is "the fundamental basis or rationale" of our evaluative concepts is to appeal to thought experiments in which one factor is present and the other absent and to appeal to our evaluative intuitions or inclinations concerning them. By prising apart factors in hypothetical cases, we force ourselves to address issues we wouldn't normally have to address if

---

31 Goldman, "Psychology and Philosophical Analysis," 150-1.

we confined ourselves to considered judgments of justification or moral worth in typical cases. In this way we are able to determine which factors are primary in our thinking about justification. Of course it's precisely this "method" that gives rise to the counterexamples to reliabilism and utilitarianism, the relevance of which Goldman wishes to discount. However, it is unclear what other method he could appeal to until he suggests some experimental evidence or tests to show what the real basis of our evaluative concepts are. Arguably, to be better naturalists we must move beyond psychology narrowly construed to anthropology, sociology, or evolutionary biology.

Goldman's naturalism, and to a lesser extent Quine's, still emphasizes the need and search for systematic norms and rules of evaluation. However, for Goldman these norms are largely norms for the external evaluation of beliefs and actions. Further, in the case of knowledge, moral or otherwise, the focus is still on beliefs and their justification. Paul Churchland, another notable naturalistic epistemologist who has recently turned his attention to moral epistemology, suggests that even these emphases are a mistake. He argues that "a normal human's capacity for moral perception, cognition, deliberation, and recognition has rather less to do with rules, whether internal or external, than is commonly supposed,"[32] and more to do with the skills that allow us to exercise these capacities well. Moral knowledge is the product of moral expertise or know-how acquired by learning over time how to recognize a wide variety of complex situations and how to respond to them. With the aid of parental instruction and commentary and much social experience, we slowly generate a hierarchy of moral prototypes, prototypical moral situations and responses, from a substantial number of relevant examples of the moral kinds at issue. Prototypes are represented by sets of features that are the most statistically common characteristics of the examples and are subject to refinement through further experience. Which prototype we take to characterize a novel situation will depend on its similarity to and degree of fit with a prototype. This applies as much as to moral recognition and response as to pattern

---

32 "The Neural Representation of the Social World," in *Mind and Morals*, ed. May, Friedman, and Clark (Cambridge: MIT Press, 1996), 101.

and object recognition and response generally, e.g., in visual perception, and thus is seen entirely appropriately as a form of moral perception. Unusually penetrating moral insight, Churchland says, requires being able to see problematic moral situations in alternative ways and to evaluate their relative accuracy and relevance. This requires both a rich variety of moral prototypes and a keen eye for ways in which a particular situation diverges from a presumptive prototype.

Churchland like many others thinks that statable moral rules capture only part of the moral wisdom possessed by a mature adult. However, even Kant thought that applying a set of rules or theory to practice requires an experienced sharpened judgment and talent that isn't itself rule governed, partly to distinguish in which cases the rules were applicable and partly to provide them with access to the will.[33] The real challenge posed by the prototype account is to explain the role rules are supposed to play in knowing how.

Let's look briefly at some reasons why rules traditionally were thought to matter. Leibniz tells us that empiricists who are guided in what they think and do by instances and their similarities are easily mistaken and tricked because they lack the demonstrative knowledge or understanding of why what they believe is true or of why what they do succeeds.[34] Like Russell's chicken whose ignorance of the principles of economics prevents him from understanding why he has been fed in the past, empiricists may be rudely awakened to have their heads placed on the chopping block. A 1946 nursing manual tells us that "the art of nursing is a skill dependent on the application of the knowledge of scientific principles" to particular situations. Without this understanding of underlying principles to explain why procedures work, the manual says, nurses will be unable to cope with "the many different and ever-changing nursing situations that arise" and be unable to

---

33 Groundwork of the Metaphysics of Morals," 45. Also "On the common saying: that may be correct in theory but is of no practice use," in *Practical Philosophy*, 279.

34 *New Essays on the Human Understanding*, ed. Bennett and Remnant (Cambridge: Cambridge University Press, 1981), 50-1, also 475.

"adjust properly to emergency situations."[35] Implicit in these worries is the idea that the success of real knowers isn't accidental and any failure is accidental. The inability of nursing aides and midwives who lack instruction in scientific theory to deal with certain types of situations shows their success in more routine situations is merely accidental and discounts its epistemic worth. Certainly one may query the relevance of these inabilities. Statistical evidence suggests that in routine births one may be better off at home with a midwife than in a hospital with doctors and nurses. Being better off here is determined not only by the standard measures of success such as reduction in maternal and infant death rates and nasty post-natal complications, but also by the less common one of quality of birth experience. Medical professionals armed with scientific credentials tend to take the failures of midwives to be more significant for an assessment of their competence than their successes.

However, Churchland provides a stronger response to this dispute: the greater success of the expert in dealing with novel situations depends largely on her repertoire of prototypes and experience-sharpened judgment rather than the deployment of principles. If Plato had only read Churchland, he would have equipped his Republic's rulers with more prototypes instead of the knowledge of the form of the Good! Indeed, Hubert and Stuart Dreyfus, arguing more from a phenomenological perspective than from an experimental one, suggest that rule followers may be the ones to worry about.[36] They outline five stages in the development of moral expertise. The fluid performance of the widely experienced expert who can see what a situation is and how to act with hardly any conscious analysis and comparison of alternatives is at the highest level. It contrasts with the bumbling performance of the novice applying instructions without benefit of recognized similarities to other situations in her experience, as well as with the

---

35 Loretta Heidgerken, *Teaching in Schools of Nursing: Principles and Methods* (Philadelphia: Lippincott, 1946), 8, 35.

36 Hubert Dreyfus and Stuart Dreyfus, "What is Morality: A Phenomenological Account of the Development of Moral Expertise," in *Universalism vs. Communitarianism*, ed. David M. Rasmussen (Cambridge: MIT Press, 1990).

middling performance of the competent but still error-prone experienced rule follower. Their model has found some confirmation in Patricia Benner's study of clinical nursing practice.[37]

Yet Benner also recognizes that even experts can find themselves in situations where their experience fails them and they must resort to slow and faltering theoretical analysis and stepwise procedures. So where do we find moral expertise, even rare, of the sort described by Churchland or the Dreyfus brothers? In the halls of the UN or Parliament? The claim would rightly be greeted with considerable derision, no matter how extensive the statesman's knowledge of human history and experience of human affairs. In the domestic, professional, or business sphere? Here seems its likely home, though even here humanity's persistent tendency to attribute its success to its virtue and its failure to bad luck or the vice of others is an equally persistent source of self-deception and should give us pause. Still, there may be wider and more detailed experience of similarities and differences dealing with individuals in the small rather than the large. Witness the problems mentioned above with comparative cultural and political history. Further, relationships in such spheres can be structured, naturally or conventionally, so that the lines of responsibility permit significant freedom of choice for some members. This freedom allows them to make decisions on their own and to experiment without having first to justify their actions to large numbers of others. They are less apt to have to defend themselves against charges of inconsistency with previous decisions or to have to get others to agree to terms of co-operation and procedures to be followed. Faced with those demands for justification, however, acting on and being able to justify oneself by appeal to rules and principles may be key. Catherine Wilson, Michael Stingl, Andy Clark, and Paul Churchland explore the role and nature of rules in moral cognition in their contributions.

In any case, what we may have to recognize is the contextual character of attributions of the epistemic worth of beliefs and decisions, a point emphasized by several of our authors. What sort of performance

---

37 P.E. Benner, *From Novice to Expert: Excellence and Power in Clinical Nursing Practice* (Menlo Park: Addison-Wesley, 1984).

we think it reasonable to expect or demand in a situation can affect our epistemic evaluations. A six-year-old who successfully counts to twenty with great deliberation, but hesitates and makes mistakes when trying to do so just before bedtime, might be said to know how to count to twenty, though we wouldn't say that of a twenty-year-old whose performance was similar. A parent whose way of making decisions concerning how to deal with his children resembled those of the statesman might be said to be a moral dummy, though in the UN chamber he might be heralded for his thoughtfulness and competence in human affairs. The search for systematic norms of epistemic evaluation, in morals or elsewhere, may seem seriously misguided.

4. The Natural and the Normative; Moral Know-how and Moral Discourse

We invited the authors of the essays to follow to write on moral epistemology naturalized just as they saw fit. Not surprisingly, their essays cover a bewildering variety of themes and issues no less complex than the literature surveyed in this introduction. Nevertheless, the ten essays appear to divide themselves evenly around two central kinds of concern. The first concern is how to accommodate the normative within the natural. Can a naturalized moral epistemology hope to preserve the normative dimensions of morality, moral knowledge, and moral theory? Though agreement exists among the authors in Part I that these dimensions can be preserved, they differ in their views about exactly what the normative dimensions are and how an epistemology that is naturalized can accommodate them. The second central concern is about the role and importance of moral discourse within a naturalized conception of morality and moral knowledge. At the one extreme is the view that the biological underpinning of morality explains all its relevant features; at the other is the view that principled moral discussion and linguistically expressible deliberation about moral choices are essential to and completely definitive of our human experience and understanding of morality. The authors in Part II defend positions between the two extremes, focusing on the contrast between biologically grounded moral know-how and the cultural expression of morality in moral discourse.

In Part I, David Copp defends moral naturalism against four objections focusing on the divergence between the apparent content and character of our moral judgments and reasoning on the one hand, and the semantics and metaphysics provided by moral naturalists. The objections, he explains, are especially important when understood in the context of naturalized moral epistemology, but can also be answered within that context. His answers draw, in part, on Goldman's reliabilism, and lead him to suggest a way moral naturalists may answer the fundamental question of naturalized moral epistemology. Why, given the way we think morally and given the truth conditions for moral judgments provided by naturalists, would our moral beliefs have any tendency to be true and our forms of moral reasoning have any tendency to yield true beliefs? Margaret Urban Walker distinguishes between two approaches to naturalized moral epistemology. One prioritizes scientific knowledge as the source of our understanding of moral knowledge; the other places as much, if not more, significance in other forms of empirical knowledge, including moral knowledge concerning how the world may be made better for us and historical perspectives on our epistemic and cultural situation. She argues that the latter approach, an alternative to Quine's and perhaps Copp's, is preferable, since it preserves the distinctive normative dimension of moral epistemology which must concern itself with whether the ways science tells us we live are ways we ought to live.

That which warrants accepting norms and thinking them true, Louise Antony argues, is the success of practices governed by them. Addressing the paradox that we need bias in order to find the truth, she defends a view of epistemic agency tailored to developments in cognitive science. In her view commitment to truth and rationality leads us not just to endorse judgments that can survive critical scrutiny and deliberation aimed at the truth. We need also to recognize and accommodate the need for ecologically valid heuristics embodying some of the shortcuts and biases to which we are naturally prone. Likewise, she argues for a naturalized Kantian conception of moral agency in which commitment to a norm of impartiality that recognizes the equal moral worth of all human beings can accommodate the need for partiality and tell us when it should be tolerated and even encouraged. Kantian moral agency is also a theme in Susan Babbitt's work. She takes up the problem of why moral facts would matter to an agent if moral naturalism is true. Christine Korsgaard, doubting naturalism's ability to meet the challenge, has argued in a Kantian vein that seeing ourselves as agents rather than as patients requires seeing our actions in a special way. One must see actions that we endorse in the context of generalizable, expected patterns of action, so that failing to endorse acting similarly in relevantly similar cases violates our self-conception. Babbitt responds that this understanding of moral agency fails to explain how we sometimes come to unify our experience and attribute importance to it in ways that conflict with our more stable background beliefs and with the expectations derived from experience of evident personal and social regularities. Drawing on Richard Boyd's realist critique of Humean regularity accounts of causal expectations, she explains normativity primarily not by practical identity itself but by our dependence as knowers on an appropriate unifying perspective. This perspective allows us to acquire a full and adequate grasp of relevant *truths* concerning human needs and goals and thus to see how we can become better persons in a better world. Finally, Lorraine Code like Walker sees a flaw in the tendency of naturalized epistemology toward scientism. Still, she sees a virtue in its self-reflexive tendency to draw attention to its own origins and seeks a naturalism devoid of scientism. For Code all factual claims have normative dimensions, but this feature need not exempt them from having objective import. Using examples from medicine, she joins Antony in framing the issue of objectivity in ecological terms.

In Part II, Catherine Wilson provides an impressive tour of relevant literature in evolutionary biology, anthropology, history, and psychology to advance what might fairly be described as a sophisticated error theory of morality. Her aim is to expose the tension that she finds between our shared, biologically based, primitive proto-moral behavioural and affective dispositions, and the varying ideational suprastructure that we express culturally in our moral discourse, institutions, and behaviour. The human mind is disposed to generate many formulas of obligation, but moral formulas differ from others, such as taboos, in that they seek to limit the personal advantage one individual or social entity has over others by dint of greater strength, intelligence, beauty, charisma, or other advantageous features. She asks where one should one place oneself for various dimensions of human activity on a gradient from a hypermoral periphery of highly compensatory principles, e.g., "Don't kill any living thing for food," to principles closer to the proto-moral core that leave much more room for opportunistic advantage taking. Wilson argues that this is a question that isn't theoretically solvable, though we are continually tempted to think that it is. Stingl seeks to defend evolutionary ethics against such error theory, especially as it has been formulated by Michael Ruse and others who see a deep mismatch between claims to moral objectivity often made by philosophers and the basis for our moral feelings and dispositions deriving ultimately from our biological evolution. Stingl, like Wilson, follows David Braybrooke in construing moral rules as having an origin in systems of intentional blocking operations. Stingl, however, diverges from Wilson in arguing that the social behaviour of chimps makes it plausible to think chimps not only perceive harms as unjustified and experience motivational oughts arising from empathy, but (non-propositionally) represent rules with moral content that have motivational force for them. Given the apparent implausibility of the error theory for chimp cognition, the error theory shouldn't be seen as the default position for human moral cognition either.

Andy Clark shares much of Paul Churchland's general outlook on the relevance of neurobiology and connectionist AI for understanding human and animal cognition. However, he argues that Churchland does not appreciate fully the significance of moral discourse for locating what is distinctively moral in human morality or for the role it plays in making moral progress possible. First, moral reasoning, decision-making, and problem-solving are quintessentially a communal and collaborative affair for which linguistically formulated moral principles, however summary, are essential tools in the co-operative exploration of moral space. Second, moral labels and summary principles are the special tool by which morally salient patterns are brought into focus for biological, pattern-based engines of reason and stay there, rather than being swamped by superficial regularities. In reply, Churchland emphasizes the similarities between the social skills of various animals whose social cognition is entirely non-discursive and the skills of us humans. For us the discursive institutions of moral language, moral argument, law and courts are external scaffolding on which our practical wisdom is efficiently off-loaded, but which don't bring moral reasoning and knowledge into existence in the first place. At the same time, it is in these off-loaded institutional structures and the increased collective success at the negotiation of increasingly complex social spaces they offer us that Churchland finds our moral progress rather than in the character of the average person. Clark finishes with two reservations. For him, discursive practices of reason-giving and public moral discussion are part of what *constitute* our practices as genuinely moral in the first instance, just as only the activity of numeral-enhanced humans is genuinely mathematical, and moral progress must consist in *enhancing* moral exchange and debate.

I. Moral Naturalism and Normativity

CANADIAN JOURNAL OF PHILOSOPHY
Supplementary Volume 26

Four Epistemological Challenges to Ethical Naturalism: Naturalized Epistemology and the First-Person Perspective[*]

DAVID COPP

Ethical naturalism is the doctrine that moral properties, such as moral goodness, justice, rightness, wrongness, and the like, are among the "natural" properties that things can have. It is the doctrine that moral properties are "natural" and that morality is in this sense an aspect of "nature." Accordingly, it is a view about the semantics and metaphysics of moral discourse. For example, a utilitarian naturalist might propose that wrongness is the property an action could have of being such as to undermine overall happiness, where happiness is taken to be a psychological property. Unfortunately, it is unclear what the naturalist means by a "natural" property. For my purposes in this paper, I shall assume that natural properties are such that our knowledge of them is fundamentally empirical, grounded in observation.[1] More

---

[*] I am grateful for helpful comments from Richmond Campbell, Janice Dowell, Bruce Hunter, Loren Lomasky, Marina Oshana, Dave Schmidtz, Walter Sinnott-Armstrong, David Sobel, and Sara Worley. Abridged versions of this paper were presented to the Departments of Philosophy at the Ohio State University, the University of Miami, and York University as well as to the 2000 Congress of the Canadian Philosophical Association. I am grateful for the suggestions and comments I received on these occasions.

1 G.E. Moore suggested a similar account when he said that naturalistic ethics holds that "Ethics is an empirical or positive science: its conclusions could all be established by means of empirical observation and induction." See G.E. Moore, *Principia Ethica* (Cambridge: Cambridge University Press, 1903), sec. 25. Naturalism is often explained differently, however, in terms of the sciences, or

precisely, a property is "natural" just in case any synthetic proposition about its instantiation can be known only *a posteriori*, or with the aid of experience.[2] Ethical naturalism is, in short, the doctrine that there are moral properties and that they are natural properties. It implies that moral knowledge is fundamentally empirical. It is committed to an empiricist moral epistemology.

This paper springs from the fact that certain unsurprising commonsense first-personal observations about our moral thinking can appear to undermine ethical naturalism by undermining the psychological plausibility of the idea that our moral knowledge is empirical.

---

in terms of the entities postulated in the sciences, or in terms of the vocabulary of the sciences, or in terms of certain favored sciences. Moore says, in *Principia*, sec. 26, "By 'nature,' then, I do mean and have meant that which is the subject-matter of the natural sciences and also of psychology." I do not see why philosophers would give a privileged place to the sciences in explicating naturalism unless they thought that the scientific method was at least an especially reliable way of acquiring knowledge *a posteriori*. Notice that, on the proposal made in the text, a naturalistic theory need not be "reductive." Notice also that a theory that is putatively naturalistic can be unsuccessful in a variety of ways. It might fail to make good on the claim that moral propositions are knowable, or that they are knowable *a posteriori*; it might propose an implausible analysis of moral propositions.

2   More would obviously need to be said in order to give an adequate account of the *a posteriori*. By a "synthetic proposition" I mean a proposition that is neither logically true nor "conceptually" true. If, for example, the concept of murder is the concept of a wrongful killing, a naturalist would not deny that we can know *a priori* that murder is wrong. But a naturalist denies that there is synthetic *a priori* moral knowledge. A naturalist would deny that we can know *a priori* that, say, killing the innocent is wrong. The notion of a proposition "about the instantiation" of a property is vague. Clearly, if a proposition implies that a property is instantiated, it counts as being "about the instantiation" of the property. A proposition is also in the relevant sense "about the instantiation" of a property if it implies a proposition about the circumstances in which the property would be instantiated. Consider, for example, the proposition that friendship is good. It is "about the instantiation" of goodness since it implies that if there is friendship, it is good. G.E. Moore therefore counts as a non-naturalist. He holds that we can know *a priori* that friendship is good. See Moore, *Principia Ethica*, secs. 112-3. He also holds that the proposition that friendship is good is synthetic. Moore, *Principia Ethica*, sec. 6.

For instance, moral belief seems more often to be a result of thinking an issue through in a way that is sensitive to morally significant considerations than a result of straightforward empirical observation or theorizing. I shall discuss four challenges of this kind. These challenges might be thought to support a kind of non-naturalistic intuitionism in moral epistemology, or perhaps to support a kind of apriorism. I shall argue that the observations that fuel the challenges are actually compatible with ethical naturalism. In the process I will be defending the idea that moral "intuition," or non-inferential spontaneous moral belief, can qualify as knowledge.

Some naturalists might be prepared to adopt the quite different strategy of disregarding objections of the kinds I will discuss on the basis of the metaphysical attractiveness of ethical naturalism. But such a strategy is not compatible with a naturalized approach to epistemology. As we will see, naturalized epistemology is undergirded by a kind of "scientific prioritism." Because of this, it blocks dismissing the objections on metaphysical grounds alone. Scientific prioritism appears also to block other kinds of responses to the objections, such as postulating a special faculty by which we acquire moral knowledge, or inferring how the psychology must work on the basis of metaphysical arguments. As we will see, naturalized epistemology gives priority to *scientific* psychology rather than to commonsense psychological observations of the kinds that fuel the objections. Hence, it would be compatible with naturalized epistemology to reject the objections if the "observations" that fuel them are empirically suspect. It might also be compatible with naturalized epistemology to reject the objections on grounds of theoretical simplicity and explanatory utility. The important point, however, is that naturalized epistemology restricts the strategies that can be used by ethical naturalists in responding to the epistemological objections. To be sure, as we will see, ethical naturalism is not *logically* committed to the doctrines of naturalized epistemology. I nevertheless find it difficult to see how a theoretical preference for ethical naturalism could be explained or justified in a way that would not equally well ground or justify a theoretical preference for at least the central doctrines of naturalized epistemology.

There are two projects for the paper. The most important is to respond to the intuitive epistemological objections to ethical naturalism. The second is to explain the relation between ethical naturalism and naturalized epistemology. Naturalized epistemology puts an important constraint on meta-ethical theory, namely, that its semantics and metaphysics must be integrated with a psychologically plausible moral epistemology. The four objections to ethical naturalism that I will discuss are grounded in an application of this constraint. On a naturalized approach to epistemology, an ethical naturalist cannot deal adequately with the objections without developing a moral epistemology that is both naturalistic, in that it shows moral knowledge to be fundamentally empirical, and compatible with a psychology of moral belief formation and moral reasoning that is plausible by the standards of psychology and the (other) sciences. I sketch such an epistemology in this paper. I will begin by presenting the objections in detail.

1. Four Epistemological Challenges to Ethical Naturalism

According to the first objection, we often seem to arrive at our moral views as a result of reflection, thought, or reasoning, rather than as a straightforward result of empirical observation or theorizing, as naturalism would seem to suggest. Observation gives us information that is morally relevant. But we can be morally perplexed, say, about euthanasia, even if we are clear that no further observation will help us to decide what to think. In such cases, reflection is called for rather than empirical theorizing about the world. Naturalism owes us an account of the nature and epistemic status of the relevant kind of reasoning or reflection and of how it gives us access to the empirical truths that it identifies with moral truths. It needs to explain how moral reasoning of this kind can give rise to knowledge if, as naturalism maintains, the basic moral facts can only be known empirically or through observation.[3]

---

3 The objection is briefly sketched in T.M. Scanlon, *What We Owe To Each Other* (Cambridge: Harvard University Press, 1998), 1. See also Robert Audi, "Intuitionism, Pluralism, and the Foundations of Ethics," in *Moral Knowledge? New Readings in Moral Epistemology*, ed. Walter Sinnott-Armstrong and Mark Timmons (New York: Oxford University Press, 1996), 101-36, especially, 114-5. For brief discussion of a similar objection, see Peter Railton, "Moral Realism," *Philosophical Review* 95 (1986): 166-8.

Second, in many cases where we draw moral conclusions as a result of conscious inferences from observations, it would on the face of it be misleading to view these as inductive inferences of any kind, such as inferences to the best explanation, although this is what might be suggested by naturalism. For instance, once we determine that an act is, say, a piece of deliberate cruelty, such as an instance of torturing just for fun, it would be appropriate for us to conclude straightaway that the act is wrong. Yet the inference to the wrongness of the action clearly is not an inference to the best explanation of the fact that the act is an instance of torturing just for fun. And it would be misleading to describe the fact that the act is an instance of torturing just for fun as *evidence* that the act is wrong. Its support for the wrongness of the act is rather stronger than and different from mere evidence of wrongness. Naturalism owes us an account of the inferences we make in such cases.[4]

Third, although in some cases we do arrive at a moral belief directly on the basis of observation, without conscious inference, it seems inaccurate to view us in these cases as observing, say, the wrongness of an action. Naturalism would seem to suggest that we do or can observe the wrongness of actions in such cases, just as we might observe the clumsiness of someone's action. To see the problem with this suggestion, consider a variation on a well-known example that was introduced by Gilbert Harman.[5] Suppose a person comes round a corner where some children are lighting a cat on fire in plain view, but suppose she does not see that what they are doing is lighting a cat on fire. Her failure might be explained by a fault in her perceptual apparatus, or perhaps by a lack of knowledge of cats. Perhaps she does not recognize that the animal being lit on fire is a cat. But suppose that although she sees and understands that the children are lighting a cat on fire, she does not "see" that what they are doing is wrong. This is no evidence at all of a fault in her perceptual faculties, nor is it good evidence that she is lacking some propositional knowledge that she need only acquire to

---

4 An argument that assumptions about moral facts are irrelevant to explaining any observations is found in chapter one of Gilbert Harman, *Morality* (New York: Oxford University Press, 1977).

5 Harman, *Morality*, 4-8.

see things rightly. It is much better evidence of a fault in her moral sensitivity. Naturalism owes us an explanation of such cases and of the nature and epistemic role of moral sensitivity.

Finally, a naturalistic theory will likely be embarrassed if it proposes informative naturalistic accounts of the moral properties. For it seems likely that there will be cases in which we take ourselves to have moral knowledge even though we have no knowledge of whether the theory's proposed naturalistic explanans of what we know obtains or not. We might have no inkling of what the proposed explanans is. And it seems likely that, in attempting to decide what to believe in a case where we are morally perplexed, we will not investigate whether the naturalistic explanans obtains, but will rather engage in a more standard kind of moral reflection. For instance, we might be morally perplexed about euthanasia. A proposed naturalistic account of the proposition that, say, euthanasia is wrong, would be a general proposition about euthanasia that we could state in purely naturalistic terms. It might be the proposition that euthanasia undermines the general happiness; or the proposition that a social rule against euthanasia would best serve the needs of our society, such as its need for peaceful social interaction; or the proposition that a rule that permitted euthanasia would be rejected by people who aimed to find principles for the general regulation of behavior that others with the same goal would not reject.[6] If we were undecided whether euthanasia is wrong, it is unlikely that we would attempt to decide what to believe about it by attempting to decide whether to believe the empirical proposition about euthanasia that a naturalistic theory would identify as stating the truth conditions of the proposition that euthanasia is wrong. We would instead engage in ordinary moral reasoning of a familiar kind. We might express these points

---

6 In this sentence I allude to three naturalistic proposals: a form of analytic consequentialism, the view I proposed in my recent book, and a close relative of the view T.M. Scanlon proposed in his recent book. See David Copp, *Morality, Normativity, and Society* (New York: Oxford University Press, 1995), and T.M. Scanlon, *What We Owe To Each Other*, 4. Scanlon does not intend to propose a form of ethical naturalism.

by saying that there is an apparent independence of moral belief from belief in the truth conditions of moral propositions that would be proposed by a naturalistic theory. Naturalistic theories need to explain this.

The four challenges form a cluster. There are cases in which we reach moral views as a result of reasoning or reflection. Naturalism owes us an account of what is going on. There are cases in which we infer a moral conclusion from an observation, but the inference does not seem to be inductive in nature. Naturalism owes us an account of what is going on in these cases. There are cases in which we come to have moral views immediately as a result of observation, but in these cases it seems it would be misleading to describe us as observing the truth of the moral claim. And, finally, it seems not to be the case that we base our moral beliefs on knowledge of the complex empirical facts that a reductive naturalism would cite as constituting the truth conditions of these beliefs. In short, naturalistic meta-ethics does not seem to cohere with a plausible moral epistemology, given commonsense observations about moral belief and moral reasoning.

There is no need to accept naturalized epistemology to appreciate the force of these four challenges. But if we accept a naturalized epistemology, we are committed to certain restrictions on acceptable responses. Most important, we must concede that the philosophical soundness of our response is hostage to its psychological plausibility. In the next section of the paper, I address the basis of this idea in naturalized epistemology. This section is optional for readers who are primarily interested in my responses to the four challenges.

2.   What is Naturalized Epistemology?

Philosophers who have discussed something called "naturalized" epistemology have had in mind different doctrines about epistemology, and they have disagreed about the plausibility of these doctrines. It is to be expected, then, that my understanding of naturalized epistemology is different from that of many other philosophers. Fortunately this does not matter for my limited purposes. For my purposes, moreover, a brief discussion of naturalized epistemology will suffice.

Quine's central concern, in his classic paper, "Epistemology Naturalized,"[7] was the failure of "traditional epistemology" to deal with skepticism about the external world. In face of this failure, Quine recommended that epistemology give up the "Cartesian quest for certainty" and instead see itself as a part of psychology, exploring empirically the relation between evidence and theory. He says, "epistemology still goes on, though in a new setting and a clarified status. Epistemology, or something like it, simply falls into place as a chapter of psychology and hence of natural science. It studies a natural phenomenon, viz., a physical human subject." It studies "The relation between the meager [sensory] input and the torrential output," which comes in the form of a description of the natural world.[8]

I think we should abandon Quine's radical idea that epistemology is rightly seen as a part of psychology. There are normative issues in epistemology that this view cannot accommodate, and we do not need to embrace the "Cartesian quest for certainty" in order to address these issues.[9] Our choice is not the stark one that Quine poses between

---

7 W.V. Quine, "Epistemology Naturalized," in *Ontological Relativity and Other Essays* (New York: Columbia University Press, 1969), 69-90.

8 Quine, "Epistemology Naturalized," 74-6, 82-3.

9 Here I agree with Barry Stroud and Jaegwon Kim. Barry Stroud, "The Significance of Naturalized Epistemology," in *Naturalizing Epistemology*, ed. Hilary Kornblith (Cambridge: MIT Press, 1985), 71-89; Jaegwon Kim, "What is 'Naturalized Epistemology'?" in *Supervenience and Mind: Selected Philosophical Essays* (Cambridge: Cambridge University Press, 1993), 216-36. Perhaps it will be objected that normative epistemological issues, properly understood, *are* psychological. On this way of thinking, we would perhaps need to rethink the import of Quine's view that "Epistemology, or something like it, simply falls into place as a chapter of psychology and hence of natural science." I take Quine to be claiming that we should give up normative epistemology as it has been practiced and instead confine ourselves to the use of scientific methodology in exploring the relation between evidence and theory. But the view that normative epistemological issues are psychological could be understood to imply instead that we should expand our conception of psychology, natural science, and the scientific method so that traditional philosophical explorations of normative issues are counted as "scientific" or "psychological." This does not appear to be a substantive suggestion. Note: The thesis that all normative properties are

Cartesianism and psychologism. But even if we give up Quine's psychologism, there remains in Quine a less radical conception of naturalized epistemology as an anti-skeptical, or at least non-skeptical, empirically informed, investigation of the grounds of knowledge. I shall take this revised conception of naturalized epistemology as my starting point.

Suppose that we reject skepticism about the external world. In so doing, we take it to be possible for ourselves, as we actually are constituted, to have knowledge about the world around us. This idea commits us to allowing that the psychological processes by which we come to have beliefs about the external world could underwrite knowledge. It commits us, that is, to placing certain psychological constraints on our philosophical account of what is necessary in order for a belief to count as knowledge. If we hold that it is necessary for us to stand in a certain relation to the world in order to have knowledge of it, or if we hold that it is necessary for us to go through a certain process of justification in order to have knowledge, then we are committed to the possibility of our actually going through this process or standing in this relation to the world, given how we actually are constituted. We are committed to constraining our philosophical epistemology by what is psychologically possible for beings like us. If we take ourselves *actually* to have knowledge of the world around us, then we are committed to a stronger thesis. For if we take ourselves to know that there are oak trees and stars, for example, we are committed to thinking that the actual psychological processes by which we come to believe such things are processes that yield knowledge, at least in some cases.

As I understand it for my purposes in this paper, then, "naturalized epistemology" is characterized by two central doctrines. First, we do have knowledge of the world around us. The actual psychological processes by which we come to have the relevant beliefs about the world

---

natural properties does not imply that normative epistemology is "a chapter of psychology"; what it implies is that any normative epistemological knowledge is fundamentally empirical. In more recent work, Quine appears to accept that epistemology is a normative discipline. See W.V.O. Quine, *In Pursuit of Truth* (Cambridge: Harvard University Press, 1990).

around us are sources of knowledge.[10] Second, in attempting to explain how these processes enable us to stand in epistemically relevant relations with the objects of our beliefs, our philosophical epistemology must be constrained by a plausible and empirically informed psychology of these processes.[11]

We know in general terms what these processes are. Perhaps most of us learn that there are oak trees and stars in the course of learning the language. We learn that the Big Dipper points to the North Star in early star gazing, at least if we live in the Northern Hemisphere. In these examples we learn from experience. Quine said, "The stimulation of his sensory receptors is all the evidence anybody has had to go on, ultimately, in arriving at his picture of the world."[12] This dictum might

---

10 This does not mean that an epistemological naturalist would ignore or reject out of hand the traditional skeptical challenge to our knowledge of the external world. Quine appears to think that science can give us a kind of response to skepticism, for, as he pointed out, science can at least hope to explain why it is that our experience leads us to have largely correct beliefs. He says, "There is some encouragement in Darwin.... Creatures inveterately wrong in their inductions have a pathetic but praiseworthy tendency to die before reproducing their kind" (W.V. Quine, "Natural Kinds," in *Ontological Relativity and Other Essays*, 126). But an epistemological naturalist might not think that this point provides an adequate philosophical response to skepticism. A variety of views about skepticism are compatible with naturalized epistemology.

11 I am grateful to Bruce Hunter for help with this paragraph. Hilary Kornblith distinguishes two questions about our beliefs. The first is, "How ought we to arrive at our beliefs?" The second is, "How do we arrive at our beliefs?" He says that "the naturalistic approach to epistemology consists in [the thesis that] question 1 cannot be answered independently of question 2." On my understanding, epistemological naturalism accepts the thesis of Kornblith's "naturalistic approach" but adds two additional doctrines. First is an explanation of *why* epistemological naturalism accepts this thesis. It does so because it is anti-skeptical or at least non-skeptical. Second, naturalism does not merely hold that the psychology of belief formation is *relevant* to normative issues in epistemology. It holds that our normative epistemology is to be *constrained* by the psychology of belief formation. See Hilary Kornblith, "What is Naturalistic Epistemology?" in *Naturalizing Epistemology*, ed. Hilary Kornblith (Cambridge: MIT Press, 1985), 1, 3.

12 Quine, "Epistemology Naturalized," 75.

need to be qualified, for we do not want to be too quick to rule out the possibility of *a priori* knowledge. But it is plausible that, "ultimately," even our *a priori* knowledge, if any, is dependent on the stimulation of our sensory receptors.[13]

The picture I have painted so far does not tell us what would be involved in naturalizing moral epistemology, for it does not tell us what would be involved in naturalizing the epistemology of a specific subject matter. Let me turn again to Quine. He says that in investigating the epistemology of science, "we are well advised to use any available information, including that provided by the very science whose link with observation we are seeking to understand."[14] This reveals that Quine is assuming that the theories of the science we are seeking to understand can be taken as a given. For he would not have said this if he had had in mind the epistemology of a theory that we take to be false, such as astrology. We could "naturalize" the epistemology of astrology, or of another false theory or discredited science, in the sense that we could study empirically how people came to accept it. But in so doing we would not use "information" provided by the science or theory in question.

These remarks point the way, I think, to a proper understanding of what would be involved in "naturalizing" the epistemology of a specific subject matter. Naturalized epistemology is characterized by a non-skeptical doctrine combined with a methodological doctrine to the effect that our philosophical epistemology must be constrained by a plausible psychology of the processes whereby we acquire knowledge. In studying the epistemology of a specific theory or body of beliefs, *T*, an epistemological naturalist would aim to arrive at corresponding specific doctrines, first, about the cognitive status of *T*, and second, about the cognitive status of the psychological processes that have led people to accept *T*. First, to simplify somewhat, the naturalist would have to decide whether or not to take *T* to be true. More

---

13 I shall leave open the question whether there is *a priori* knowledge, and if so, how it should be understood. Nothing in this paper turns on our having an answer to the question.

14 Quine, "Epistemology Naturalized," 76.

realistically, her decision might be more nuanced. She might decide, for example, that some of the beliefs or some of the propositions in *T* are true and some are not. In many cases, the issues here will be philosophically subtle and controversial. Second, depending on what she decides about the cognitive status of *T*, she will reach corresponding or at least compatible conclusions about the cognitive status of the processes that have led people to accept *T*. If she takes *T* to be true, or parts of *T* to be true, then, depending on her normative epistemology, she presumably would take at least some of the psychological processes by which we come to accept *T* as sources of knowledge. And if so, then as Quine suggests, she can use or assume *T* or the known parts of *T* in studying these processes. If she takes *T* not to be true, then she must allow that these processes are potential sources of error, and she cannot use *T* or assume *T* in studying the processes. In more nuanced cases, her views about the cognitive status of the mechanisms that have led to acceptance of *T* will need to be more subtle and nuanced. A plausible naturalized epistemology of astrology would be built on the premise that the fundamental doctrines of astrology are false and not known. But a plausible naturalized epistemology of mathematics would instead be built on the premise that the theorems of mathematics are known. A naturalist would presumably take a more nuanced view of theoretical physics, given that even the best theories in physics are sensibly taken to be open to revision.

In order to get the project of naturalizing *moral* epistemology off the ground, the naturalist must decide whether we have moral knowledge, and, if she decides that we do, she must decide what it is that we know, at least within broad limits. She has to decide the truth conditions of our moral beliefs. The problems here are the familiar problems of moral philosophy. The main contribution made by the epistemological naturalist would be the idea that our theories of what it is that we know, in having moral knowledge, and our theories of how it is that we know these things, must mesh with a plausible psychology of moral belief. An acceptable moral semantics and metaphysics must fit with an acceptable moral epistemology and an acceptable moral epistemology must fit with an acceptable empirical psychology of moral belief.

This is a familiar subtext in recent moral theory. According to non-naturalism, moral properties are not natural properties, so our knowledge of their instantiation is not empirical. It is widely agreed that non-naturalism owes us an explanation of how we can come to know that such properties are exemplified. How can we come to know that torture is wrong, for instance, unless wrongness is a property we can be acquainted with or otherwise related to in the natural world? How can we come to be in epistemically significant relations to non-natural properties given that, ultimately, all our knowledge is grounded in observation of the natural world? The non-naturalist might posit a special faculty by which we can detect the wrongness of torture.[15] But according to epistemological naturalism, such a view is tenable only if there are independent psychological grounds for supposing the existence of such a faculty – or no independent psychological grounds for supposing its non-existence. According to the epistemological naturalist, our psychological holdings cannot properly be amended to serve the needs of our philosophical theories. Rather, our epistemology is properly constrained by the holdings of empirical psychology.

Of course, at any given time, the "holdings" of psychology are open to revision. Science is fallible, and there is never going to be a "finished" psychology. There are controversies within psychology. We might view some of the tenets of a certain psychological theory, as we find it at a given time, to be empirically or otherwise scientifically suspect. Because of this, the characteristic doctrine of naturalized epistemology needs to be interpreted with care. It is too crude to hold that our

---

15 The intuitionism proposed by Robert Audi does not postulate a special faculty. See Audi, "Intuitionism, Pluralism, and the Foundations of Ethics," 121, 124. J.L. Mackie challenged any theory that postulates the existence of moral properties to provide a plausible epistemology of those properties. If a theory postulates the existence of a property of wrongness, for example, Mackie challenges it to provide a plausible account of how it is that we "discern" the wrongness of actions that we believe to be wrong, and of how it is that we "discern" the link between the actions' feature of wrongness and the natural features, such as deliberate cruelty, that we believe the wrongness of the actions to be "consequential" to. He appears to think that no such account will be as comprehensible and as simple, and as plausible psychologically, as the idea that we are not perceiving a property of wrongness at all, but are rather simply responding subjectively and negatively to the natural features in question. See J.L. Mackie, *Ethics: Inventing Right and Wrong* (Harmondsworth: Penguin, 1977), chap. 1, sec. 9.

epistemology is to be constrained by the "holdings" of psychology. Instead, we should say this: If we take it that a given thesis is settled in current psychology and is not scientifically doubtful, then our epistemology must be compatible with that thesis. The doctrine is roughly that our epistemology must be constrained by what we take to be the settled results of empirical psychology regarding the formation of our beliefs.

This doctrine is not uncontroversial. It rules out amending the results of psychology in the interest of explaining the possibility of our having knowledge of a specific subject matter. Paul Benacerraf used an argument of this kind against Kurt Gödel's mathematical intuitionism.[16] The doctrine could also be used in arguments against analogous intuitionist or special faculty views in moral epistemology and in the

---

16 Benacerraf argued that "the concept of mathematical truth ... must fit into an over-all account of knowledge in a way that makes it intelligible how we have the mathematical knowledge that we have. An acceptable semantics for mathematics must fit an acceptable epistemology." See Paul Benacerraf, "Mathematical Truth," *Journal of Philosophy* 70 (1973): 667. Benacerraf then went on to argue that the standard "platonistic" account of mathematics, according to which numbers are abstract objects, "makes it difficult to see how mathematical knowledge is possible," given a familiar causal account of knowledge (Benacerraf, "Mathematical Truth," 673, 671-3). On any acceptable epistemology, he suggests, there must be some "link between our cognitive faculties and the objects known." For "We accept as knowledge only those beliefs which we can appropriately relate to our cognitive faculties." To fill this gap, one might postulate the existence of a special cognitive faculty, which we could call "mathematical intuition." Benacerraf notes that Kurt Gödel postulated the existence of just such a faculty to account for mathematical knowledge, but he says, "the absence of a coherent account of how our mathematical intuition is connected with the truth of mathematical propositions renders the over-all account unsatisfactory" (Benacerraf, "Mathematical Truth," 674-5). Benacerraf does not explicitly say that a satisfactory epistemology of mathematics would have to mesh with an empirically plausible psychology of mathematical belief. But the idea is implicit in his response to Gödel's intuitionism. He appears to rule out the soundness of an argument from metaphysics and epistemology to the existence of a psychological faculty. He therefore appears to accept tenets that would be characteristic of a naturalized mathematical epistemology. For similar views, Benacerraf cites Mark Steiner, "Platonism and the Causal Theory of Knowledge," *Journal of Philosophy* 70 (1973): 57-66.

epistemology of theological belief. But it is not clear what argument could be given in support of the doctrine. Suppose that certain philosophical theories in mathematical and moral epistemology and metaphysics are in tension with what the settled psychology of a given period tells us about mathematical and moral belief formation. The thesis that, in this case, it is the philosophical theories that must give way, not the psychology, is itself a philosophical thesis. It is presumably derived from a more general doctrine to the effect that philosophy must be constrained by the results of science. We could call this doctrine "scientific prioritism," since it gives methodological priority to science. Of course, at any given time, the "results" of science are open to revision, for science is fallible, and it is never going to be "finished." With this understood, the doctrine of scientific prioritism should be understood to say, roughly, that our philosophical theorizing must be constrained by what we take to be the settled results of empirical science. It is not clear what arguments could be given in support of scientific prioritism, but it is nevertheless characteristic of naturalized epistemology as I understand it.[17]

I also believe that any ethical naturalist would be tempted by scientific prioritism, given what I take to be the underlying epistemological motivation of naturalism. But it is not the case that an ethical naturalist is logically committed to naturalized moral epistemology. Ethical naturalism is the view that moral properties are natural properties. The parallel view in epistemology is the view that normative epistemological properties are natural properties. An ethical naturalist is not even logically committed to this latter thesis, and, anyway, it is distinct from naturalized epistemology. Naturalized epistemology is a position about the methodology of epistemology rather than a view about the metaphysics of normative epistemological properties. Ethical naturalism and naturalized epistemology are therefore

---

17 Richmond Campbell objected, in personal correspondence, that epistemology and psychology are interdependent, since psychological methodology reflects certain assumptions about epistemology, and since epistemological theory depends on certain assumptions about psychology. But I don't see this independence as a decisive objection to scientific prioritism. It may still be true that epistemology must be constrained by what we take to be the settled results of empirical science.

logically independent of one another.[18] They do nevertheless appear to be intellectual cousins. So it is important to consider whether ethical naturalism can adequately respond to the four epistemological challenges I described earlier in the paper without running afoul of scientific prioritism or any of the other tenets of naturalized epistemology.

Indeed, the four challenges can now be seen to be commonsense instances of a more general theoretical challenge to ethical naturalism from naturalized epistemology. The four challenges suggest that there is evidence in commonsense reflection and observation that the nature of moral reasoning, moral inference, and moral observation are not what we would expect if ethical naturalism were true. That is, the metaphysics and semantics of ethical naturalism seem not to cohere with commonsense observations about moral belief. Naturalized epistemology adds that although common sense is not decisive, empirical psychology (among other things) can be decisive in assessing the tenability of a moral epistemology. Any given naturalistic meta-ethical theory must show that the psychological mechanisms that *actually* account for our moral beliefs, in cases where the theory implies that the beliefs are true and so might constitute knowledge, are such as to give us knowledge-enabling access to the facts that, according to the theory's semantics and metaphysics, make the beliefs in question true. More briefly, an acceptable moral epistemology must fit with the psychological facts about how we come to have moral beliefs.

3. Summary of a Naturalistic Theory

Before we can attempt to deal with these epistemological challenges, we need to bring ethical naturalism into clearer focus. For, to deal with the challenges, we need to show that there is at least a defensible and

---

18 Naturalized epistemology is not committed to ethical naturalism for it is not committed to the idea that moral knowledge is empirical. It is compatible with naturalized epistemology to hold that we do not have moral knowledge, or to hold that our moral knowledge is not empirical. Similarly, it is compatible with naturalized epistemology to deny that we have mathematical or theological knowledge, or to hold that such knowledge is not empirical.

coherent form of ethical naturalism, and an accompanying moral epistemology that meshes suitably with commonsense observations about moral reasoning, moral inference, and moral observation and with the psychology of moral belief formation. To show this, we need to specify a naturalistic theory. In this section of the paper, I will sketch such a theory. Fortunately, it is not necessary that I try to establish its truth. It will be enough to formulate it and to urge that it is defensible. For obvious reasons, the theory I will present for consideration is a naturalistic theory that I have proposed and defended in detail elsewhere.[19] I have called it "society-centered moral theory."

To a first approximation, the central idea is that a basic moral *proposition* is true only if a corresponding moral *standard* or *norm* is relevantly justified or authoritative.[20] By a "standard," I mean a content expressible by an imperative. For example, it is wrong to torture just for fun just in case (roughly) a standard or rule prohibiting people from torturing just for fun is relevantly justified.[21] A moral standard is relevantly justified just in case (roughly) its currency in the social code of the relevant society would best contribute to the society's ability to meet its needs – including its needs for physical continuity, internal harmony and co-operative interaction, and peaceful and co-operative

---

19 Copp, *Morality, Normativity, and Society*. For a brief introduction to the view, see David Copp, "Does Moral Theory Need the Concept of Society?" *Analyse & Kritik* 19 (1997): 189-212. For a reply to some objections, see David Copp, "Morality and Society – The True and the Nasty: Reply to Leist," *Analyse & Kritik* 20 (1998): 30-45.

20 A basic moral proposition is such that, for some moral property M, it entails that something instantiates M. An example is the proposition that capital punishment is wrong. Among non-basic moral propositions are propositions such as that nothing is morally wrong and that either abortion is wrong or $2 + 2 = 4$. In Copp, *Morality, Normativity, and Society*, I called basic moral propositions "paradigmatic."

21 In a fuller discussion of society-centered theory, I would qualify this claim. It is correct that a basic moral claim is true only if a corresponding standard is relevantly justified, but there are other conditions necessary for the truth of some moral claims. Some details are set out in Copp, *Morality, Normativity, and Society* at, for example, 24-6, 28-30.

relations with its neighbors. This semantics treats moral properties as relational. If torture is wrong, it is wrong in relation to a given society, a society in which the currency of a standard prohibiting torture would best contribute to the society's ability to meet its needs. The moral standards with currency in a society form the social moral code of the society; a social moral code is a system of moral standards or rules that has currency in a society. Not all possible codes of this kind are relevantly justified or authoritative, of course. Moral claims are true or false depending on the content of the relevantly justified and relevantly local moral code.

Society-centered theory raises a number of difficult questions, including questions about its semantics and its metaphysics of moral properties. There are perhaps two sets of issues that are especially pressing. First are issues raised by the theory's treatment of moral properties as relational to societies. What distinguishes societies from other kinds of collective entities? Which society is the relevant one for assessing the truth of a given moral claim? Which society is the one, the needs of which determine my duties, for instance? Second are issues raised by the idea that the truth value of a moral claim is determined by the nature of the moral code the currency of which would best enable a society to meet its needs. What in detail are the needs of societies? Is there in general a *single* code the currency of which would *best* enable a society to meet its needs? I have addressed many of these questions in previous writings and I have introduced clarifications, qualifications, and amendments to the basic idea of the theory in order to deal with them.[22] This is not the place to go into detail, or to attempt to explain why I find the theory plausible. Some of the details are less important than others for my purposes. In this paper, I merely want to let the theory serve as an example of ethical naturalism.

According to society-centered theory, moral properties relate actions, persons, traits of character, institutions, and the like to the requirements of the moral code that is relevantly justified in relation to a relevant society. For my purposes, the important point is that moral

---

22 Copp, *Morality, Normativity, and Society*, chaps. 6 through 11. Copp, "Does Moral Theory Need the Concept of Society?"

properties are natural properties according to the theory. I proposed before that a property is natural just in case our knowledge of it is fundamentally grounded in observation and inference from observation. More accurately, a property is "natural" just in case any synthetic proposition about its instantiation can be known only *a posteriori*, or with the aid of experience.[23] So in order to show that moral properties are natural according to society-centered theory, I need to show that our knowledge of them is fundamentally empirical.

Consider the property of wrongness, for example. To show that wrongness is a natural property, according to the theory, I need to show that, according to the theory, any knowledge we have about its instantiation is fundamentally empirical. The theory implies that the property of wrongness – in relation to society S – *is* the property of being forbidden by the social moral code the currency of which in society S would best enable S to meet its needs. Call this the "S-ideal moral code." That is, in a context in which society S is the morally relevant one, the term "wrong" picks out the property that would also be picked out by the complex description, "the property of being forbidden by the S-ideal moral code." Call this property "society-centered wrongness," or "SC-wrongness." I take it to be obvious that we could not know anything substantive about *this* property, such as whether or not some action has the property, except with the aid of experience. Except with the aid of experience, for example, we could not know that capital punishment has the property of being SC-wrong. We surely could not know *a priori* that capital punishment has the property, for some society S, of being forbidden by the moral code the currency of which in S would best enable S to meet its needs.

According to society-centered theory, every moral property is identical to some relation between things that have the property and the requirements of the S-ideal moral code. I have used the

---

23 The issue is what human beings could know, given their nature. Perhaps a god could know *a priori* things that humans could only know through experience. If some humans can know certain things *a priori*, then these things are knowable *a priori* regardless of whether some other humans would need to rely on experience in order to know them.

term "*SC*-wrongness" to pick out the property that the theory implies to be identical to wrongness. We can understand the terms "*SC*-virtue," "*SC*-justice," "*SC*-rightness," and so on, in corresponding ways. On this account, for instance, the *SC*-virtues – in relation to society *S* – are, roughly, the states of character that all adults would be enjoined to exhibit by the *S*-ideal moral code. Since every moral property is like wrongness in the relevant way, every moral property is natural.

Given what I have said so far about society-centered theory, the theory might seem to imply that, in order to have any moral knowledge, we would have to be virtuoso sociologists. For example, to know that capital punishment has the property of being *SC*-wrong in relation to society *S*, it will seem that we would have to know a great deal about *S* and its circumstances so that we could know what a moral code would have to prohibit in order to best serve as the social moral code in *S*. So understood, society-centered theory will seem to be open to the epistemological challenges that we looked at before, as I will now explain. This should be no surprise. Naturalism attracts the challenges because it claims that moral properties are natural, and society-centered theory, as a kind of naturalism, makes precisely this claim. With society-centered theory on the table, then, let us go through the challenges one by one and ask ourselves how a defender of the theory might respond, compatibly with the constraints of naturalized epistemology.

4. Moral Belief and Naturalistic Truth Conditions

I begin with the fourth challenge. According to this challenge, if a naturalistic theory claims to provide informative reductive accounts of the truth conditions of moral propositions, there are the following two problems. First, there will be cases in which we take ourselves to have knowledge that *p*, for some moral proposition *p* held by the theory to have truth conditions *q*, even though we do not believe that *q*, and even though we have no idea that *q* might express the truth conditions of *p*. Second, even in cases in which we arrive at a moral belief *p* as a result of deliberation, where *p* is held by the theory to have truth conditions q, it typically is not the case that we base our belief that p on knowledge that q, or even on a belief or evidence that q.[24]

According to society-centered theory, for example, capital punishment is wrong just in case it is *SC*-wrong. And this is true just in case it has the property of being forbidden by the *S*-ideal moral code. The latter property is quite a complex empirical property. It appears that we might believe that capital punishment is wrong without believing that capital punishment has this complex property. And it appears that people typically do not base their beliefs about the wrongness of capital punishment on knowledge of or evidence of such a complex fact about capital punishment as whether it is *SC*-wrong. To be sure, people sometimes argue that capital punishment is wrong on the ground that it does not deter murder. And this claim is at least *relevant* to the issue of whether the currency of a prohibition of capital punishment in the social moral code would affect the ability of a society to meet its need for internal harmony. But the connection to issues about the ability of society to meet its needs is not often drawn. And many people who are morally opposed to capital punishment at bottom simply view it as abhorrent for the state to take someone's life when that person is in custody and therefore poses very little threat to anyone. Similarly, many people who take capital punishment not to be wrong have at bottom a rather visceral belief that a person who is guilty of murder deserves a similar fate. There appears, then, to be a lack of connection between the grounds of moral belief and the truth conditions of moral propositions that are proposed by society-centered theory.

This is no objection in cases in which it is plausible that a person's moral beliefs do not qualify as knowledge. Suppose for example that someone believes capital punishment is wrong on superstitious grounds. Suppose the ouija board told him that capital punishment is wrong. In this case, we would not be tempted to think that the person knows capital punishment to be wrong. Hence, it is no objection to point out that his belief is not grounded in any belief that, by the lights of society-centered theory, would support the truth of the proposition that capital punishment is wrong.

---

24 The objection raises issues about the individuation of propositions that I cannot address here.

The sharp end of the objection turns on the claim that our moral beliefs can *qualify as knowledge* in many cases where we do not believe, or have evidence or reason to believe, that the proposed society-centered truth conditions of our beliefs obtain. This seems to imply that the truth conditions proposed by society-centered theory are not correct. How could it be that moral propositions have the truth conditions that society-centered theory claims them to have if we can know a moral proposition to be true without having any evidence that, or believing that, or even having any inkling whether, the theory's proposed truth conditions for the proposition obtain?[25]

A defender of the society-centered view might reply that a moral belief does *not* qualify as knowledge *unless* it is grounded in evidence that the truth conditions of the proposition obtain according to the account given in the theory. This would mean that moral knowledge requires detailed sociological evidence regarding the content of the S-ideal moral code. The theory certainly suggests that we *can* acquire moral knowledge in this way, at least in principle. I myself have presented armchair sociological arguments in an effort to ground some specific moral judgments directly in society-centered theory.[26] But we rarely deliberate about whether or not the proposed society-centered truth conditions of moral propositions obtain, and it appears that we rarely have any inkling of whether the proposed truth conditions obtain. I think that we have moral knowledge in many more than these rare cases.[27] How could this be, if society-centered theory is correct?

This is a serious challenge, and I think that a corresponding challenge could be developed for any naturalist theory that proposed substantive

---

25 I take it that this objection is an epistemic variation on the famous "open question argument." See Moore, *Principia Ethica*, sec. 13.

26 See the discussion of moral issues, including abortion and cruelty to animals, in Copp, *Morality, Normativity, and Society*, 201-9, 213-6.

27 See Copp, *Morality, Normativity, and Society*, 237-40. See also David Copp, "Moral Knowledge in Society Centered Moral Theory," in *Moral Knowledge? New Readings in Moral Epistemology*, ed. Walter Sinnott-Armstrong and Mark Timmons (New York: Oxford University Press, 1996), 243-66.

truth conditions for moral propositions. I now want to argue that the challenge can be met. To do so, I need to show, or at least to make plausible, that moral belief is relevantly analogous to beliefs in other areas where we observe similar phenomena.

Consider our "economic beliefs," which have complex truth conditions analogous to the truth conditions attributed to moral beliefs by society-centered theory. Ordinary people would have difficulty explaining the truth conditions of their economic beliefs in any substantive way. Consider the proposition that I have a U.S. one dollar bill in my hand. On reflection, I hope it will be obvious that the truth conditions of this proposition are enormously complex. In order for this piece of paper to be a one dollar bill, there must be a complex disposition among the relevant officials and among the bulk of the population of the United States to exchange the piece of paper for goods or services priced at one dollar. But what must obtain in order for the given population to be the population of the United States? What must obtain in order for goods or services to be "priced" at "one dollar"? What must obtain in order for a person to be one of the "relevant officials"? Plainly, we can know immediately, on inspection, that the thing in my hand is a U.S. one dollar bill, and we can know this without having more than a vague idea of the truth conditions of the proposition that it is a one dollar bill. Indeed, one dollar bills could not fulfill their function in the economy if this were not the case.[28] Our beliefs about the presence of dollar bills in our immediate visual field are reasonably reliable even though, remarkably, the property of being a one dollar bill is a highly complex theoretical property in a theory that few of us know.

Given the example of the one dollar bill, it seems clear that we can know something even if there is a proposition that expresses its truth

---

28 This was pointed out to me by Elijah Millgram. If one dollar bills were counterfeited very commonly then matters would be different. In that case, the one dollar bill would not serve very well its intended function in the economy.

conditions and we do not know that it is true.[29] The example did not involve deliberation, however, and one might think that this is significant. But one can know something as a result of deliberation while having no inkling about its truth conditions. If you see that I have both a one dollar bill and a five dollar bill in my hand, you can perform a simple mathematical calculation and conclude that I have at least six dollars without knowing the truth conditions of what you know as they are laid out in economics. This is no objection to the economic theory of the truth conditions of propositions about money. Perhaps, then, it is no objection to a meta-ethical theory that we can have moral knowledge without having any idea of the truth conditions of our moral beliefs as they are laid out by the theory.

The familiar "reliabilist" strategy for responding to skepticism about the external world is basically to argue that we can have knowledge about the physical objects around us in circumstances in which we are detecting the objects by means of a reliable belief-generating mechanism. We can have such knowledge even if we cannot justify our beliefs about the objects by inferring them from data given in our sensory experience.[30] This strategy implies that knowledge is possible in cases in which we do not have knowledge of relevant truth conditions. But it does not follow that knowledge is possible without knowledge of truth conditions in a case in which the relevant belief is *not* produced by a reliable belief-generating mechanism.

Reliabilism therefore suggests a problem for our response to the objection about knowledge of truth conditions. We might concede that it is possible to know a proposition to be true without having any inkling of its truth conditions in cases in which the relevant belief is produced by a reliable belief-generating mechanism. We are reasonably

---

29 To give a second example, it is clear that we can know various propositions about water without knowing, believing, or having any idea of, the chemical truth conditions of the propositions. And the grounds of our "water beliefs" need not include any grounds to believe corresponding propositions about H_2O that constitute the truth conditions of our water beliefs.

30 One of the first to propose and defend "reliabilism" was Alvin I. Goldman, "What is Justified Belief?", *Justification and Knowledge*, ed. George S. Pappas (Dordrecht: Reidel, 1979), 1-23.

reliable, in at least a wide range of circumstances, in forming true beliefs about dollar bills. But, one might say, given the moral disagreement we see in the world, it is not plausible that there is a similarly reliable psychological process for generating moral beliefs. If this is correct, then to defend society-centered theory, either we must argue that there *is* a reliable mechanism for generating moral beliefs, or we must after all deny that moral knowledge is possible without evidence as to the obtaining of the proposed society-centered truth conditions.

The best response to this objection, I think, is to argue that, at least in certain contexts, some people can be quite reliable in arriving spontaneously at true moral beliefs and, moreover, their reliability in these contexts can be explained in a way that is compatible with naturalism. This is what I shall now argue.

5. Moral Sensitivity

In Harman's example, we imagine ourselves coming around a corner and seeing some children lighting a cat on fire right in front of us.[31] If we recognized what was going on, we naturally would know right away that what the children were doing was wrong. In contexts of this kind, we arrive immediately at a moral belief, and our belief might qualify as knowledge – assuming we are correct in our perception of what is going on. We might have no more than a vague and unhelpful idea of the complex truth conditions that would be assigned to the belief by society-centered theory. The example of the dollar bill suggests that this is no objection to the theory. But to cement this response, I need to explain *how* we can be reliable in such contexts in arriving at true moral beliefs *given* the truth conditions assigned to moral beliefs by society-centered theory, and *given* what psychology tells us about processes of belief formation. In other words, I need to show that there is or can be an epistemically relevant connection between our moral beliefs and the moral facts, given the society-centered account of what

---

31 Harman, *Morality*, 4-8.

those facts consist in. I will return to this issue after discussing the remaining three challenges to ethical naturalism.

To begin, I need to discuss the nature of the "moral sensitivity" that, according to the third of the four challenges, is crucially involved in leading us to our beliefs in cases like the cat example. In the cat example, even if the person sees that the children are lighting a cat on fire, she might not take it that what they are doing is wrong. This would be evidence of a lack of moral sensitivity. Ethical naturalists need to explain the nature and epistemic role of moral sensitivity.

It seems to me that there are three aspects to what we have in mind when we speak of moral sensitivity. One is a heightened tendency to notice morally relevant features of a situation. In the cat example, a morally sensitive person will not fail to notice that an animal is being tortured, or that it is screaming or fighting to get away from the children, or that it is terrified. A less sensitive person might not notice these facts about the situation. He might see that the children are lighting the cat on fire without understanding what this will mean for the cat. The second aspect of moral sensitivity is a reliable tendency to draw the correct moral conclusion from the noticed morally relevant features of situations, and to draw this conclusion as promptly as is morally appropriate. In many circumstances, this drawing of the correct conclusion would not involve conscious reasoning. In fact, in some circumstances, a need to reason consciously from morally relevant features of a situation to the moral conclusion would be a sign of moral insensitivity. In the cat example, a morally sensitive person who could see what was happening would immediately realize that it was morally unacceptable. In other circumstances, although some reasoning would be appropriate, protracted reasoning would be untoward. This explains why I say that moral sensitivity involves a tendency to draw the correct conclusion "as promptly as is morally appropriate." The third aspect of sensitivity is a reliable tendency to be motivated in the morally appropriate way. A morally sensitive person in the cat example would want to stop the children from hurting the cat.

These features can come apart, but in a morally sensitive person they do not come apart. A morally sensitive person in the cat example would notice that a cat is being hurt, draw the obvious conclusion that the children are doing something quite wrong, and he would want to help the cat. A less sensitive person might notice that a cat is being hurt without drawing the obvious conclusion that the children are doing something quite wrong, or this conclusion might dawn on him several minutes later, or he might promptly draw the conclusion but callously walk away.

The epistemic significance of moral sensitivity should be obvious. The first and second aspects are kinds of epistemic sensitivity. They are tendencies to notice morally relevant things and to draw correct conclusions. There are analogous epistemic sensitivities with respect to other subject matters. There are sensitivities to garden variety facts, such as horticultural, geographic, fiscal, and emotional facts. Some people notice flowers and pay attention to their names. They readily recognize flowers when they see them. Some people have a "geographic sensitivity." They are keenly aware of where they are and where they are going. Other people are noticeably lacking in geographic sensitivity, getting lost quite easily, having difficulty orienting themselves to maps, not knowing which way is north and which way is back the way they came. Children and many adults in our society have a sensitivity to dollar bills, having a keen tendency to notice unattached bills – bills lying on the sidewalk, for example – and to grab them when possible. Some people have a keen awareness of the emotions of other people, being quite well attuned to the symptoms of how others are feeling and being quite accurate in the conclusions they draw about their feelings. People who lack this kind of sensitivity to emotions might not notice when a friend is feeling embarrassed or uncomfortable or self-satisfied or content. Moreover, emotional sensitivity is clearly an empirical sensitivity, since the emotions are empirical phenomena. Of course, since the emotions are morally relevant, moral sensitivity will involve emotional sensitivity, but the two kinds of sensitivity are nevertheless distinguishable since one could conceivably be emotionally sensitive without being morally sensitive.

There are motivational aspects of some of the garden variety sensitivities that are analogous to the motivational aspect of moral sensitivity. People with a horticultural sensitivity care about flowers. People with a geographic sensitivity might feel uncomfortable if they do not know where they are or which way is north. People with a keen sensitivity to available dollar bills typically are motivated to grab the bills, and this motivation partly explains their sensitivity. Emotional sensitivity also has a motivational aspect. A person who is sensitive to the emotions of others does not merely detect these emotions with unusual accuracy. She also responds to them in appropriate ways. If someone who is keenly aware of the fear that other people feel uses her awareness to make herself a more efficient torturer, we would not want to describe her as "emotionally sensitive." We reserve the term "emotionally sensitive" for people who not only have a keen and accurate awareness of people's emotions, but who respond to the emotions they perceive with appropriate concern and compassion. This terminological restriction does not change the fact that emotional sensitivity is a sensitivity to an empirical aspect of persons.

It appears, then, that the existence, epistemic significance, and motivational aspects of moral sensitivity are no problem for ethical naturalism. The basic idea is this. We can acquire knowledge or conceptual frameworks, the having of which enables us, in noticing things, to conceptualize them relevantly and to draw correct conclusions about them. We can also come to care about the relevant kinds of things. The example of "dollar bill sensitivity" illustrates this basic idea, and, according to society-centered theory, "dollar bill sensitivity" is relevantly analogous to moral sensitivity. This basic idea will be articulated more fully in what follows.

6. Moral Reasoning

The first two challenges to naturalism turn on the claim that moral reasoning is not a kind of empirical theorizing of the sort that we would expect if naturalism were true. In order to address these objections, I need to begin with a discussion of moral learning.

On any plausible view, we acquire our initial moral attitudes and beliefs early in our lives, through familiar kinds of teaching, training, and experience. We are taught to believe what our parents and other teachers believe, and of course their beliefs are affected by the moral culture of the society. There are constraints on the process that are set by our psychological and other characteristics, and these constraints presumably have an evolutionary explanation. This need not concern us provided that the explanation, whatever it is, does not undermine our justification for believing that the behavioral and judgmental dispositions that we come to have, as a result of the process, can be reliable in leading us to form true moral beliefs.[32]

One quite important factor is that humans have limited psychological and intellectual capacities. We are better able to understand and apply rather simple general maxims than to understand and apply more complex ones, and there is a limit to how many such maxims we can usefully be taught to use or trained to follow. Because of these limits, and because also of the variable circumstances we encounter from time to time, we could not be explicitly taught to have all the particular moral beliefs that it will from time to time be appropriate for us to bring to mind. We need either to be taught general rules or to be trained to have certain key judgmental dispositions. We might be taught that torture is wrong, for example, and be taught also to have an aversion to animals being in pain, so that when we see a cat being caused terrible pain we would both have an aversion to this and tend to judge it to be wrong. We would almost certainly be taught simply that torture is wrong rather than being explicitly taught, for each kind of animal that could be tortured, taken one at a time, that it is wrong to torture animals of that kind. That is, we need to be given a relatively small but not insignificant number of rather general behavioral and judgmental dispositions as well as to be brought to believe a number of corresponding general moral maxims or principles. It is reasonable therefore to suppose that the *S*-ideal moral code would consist of a number of general principles and maxims.[33]

The behavioral and judgmental dispositions I have been discussing ground our moral sensitivity, which is our tendency in some

---

32 Walter Sinnott-Armstrong pointed out, in correspondence, that evolutionary explanations of processes of belief formation can explain why these processes are sometimes not reliable, as in the case of explanations of visual and cognitive illusions.

33 The *S*-ideal code obviously would not consist solely of a master standard calling on people to act on the standard or standards, whatever they are, that would be part of the moral code whose currency in the society would best enable the society to meet its needs. If it consisted solely of a master standard, it would be rather more familiar, substantive, and concrete standard, such as, perhaps, a utilitarian standard.

circumstances, such as in the cat example, to respond immediately with a moral judgment and an emotional stance. The third challenge to naturalism drew attention to moral sensitivity. The dispositions in question also underwrite our tendency to have moral beliefs even if we are unable to state their truth conditions in helpful terms. The fourth challenge to naturalism doubted that we could have knowledge in such cases.

Let me now turn to the first and second objections, the objections about moral reasoning. The general principles we come to believe license us to draw relevant inferences. The second challenge drew our attention to the immediacy of many such inferences and argued that they are not inferences of the kinds we find in empirical reasoning. We might reason, for instance, that if thus and so were done to a cat, it would experience enormous pain, and so it would suffer torture, and, since torture is wrong, it would be wrong to do thus and so to the cat. We can call this reasoning "subsumption" since it is a matter of subsuming cases under general rules or principles. The first challenge drew our attention to the kind of reflection we engage in when we encounter cases to which our principles do not straightforwardly apply, including cases of special complexity and cases of a kind we have not encountered before. Moral reflection can lead us to extend or to amend our principles, or to refine them in the face of anomalies, such as failures of coherence among our principles, or between our principles and the non-moral facts when principles have non-moral presuppositions. We can reflect on our overall moral view with the goal of increasing its coherence. Reasoning of this kind is given an idealized characterization in Rawlsian wide reflective equilibrium theory, according to which the aim of moral theorizing is to arrive at moral principles that we would accept in a "wide reflective equilibrium."[34] The first of the challenges asserts that moral reflection of this kind is not empirical. It is not an instance of empirical theorizing or reasoning.

----

34 See John Rawls, *A Theory of Justice* (Cambridge: Harvard University Press, 1971). See also Norman Daniels, "Wide Reflective Equilibrium and Theory Acceptance in Ethics," *Journal of Philosophy* 76 (1979): 256-82.

The first two challenges to naturalism claim, then, that the characteristic kinds of moral reasoning are not instances of empirical reasoning. They are not instances of ordinary inductive inference, inference to the best explanation, or empirical theorizing. They are rather cases of subsuming a case under a general rule, of seeing a particular as an instance of a kind, or of drawing connections among general principles and refining our principles in order to increase the coherence of our overall view. But these are exactly the kinds of moral reasoning that we should expect, if the *S*-ideal moral code consists of a plurality of moral principles, as it seems likely that it does. The principles need to be applied to specific cases. Hence subsumption reasoning is to be expected. Moreover, if the principles are akin to those that make up commonsense morality, they can come into conflict and they do not always apply in straightforward ways to unfamiliar situations. We might need to reason about unusually complex moral problems, to extend our views to new kinds of cases, and to refine our views when we notice failures of coherence. Hence, reasoning toward equilibrium is to be expected. In short, if society-centered theory is true, we should expect moral reasoning to include at least subsumption reasoning and reasoning toward equilibrium. It is false that these kinds of reasoning are not to be expected.

Reasoning that is somewhat similar is found in areas that are uncontroversially empirical. For example, in economics we might reason that since recessions occur in thus and so circumstances, and since we are in circumstances of that kind, we are likely to experience a recession. This is an example of subsumption reasoning. In this case, the reasoning itself is perhaps *a priori*, but the premises are empirical. Also in economics, someone might prove a theorem showing that a certain kind of economy would reach an equilibrium in which all markets clear. This reasoning is analogous to moral reasoning toward coherence since it draws connections among various economic principles just as moral reasoning does among moral principles. In this case, again, the reasoning is *a priori*, but in order to use the theorem to cast light on any actual economy the premises must be at least approximately true of that economy. And our knowledge that this is so would be empirical. Accordingly, the fact that analogous kinds of reasoning are characteristic of moral reasoning is not an objection to naturalism. The mistake that lies behind the two objections about moral reasoning is to have an overly simple understanding of how we reason about empirical matters.

Of course, as we saw before, society-centered theory suggests that we *can* acquire moral knowledge by acquiring detailed and complex sociological evidence regarding the content of the *S*-ideal moral code and then inferring various moral propositions from the content of that code. It would not be plausible to hold that *all* moral knowledge is arrived at in this way. Yet if the theory is true, people surely must sometimes deliberate about a moral claim by asking themselves whether a corresponding standard would be part of a moral code that would serve well the needs of society. This point might suggest two additional objections. First, it might seem that if the theory were true, deliberation of this kind would be common. Yet it is not common, and when it does occur, it is not taken to be obviously probative.[35] Second, it might seem that if the theory were true, then since we could acquire moral knowledge through complex sociological theorizing, there ought to be a kind of professional moral expertise just as there is, or to the extent that there is, expertise in economics. Yet even if we agreed that moral expertise is possible in principle, we would not expect it to be more common among sociologists than among people in other occupations, and we would not defer to putative moral experts in the way we defer to experts in economics.[36]

Let me begin with the first objection. It is true that people do not commonly deliberate about whether the content of a moral code would serve the needs of society. Society-centered theory is not widely accepted, nor is it intuitively obvious. Some people accept theories that conflict with it, and have had their intuitions tutored by their theoretical commitments. But with these qualifications understood, I suggest that deliberation about the content of the *S*-ideal moral code does not seem intuitively irrelevant when it is couched in ordinary terms rather

---

35 Richmond Campbell urged me to discuss this objection.

36 This objection was suggested by comments made by Justin d'Arms and Walter Sinnott-Armstrong, in personal communications.

than the technical terms of the theory. I cite a newspaper article by an English vicar who argues explicitly for "the old moral universals" on the basis of the impact of their currency on the needs of society.[37] Anthropologists have argued in similar ways.[38] I myself have argued for various moral views, including views about the treatment of animals, abortion, civil liberties, and the legitimacy of the state, from the basic society-centered theory.[39] Arguments of this kind admittedly are rather rare. But society-centered theory suggests why they are rare and suggests that they will be rare even in ideal circumstances. For, in ideal circumstances, the S-ideal moral code would have currency in society S, and this means that people in S would generally have internalized its standards and would tend to reason from them in deciding what to do rather than to reason directly from society-centered theory. Even in less than ideal circumstances, as I have been arguing, we are taught rather general moral rules and tend to reason from them to the extent that we have internalized them.

As for the second objection, I want to insist, to begin with, that the idea that there can be moral expertise is not alien and should not be surprising. Millions of Christians and Muslims in the world believe there is moral expertise and defer to the views of the people they take to be experts. Nor is the idea of moral expertise necessarily based in religious views. Indeed, the idea that there can be moral expertise should be no more surprising than the idea that there can be moral obtuseness. Some people are morally vicious and insensitive, and it is possible, at least in principle, that there are people who are especially virtuous and who are unusually sensitive to morally significant

---

37 Peter Mullen, "What's Wrong Can Never Be Right," *Manchester Guardian Weekly* (December 4, 1983): 4.

38 D.F. Aberle, A.K. Cohen, A.K. Davis, M.J. Levy, Jr., and F.X. Sutton, "The Functional Prerequisities of a Society," *Ethics* 60 (1950): 100-11. They discuss sexual abstinence in relation to the needs of society (103-4).

39 See the discussion of moral issues in Copp, *Morality, Normativity, and Society*, 201-9, 213-6. See also David Copp, "The Idea of a Legitimate State," *Philosophy and Public Affairs* 28 (1999): 3-45.

considerations so that they are better judges of right and wrong than the rest of us. It seems to me that it would be difficult to deny this. Indeed, it seems to me that the denial that there can be moral expertise would have to be grounded in an antirealist meta-ethical view such as, perhaps, J.L. Mackie's error theory.[40] Not even noncognitivist or expressivist theories such as the theories of Simon Blackburn and Allan Gibbard are committed to denying the possibility of moral expertise.[41] And typical normative theories, such as utilitarian and Kantian theories, imply that it is possible in principle for some people to be better judges of right and wrong than the rest of us. It is true that we are morally responsible for our own decisions. We cannot avoid this responsibility by deferring to a putative expert. If we decide to accept someone's advice, we can be held responsible both for our choice of advisor and for acting on the advisor's advice. If we act on bad advice, we can be blameworthy for doing so, although if we acted in good faith and were careful in choosing an advisor, the blame might be mitigated. In any event, the important point is that it should not be surprising that my position implies there can be moral expertise, nor is this an objection to it.

It is true of course that a sociologist is no more likely to exhibit moral expertise than is anyone else. This is because the moral education and experience of sociologists, and their moral views, are of the same kind as the moral education and experience, and the moral views, of people in other occupations. According to society-centered theory, sociological evidence can be especially relevant to assessing the content of the S-ideal moral code, but the evidence has not been assembled, and, moreover, sociologists are not more likely to accept the society-centered theory than are other people.

---

40 Mackie, *Ethics: Inventing Right and Wrong.*

41 Simon Blackburn, "How to Be an Ethical Antirealist," *Midwest Studies in Philosophy,* vol. 12, *Realism and Antirealism,* ed. P.A. French, T.E. Uehling and H.K. Wettstein (Minneapolis: University of Minnesota Press, 1988), 361-75; Simon Blackburn, *Essays in Quasi-Realism* (New York: Oxford University Press, 1993); Allan Gibbard, *Wise Choices, Apt Feelings* (Cambridge: Harvard University Press, 1990).

7.   How are Moral Beliefs Linked to the Moral Facts?

Earlier, I set aside questions about the existence of an epistemically relevant connection between moral beliefs and the moral facts, and I also set aside questions about the epistemic credentials of the psychological processes by which we come to have moral beliefs. These questions now need to be answered. The problem is to explain how our capacity for moral sensitivity, as well as our capacity to reason about moral facts, come to be linked to what are *actually* moral facts rather than merely to the facts taken in a given society to be morally relevant. The problem is not merely academic, for there have been unjust societies in which corrupt moral beliefs were widespread. The underlying issue is to explain how our moral beliefs come to be linked epistemically to what are actually moral facts in a way that underwrites the possibility of moral knowledge. This is the central problem for moral epistemology.

We accept a number of moral principles. Our acceptance of them is a result of the initial moral teaching we were given combined with subsequent experience and reasoning. The principles we accept might or might not be true. And even if some principle we accept is not true, it might be an approximation to the truth. For example, we might come to think that torture is wrong except for the torture of non-human animals. I take it that this is at least an approximation to the truth, even though there is no justifiable exception that permits the torture of non-human animals, for, I assume, torture *is* wrong.[42] Suppose then that the moral principles we believe as a result of this process of initial teaching and subsequent experience and reasoning are true or approximately true, and suppose that the judgmental dispositions we have as a result of these processes tend to lead us to make true judgments. If these suppositions are true, then, I believe, the true moral beliefs we may come to have as a result of reasoning from the principles we accept, or as a result of appropriate exercises of our moral sensibility, might count

---

42 For an argument that society-centered theory supports a prohibition on cruelty to animals see Copp, *Morality, Normativity, and Society*, 204-7.

as knowledge. The explanation for the truth of the suppositions must be of the right kind, however. That is, the truth or approximate truth of the moral principles we accept, and the accuracy of our judgmental dispositions, must be due at least in part to the existence of an appropriate kind of causal connection between the moral facts and the truth or approximate truth of the relevant beliefs. Can we make it plausible that there might be such a connection?

The chief problem here for society-centered theory is to explain how it could be that the truth or near truth of our moral perspective might be due in part to the fact that the corresponding moral code is, or approximates to, the *S*-ideal moral code. To begin with, it seems unlikely that the truth or near truth of a moral perspective would be entirely accidental. If the principles we believe are true or approximately true, and if a large proportion of our basic moral beliefs are true as a result, this is *not* likely to be purely coincidental. It is likely to be a result, at least in part, of the fact that the truth conditions of the beliefs do in fact obtain. Indeed, on the assumption that society-centered theory is correct, it is likely to be a result, at least in part, of the fact that the standards corresponding to our beliefs would belong to, or be approximations of standards that would belong to, the *S*-ideal moral code. But even if all of this is plausible, a naturalist still needs to explain the nature of the mechanism or mechanisms, the operation of which could bring it about that our moral perspective approximates to the *S*-ideal moral code of our society.

There is, first, I suspect, a comparative mechanism. If society-centered theory is correct, societies do better at coping with their problems, other things being equal, to the extent that their members have true moral beliefs and subscribe to corresponding moral standards. And over time, other things being equal, we can expect the societies that are more successful at meeting their needs to thrive. Societies in which a large proportion of people's moral beliefs are true or approximately true and in which people subscribe to corresponding standards should do better at meeting their needs in their ecological circumstances than otherwise would be the case, other things being equal. Such societies should tend to absorb the populations of societies in the same or similar ecological circumstances in which the moral culture is less accurate to the underlying *S*-ideal moral code. Or the moral cultures of such societies should tend to be exported to societies in similar circumstances that are doing less well at meeting their needs because of the content of their societal codes. Moreover, many of the standards that would usefully be subscribed to are obviously so, and subscription to them by the members of many smaller groups would also contribute to the success of these other groups. For these reasons, it is likely that, with time, in at least some societies, and other things being equal, the prevailing moral outlook will tend toward the *S*-ideal code, the currency of which would best enable the society to meet its needs.

I believe there is also likely to be a feedback mechanism, a mechanism that involves a feedback between the dominant moral perspective or perspectives of a culture and the corresponding society's ability to meet its needs. In favorable circumstances – but, unfortunately, not in all circumstances – the mechanism would tend to bring about changes in the direction of the *S*-ideal moral code in cases in which the society's ability to meet its needs could be improved by such changes. And it would tend to stabilize the dominant moral perspective in cases in which the corresponding code approximated sufficiently to the *S*-ideal code.[43]

I take it that we have observed moral progress in the dominant moral perspective in American society over the past century. We have seen improvements in people's attitudes in race relations, in gender relations, in reproductive matters, in treatment of youth, and so on. And I would argue that these changes are improvements when judged by the criterion proposed by society-centered theory. The pressing question is whether these changes were due at least in part to the effect on the moral culture of the fact that the society was better able to meet its needs after the changes than before. This is a large issue that goes beyond the scope of this paper. But I think there is evidence that this was so. Race relations and gender relations improved at least in part, I believe, because the society could ill afford to waste the talent of African Americans and women who were often shunted into demeaning or undemanding jobs or unpaid work. In order to draw from these talented

---

43 For a more thorough discussion of a similar proposed feedback mechanism, see Railton, "Moral Realism," 192-7, 204-7.

people the benefits that their full participation could offer to the society, social attitudes needed to change so that full participation would be accepted. I think that many people understood these facts. Of course, they perhaps would have described themselves, and not inaccurately, as seeing the injustice of discrimination. And, partly for this reason, efforts were made to change people's attitudes, partly through legal reform and partly through more diffuse social channels. The exact mechanisms are perhaps poorly understood, and it is certainly true that there is a level of description on which the mechanisms have little to do with the needs of society. I believe, however, that there is also a level of description on which the mechanisms are affected by the needs of society, as I have attempted to illustrate.

The argument I have been giving depends on two suppositions. First is the supposition that the moral principles we accept as a result of the processes of moral teaching, reasoning, and experience are true or approximately true, and second is the supposition that the judgmental dispositions we have as a result of these processes tend to lead us to make true judgments. I argued that, if these suppositions are true, the explanation for this might well be of the right kind. It might well be that the comparative and feedback processes I described have resulted over time in the truth or approximate truth of our moral perspective. And, if this is so, then, I claim, true moral beliefs we have as a result of moral reasoning, or as a result of exercises of our moral sensibility, might count as knowledge. This is not to say, of course, that they *would* count as knowledge. It might be, for instance, that we believe truly that capital punishment is wrong, and the explanation for this might be of the right kind, but if we ignore the contrary beliefs of reasonable people who disagree with us, and if we have no response to their objections, then we should not be said to have *knowledge* that capital punishment is wrong.[44] My claim is simply that, under favorable conditions, we *can* have moral knowledge.

44　For discussion of such cases, see Copp, "Moral Knowledge in Society Centered Moral Theory," 262-4.

8. Naturalized Epistemology Revisited

We have now addressed the four challenges to naturalism. And I have argued that ethical naturalism has nothing to fear from naturalized epistemology. The main lesson of naturalized epistemology, I said, is that a semantical and metaphysical theory of a given subject matter can be plausible only if it meshes suitably with a psychologically and philosophically plausible epistemology. It would indeed be difficult to deny this.

There are philosophers who deny it, in effect, since they postulate a special faculty of "intuition" by which we acquire moral knowledge. They might postulate such a faculty, despite the lack of any psychological evidence that one exists, on the basis of arguments to the effect that such a faculty is required if we assume that there is moral knowledge. Moves of this kind run afoul of the scientific prioritism that is implicit in naturalized epistemology. I conceded that I know of no arguments for prioritism that would convince someone inclined to reject it, but naturalists will want to accept it. The bare idea that some of our moral beliefs are justified non-inferentially does not run afoul of scientific prioritism, however, and this idea might be viewed as a weak form of intuitionism. Since I think that true beliefs we come to have as a result of appropriate exercises of our moral sensibility can count as non-inferential knowledge, my arguments appear to support a minimal form of naturalistic "intuitionism."[45]

Naturalized epistemology does imply that the acceptability of my responses to the four epistemological challenges depends on their psychological plausibility. Of course, their psychological plausibility is an empirical matter that is beyond the scope of my work, but the kind of psychological considerations that would undermine

---

45 Robert Audi describes a "modified" form of ethical intuitionism in Audi, "Intuitionism, Pluralism, and the Foundations of Ethics." Given the restrictions he imposes on the idea of an "intuition," I do not know whether he would describe my view as intuitionistic.

my responses should be clear. I shall discuss one example, a theory in cognitive science that might appear to conflict with society-centered theory.

Society-centered theory makes prominent use of the ideas of a moral standard and a moral code, where a moral standard is a kind of rule, and a moral code is a system of such rules. I argued, moreover, that the processes of moral learning result in our accepting a number of general maxims or principles, which might also be called "rules," and I described moral reasoning as involving, among other things, subsuming cases under such principles. These features of my view might appear to put it in conflict with accounts of cognitive processing that Paul Churchland and Alvin Goldman think are supported by research in cognitive science and artificial intelligence. On the basis of "prototype" theory, Churchland has suggested that moral concepts should be construed as "prototypes" rather than as packages of necessary and sufficient conditions. Echoing particularists, he says that "One's ability to recognize instances of cruelty, patience, meanness, and courage, for instance, far outstrips one's capacity for verbal definition of these notions." Hence, he suggests, "it is just not possible to capture, in a set of explicit imperative sentences or rules, more than a small part of the practical wisdom possessed by a mature moral individual." He concludes that "a rule-based account of our moral capacity" is mistaken and should be replaced with an account that exploits the idea of a "hierarchy of learned prototypes."[46] Alvin Goldman describes a view he calls the "exemplar view" in a similar way as holding that "concepts are (sometimes) represented by one or more of their specific exemplars, or instances, that the cognizer has encountered." On the basis of the exemplar view, he argues that moral learning might consist primarily in "the acquisition of pertinent exemplars

---

46 Paul Churchland, "Neural Representation and the Social World," *Mind and Morals: Essays on Cognitive Science and Ethics*, ed. Larry May, Marilyn Friedman, and Andy Clark (Cambridge: MIT Press, 1996), 91-108. The quotations are from pp. 101, 102, 106. For particularism, see, for example, Jonathan Dancy, *Moral Reasons* (Oxford: Blackwell, 1993).

or examples" rather than the learning of rules.[47] It appears, then, that if Churchland and Goldman are correct, exemplar or prototype theory threatens my account of moral learning and reasoning, and might even threaten society-centered theory itself.

Let me set aside questions about the theoretical plausibility of prototype or exemplar theory, and about the evidential support they enjoy. This is not settled science. The important point, however, is that we do not have to choose between exemplar or prototype theory and the idea that we accept moral rules any more than we have to choose between these theories and the idea that we have concepts. The theories provide accounts of what concepts are, or of how they are represented. They do not imply that we have no concepts. Similarly, we should view the theories as offering accounts of how moral rules are represented, or what their acceptance consists in, rather than as showing that we do not accept any moral rules. Perhaps, for example, a person who accepts a "rule" that prohibits cursing has a concept of cursing that either is, or is represented by, a prototype or exemplar, and perhaps the rule is best construed as prohibiting actions that are relevantly similar to the prototype. On this understanding, the currency of moral code would depend on our having sufficiently similar prototypes. For example, the currency of a moral code calling for patience with children and precluding cruelty to animals might depend on our having sufficiently similar prototypes of patience and cruelty. But none of this is an argument against the idea that we accept moral rules, and none of it constitutes an objection to anything I have said.

In any event, I believe that ethical naturalism has nothing to fear from naturalized epistemology. I have argued that the moral epistemology I relied on, in responding to the four epistemological challenges

---

47 Alvin I. Goldman, "Ethics and Cognitive Science," *Ethics* 103 (1993): 340-1. Goldman cites Stephen Stitch, "Moral Philosophy and Mental Representation," in *The Origin of Values*, ed. Michael Hechter, Lynn Nadel, and Richard E. Michod (Hawthorne, NY: Aldine de Gruyter, 1993), 215-28; Douglas Medin and M.M. Schaffer, "A Context Theory of Classification Learning," *Psychological Review* 85 (1978): 207-38; William Estes, "Array Models for Category Learning," *Cognitive Psychology* 18 (1986): 500-49.

to naturalism, is relevantly similar to the epistemology of various other subject matters. Let me conclude by spelling out some of the details.

9. Conclusion

As we saw, society-centered theory holds that true basic moral claims are true in virtue of the obtaining of relevant facts about the content of the *S*-ideal moral code. But our moral beliefs are not typically grounded in evidence regarding the content of the *S*-ideal moral code. Few people accept society-centered theory, and few of us are in a position to decide what to believe morally on the basis of evidence regarding which moral standards would be part of the *S*-ideal moral code. Our early moral training and subsequent experience and reasoning do not typically give us any direct evidence about the content of the *S*-ideal moral code. Yet, if I am correct, we can have moral knowledge even if the relevant beliefs are not grounded in evidence that relevant corresponding moral standards would be part of the *S*-ideal moral code, and even if no one in the causal ancestry of the relevant beliefs has ever had such evidence. In this respect, moral knowledge is similar to empirical knowledge in many other areas of thought. You can know that dollar bills are green even if you do not believe this on the basis of articulated evidence that its scientifically explicit truth conditions obtain, and even if no one in the history that led to your believing it believed it on such a basis. All of this is compatible with society-centered theory.

Whether a given moral belief qualifies as knowledge depends on whether there is an epistemically relevant link of the right kind between the belief and the facts in virtue of which it is true. In cases where we have moral knowledge, the epistemically relevant link between our moral belief and the natural fact in virtue of which it is true is brought about through the genesis of the belief, which traces to our early moral learning and to subsequent experience and reasoning. If the moral perspective we have acquired through these mechanisms is true or approximately true, and if this is non-accidental and due at least in part to the fact that the corresponding moral code is, or approximates to, the *S*-ideal moral code, then a true moral belief that we have at least partly as a result of having this moral perspective might qualify as knowledge.

I argued before that the *S*-ideal code likely would include a variety of general moral principles rather than a single master principle. So, if our outlook approximates to the *S*-ideal code, we accept a variety of principles. In some circumstances, these principles might point us in different directions. When they do, we need to look for a single prescription, and we can do so by reasoning in the familiar way that begins with principles and prescriptions that we accept and looks for a prescription for the case at hand that best coheres with them. What is to be expected is that we have certain dispositions to judge, respond, and reflect, the nature of which is due to the combined effect of our initial moral teaching and training and subsequent experience and reasoning. Our dispositions to judge and respond enable us to have a special moral sensitivity to the morally relevant characteristics of situations. Together with dispositions to reflect, they explain how moral perception is possible, how immediate inferences are grounded in general moral beliefs or dispositions to believe, and they explain why reasoning that tends toward wide reflective equilibrium is characteristic of moral reasoning.

Suppose then that your belief that capital punishment is wrong is in fact true. You believe this about capital punishment, let us say, on the basis of reasoning from moral premises your acceptance of which traces back ultimately to a moral outlook that you were taught in childhood. Suppose that this reasoning has in fact made your overall outlook more coherent than it would otherwise have been and has also made it a closer approximation to the *S*-ideal moral code, and suppose that the moral outlook you were taught in childhood also approximated to the *S*-ideal code and did so partly as a result of the operation of feedback and comparative mechanisms of the sort that I have described. Under these circumstances, I think your belief could qualify as knowledge. If it did, it would qualify as empirical knowledge since it would rest on your experience and on the experience and observations of others and on the existence of a mechanism that tends to bring our moral perspective into line with the *S*-ideal moral code.

From the first-person perspective, matters seem different than they do from the perspective of meta-ethical theory. It seems that we can sometimes just *see* what would be right or wrong, without being aware of drawing any inferences at all. From the first-person perspective as well it seems that we can draw immediate inferences that are not like the inferences we make in empirical reasoning. Moreover, it seems that we can be morally perplexed even when all the facts are in. And in such cases of perplexity, it seems that our reasoning about what to do is rather more like *a priori* reasoning than it is like the reasoning we should expect to be engaged in if the issues were fundamentally empirical. These phenomena can all seem to undermine naturalism, yet I have argued that naturalism can make sense of them. Indeed, among cognitivist positions, it seems that ethical naturalism is the only kind of view that can make sense of all of this within the strictures of naturalized epistemology.

CANADIAN JOURNAL OF PHILOSOPHY
Supplementary Volume 26

Naturalizing, Normativity, and Using What "We" Know in Ethics

MARGARET URBAN WALKER

The provenance of "naturalized epistemology," so called, is too recent for the hand of Quine not to be still heavily upon it. But like its older relative, "naturalism," it is an idea rich enough to be coveted, and protean enough to be claimed, by diverse comers with different things in mind. While Quine's version of naturalized epistemology of science inevitably furnishes the backdrop for current discussion of naturalizing moral epistemology, it is important to pause over what "naturalized epistemology" can and should mean in ethics. To what extent is Quine's example of an epistemology *of* science that helps itself *to science* the model for understanding knowledge of and in morality? Does it require a view of moral knowledge as reducible to, or in a fundamental way furnished by, science? Or a view of moral theory as sciencelike in some way? I argue that the appropriate analogy is instead a holistic and reflexive epistemology of morality that helps itself to moral judgments and standards seen as answerable to the experience of the kinds of shared lives they make possible and necessary. This approach neither privileges nor rejects wholesale what scientific inquiries might have to say. In the spirit of naturalized epistemology, the importance of science to moral understanding is held subject to what else we think we know, including what we know morally.

My aim is to show that there are choices here that are deeply enmeshed in views about science, knowledge, and morality. I take morality, and hence the object of moral theorizing and moral epistemology, to be real-time, culturally embedded practices of responsibility. I see moral philosophy as a reflective but (for that reason) empirically burdened theoretical practice that is epistemically reflexive and normatively critical.[1] There is no question here of trying to defend the view as a whole; instead I want to illustrate how it exemplifies some features of a naturalized conception, with the effect of steering attention in directions that moral philosophers have been slow to go, and perhaps resistant to going.

My specific, interested, and constructive appropriation of naturalized epistemology is as loaded as anyone else's is going to be. But this is only "natural," in the relevant epistemological sense: there is no epistemic position outside (a great deal of) our knowledge. But *where* – that is, on what knowledge – we stand as we seek new understanding or revisions in the understanding we possess, and what some of "us" think of as "our" knowledge, is a question that must be opened. I am going to suggest our response to it should be morally and politically self-conscious, as well as epistemologically freewheeling.

1. How Quine "Naturalized" Epistemology

In "Epistemology Naturalized," Quine argued that, with the failure of reduction programs that promised firm foundations for mathematical and scientific knowledge, science might just as well explain itself.[2] "Epistemology, or something like it, simply falls into place as a chapter of psychology and hence of natural science" (82), whose job is to study the actual construction of a picture of the world from scant sensory inputs. Quine is unconcerned about the circularity of using empirical science to validate empirical science, since there is no alternative knowledge of our knowledge. "We are after an understanding of science as an institution or process in the world, and we do not intend that understanding to be any better than the science which is its object" (84).

This move immediately and persistently raised the question whether Quine's naturalized epistemology recaptured the *normative* mission of

---

1 My view is developed in Margaret Urban Walker, *Moral Understandings: A Feminist Study in Ethics* (New York: Routledge, 1998).

2 W. V. Quine, "Epistemology Naturalized," in *Ontological Relativity and Other Essays* (New York: Columbia University Press, 1969).

traditional epistemology to explain what constitutes *adequate* justification and *real* knowledge. The role of norms in scientific knowledge in Quine's naturalized epistemology is debatable.[3] Quine's view seems to be that the cognitive equipments of human creatures disciplined by "pragmatic" inclinations, like conservatism in theory change, simplicity of laws, and of course the ultimate "empiricist discipline" of predictive success, are quite good enough. Our inquiry into "how it is done" *in science* will reveal what it is like for it to be done *well*, for science is our best case of natural knowledge. Its practice embodies what is *to be done*, as well as what is done, in this pursuit.

---

3 Richmond Campbell claims that Quine views science as "free of" the effect of value judgments, but acknowledges that Quine in at least one context speaks of empiricism as a theory of evidence that "has both a descriptive and a normative aspect" ("On the Very Idea of a Third Dogma," in *Theories and Things* (Cambridge: Harvard University Press, 1981), 39, and 41 on the "empiricist discipline" that makes for "more or less responsible science"). See Richmond Campbell, *Illusions of Paradox* (Lanham, MD: Rowman & Littlefield, 1998), chap. 5. A useful discussion that rejects the "no normativity" view but recognizes ambiguity in Quine's position about normativity is Richard Foley, "Quine and Naturalized Epistemology," in *Midwest Studies in Philosophy*, vol. 19, *Philosophical Naturalism*, ed. Peter A. French, Theordore E. Uehling, Jr., and Howard K. Wettstein (Notre Dame: University of Notre Dame Press, 1994). Certainly for Quine it is no business of science to judge how the world ought to be, but this is not the same as judging what science ought to do in constructing and revising its picture of the world. And Quine invokes predictive success, conservatism in accommodating recalcitrant experiences, and simplicity of laws, as considerations in revising our web of belief (see, for example, W. V. Quine, "Two Dogmas of Empiricism," *Philosophical Review* 60 (1951): 20-43). Quine seems to like to label these appeals "tendencies" and "inclinations," but this doesn't disguise the fact that they are normative, i.e., parts of the practice of doing *good* science. See, finally, Quine's later discussion in *Pursuit of Truth* (Cambridge: Harvard University Press, rev. ed., 1992), chap. 1, 19-21, which calls naturalized epistemology a "chapter of engineering: the technology of anticipating sensory stimulation" (19) concerned with heuristics, with "the whole strategy of rational conjecture in the framing of scientific hypotheses" (20). Here Quine considers the constraint of predictive power not normative but constitutive of a "language-game" of science. I believe it is Quine's earlier views that have set the tone for dominant conceptions of what "naturalizing" is.

In the conclusion of another essay from the same period, Quine's triumphal teleology of natural science emerges unabashed. As he has it there, we pass from reliance on our innate similarity sense, through intuitive understandings of similarity, and then on to the scientific definition of theoretical kinds with explanatory significance, which need not owe anything to the innate similarity sense. So, "the animal vestige is wholly absorbed in the theory," providing us a "paradigm of the evolution of unreason into science." It is also an example of natural knowledge that spurs further knowledge which in turn rejects or corrects the original knowledge, or puts it into its newly discovered place. Yet this looping process by which what we (think we) know is corrected as we go farther on its very basis, has for Quine a *direction*. Even as we "live by bread and basic science both," it is science to which human sapience "rises."[4]

In naturalized epistemology as Quine first styled it under that name, we have the usually remarked elements of holism (the "web of belief" vs. foundationalism), fallibilism (any of our previously credited beliefs could be found in need of rejection or revision) and naturalism (there is knowledge of the world only through its limited sensory impacts on us, no knowledge *a priori*). These together disqualify an *indefeasibly privileged epistemic position* that epistemology as normative tribunal of all knowledges would have to occupy. But there is also the *scientism*, the vision of science as the mature culmination of all natural knowledge, science as that

---

4 W. V. Quine, "Natural Kinds," in *Ontological Relativity and Other Essays* (New York: Columbia University Press, 1969), 138. See also "Five Milestones of Empiricism," in *Theories and Things* (Cambridge: Harvard University Press, 1981), 72. Peter Hylton makes a good case that Quine's naturalism can go so far as to reject *empiricism* if science, improbably, validated nonsensory forms of knowledge like telepathy and clairvoyance (the examples are Quine's own). See Peter Hylton, "Quine's Naturalism," in *Midwest Studies in Philosophy*, vol. 19, *Philosophical Naturalism*, ed. Peter A. French, Theordore E. Uehling, Jr., and Howard K. Wettstein (Notre Dame: University of Notre Dame Press, 1994).

knowledge in and of the world than which there is not any better.[5] This makes science the operative normative tribunal for other kinds of knowledge of the world as well as all of its own parts (but never, of course, all at once).[6]

2. The Science Question in Moral Epistemology

Quine's founding discussion of naturalizing epistemology suggests a certain prototype of that enterprise: a global scientifically regimented holism and a particularly scientific naturalism. I argue now that this is but one option, and not the best one, for naturalizing *moral* epistemology. Here is a generic prototype version (NE) of a broadly "Quinean" argument for naturalizing the epistemology of scientific knowledge. Without vexing the question about Quine's views, I build into this prototype the demand that epistemology have a *normative dimension*. I build this in because I think even philosophers who place themselves far distant from the search for foundations of knowledge are nonetheless

---

5 Lorraine Code presents a detailed diagnosis and critique of the tendentious and unsupported assumptions about science, scientific psychology, and nature that structure Quinean naturalized epistemology. Although she does not discuss naturalized moral epistemology, her critique powerfully exposes the non-scientific ethos of *scientism* at several levels. See "What is Natural About Epistemology Naturalized?" *American Philosophical Quarterly* 33 (1996): 1-22. See also, Tom Sorrell, *Scientism: Philosophy and the Infatuation with Science* (London: Routledge, 1991), cited by Code.

6 Quine's own meager views on ethics confirm that science will be judge of ethics, at least: ethics is "methodologically infirm," because "lacking in empirical checkpoints" for those ends that cannot be shown instrumental (Quine says "causally reduced") to others. Our moral judgments, as also our propensity to extrapolate from some applications of ethical standards to others, can only answer back to our "unsettled" moral standards themselves, so "coherence" only and "no comparable claim to objectivity" is the lot of ethics. See "On the Nature of Moral Values," in *Theories and Things* (Cambridge: Harvard University Press, 1981), 63-5. Below I return to the idea that moral standards answer back to moral standards, although also to the experience of the world of those who live in social worlds in which these standards have authority.

reasonably disinclined to view anything as an epistemology that does not issue in at least, to use Hilary Kornblith's generous phrase, "constructive advice on the improvement of our epistemic situation."[7] Of course, in a naturalized epistemology, normative insight must be compatible with epistemology's being a kind of natural knowledge within the world, available through uncontroversial human cognitive capacities; the normative dimension must not interject itself from somewhere else, or enter through claims to insight prior to or beyond all experience. A normative dimension does not require that epistemology introduces some *sui generis* constraints, values, or standards from somewhere outside actual epistemic practices of several kinds. It might, for example, reflectively retrieve standards immanent in epistemic practices and try to understand relations of those standards to the practices themselves and to other standards of those practices, as well as to standards of other practices. I also use "real knowledge" as a dummy expression for whatever conditions for beliefs' being warranted one wants to plug in.[8] I am interested in exploring a structural parallel here, and I try to leave this schematic prototype extremely general. This will allow us to study some options for naturalizing moral epistemology in extremely simplified and broad form, as well as to see where the "normative" element reappears differently in the case of moral understanding.

> NE: The epistemology of science seeks to tell us under what conditions we have real knowledge of the world.
>   So, epistemology must have a normative dimension, its inquiries must distinguish conditions under which we are

---

7 Hilary Kornblith, "A Conservative Approach to Social Epistemology," in *Socializing Epistemology: The Social Dimensions of Knowledge*, ed. Frederick F. Schmitt (Lanham, MD: Rowman & Littlefield, 1994), 96.

8 I'm using "warranted belief" here in the fairly open sense that Michael DePaul does as "meeting standards that identify what would be epistemically good, excellent, or best." See Michael DePaul, *Balance and Refinement* (New York: Routledge, 1993), 74.

likely to have genuine knowledge of the world from those under which we have something else (belief that is not warranted).

There is no kind of purely nonempirical knowledge that could validate scientific knowledge.

There is no empirical knowledge with validity superior to scientific knowledge.

So, there is no kind of knowledge that does not include scientific knowledge that can be used to establish the validity of scientific knowledge.

So, the account of how we have real knowledge of the world must itself become another application of science. That is, we will have to use (presumptively genuine but always in principle fallible and revisable) scientific knowledge (our best knowledge and its methods) to explain the conditions under which we come to have such a thing as genuine scientific knowledge.

Now let's explore straightaway one direct extension of this prototype for naturalizing epistemology in the case of moral knowledge (NME1).

NME1: The epistemology of moral knowledge tells us under what conditions we have real knowledge of how we ought to live.

Moral epistemology must have a normative dimension, its inquiries must distinguish conditions under which we have genuine knowledge of how we ought to live from those under which we have something else (beliefs about how to live that are not warranted).

Moral knowledge is one kind of knowledge about the world (rather than about a transcendent or non-natural realm).

Moral knowledge is knowledge about which understandings of how to live are "valid" (true/right/acceptable/deserving of authority).

So, there is no kind of purely nonempirical knowledge that could validate moral knowledge.

> There is no kind of empirical knowledge about the world, including moral knowledge, with validity superior to scientific knowledge.
>
> *So, there is no kind of knowledge outside of scientific knowledge that can better be used to establish the validity of moral knowledge.*
>
> So, the account of how we have real knowledge of how we ought to live becomes another application of science. That is, we will use some (presumptively genuine but always in principle fallible and revisable) scientific knowledge (our best knowledge and its methods) to explain how we come to have such a thing as genuine knowledge of how we ought to live.

I have represented the matter of moral knowledge here under the generic idea of "how we ought to live." I assume this place holder can accommodate views with deontological, consequentialist, virtue and other elements, so long as these are views about how we ought to live. I have for the purposes of this discussion assumed that people express, defend, wonder and argue about, and teach their children beliefs about how to live, and that the question about moral knowledge involves asking whether such beliefs are or could be warranted.[9] I have included the "naturalistic premise" that moral knowledge is a kind of knowledge about this, our actual, world. Although a naturalist need not go in for naturalizing epistemology in morals or elsewhere, it is hard to imagine anyone interested in naturalizing moral epistemology not being some kind of naturalist about morality. But the idea that moral knowledge is in and of the world is meant in a fairly undemanding sense. It does not imply narrower naturalist commitments about moral

---

9 I like to think that this model could be adapted to characterize the justification of certain moral sensibilities, attitudes, or endorsings of norms if moral judgments are explained as expressive rather than descriptive, but I do not attempt to show this here. See Alan Gibbard, *Wise Choices, Apt Feelings: A Theory of Normative Judgment* (Cambridge: Harvard University Press, 1990) and Simon Blackburn, *Ruling Passions: A Theory of Practical Reasoning* (Oxford: Oxford University Press, 1998) for expressivist views.

properties or facts; it only suggests, on a parallel with NE above, that such knowledge as we may have of how to live is gotten in the world by ordinary cognitive capacities from our experiences of the world, which include our experiences of living with others and thinking about how we and others act and live.[10] Finally, I leave open the characterization of the validity of beliefs about how to live in order to leave open the possibility that multiple ways in which to live might be "validated" by inquiries into morality, and that there are different forms that this "validation" might take. Again, I think this allows for the structural parallel to emerge at a high level of generality.

This model raises a problem widely associated with scientifically naturalized moral epistemology, the "loss of normativity." Scientific theories with explanatory power and predictive value may tell how morality arises, is seated in our native capacities, and is transmitted in communities with more or less continuity, *without* being able to say whether any extant forms of morality are *morally* better or worse than others.[11]

---

10 I neither affirm nor deny "a" or "the" fact/value distinction, being uncertain what it means but certain that it means different things to different people. I consider ethical propositions *bona fide* propositions; but ethical propositions have distinctive and, I believe, multiple roles to play within practices of responsibility structuring social life. These roles include descriptive, expressive, directive, and perhaps other aspects.

11 The empirical-scientific study of morality is, of course, not a "value-free" enterprise. Few today will deny that scientific knowledge is imbued with epistemic norms, if not other kinds. Feminist epistemology has produced the most sustained contemporary philosophical defense (in varied forms) of the claim that scientific knowledge is also inescapably constrained or driven either by non-epistemic (for example, social, moral, and political) norms. For two good samplers, see *Feminist Epistemologies*, ed. Linda Alcoff and Elizabeth Potter (New York: Routledge, 1993) and *A Mind of One's Own: Feminist Essays on Reason and Objectivity*, ed. Louise Antony and Charlotte Witt (Boulder, Colo.: Westview Press, 1993). Some classics are: Lorraine Code, *What Can She Know?* (Ithaca: Cornell University Press, 1991); Sandra Harding, *The Science Question in Feminism* (Ithaca: Cornell University Press, 1986); Helen E. Longino, *Science as Social Knowledge* (Princeton: Princeton University Press, 1990); Lynn Hankinson Nelson, *Who Knows?* (Philadelphia: Temple University Press, 1990); Donna Haraway, *Simian, Cyborgs, and Women* (New York: Routledge, 1991); and Naomi Scheman, *Engenderings* (New York: Routledge, 1993). See also Richmond Campbell, *Illusions of Paradox* (Lanham, MD: Rowman & Littlefield, 1998) for a recent defense of feminist empiricism.

Naturalized epistemology of science might at least plausibly claim to have recaptured epistemology's normative role from *within* science, to the extent that sciences are *successful* practices of knowledge of how the world in fact is in some respects. In their respective domains with respect to the kinds of explanatory and predictive powers for which we want that kind of knowledge, sciences deliver what we want. We want to know how things work, in particular how the structures of things explain how they work; where applicable, we hope by knowing how things work to anticipate what they do, and make them do what we want them to, and not what we don't. Well-developed bodies of scientific theory deliver this, and deliver more of it as they are extended and refined. Thus many of us are already as sure as we can be (having given up on Cartesian certainty) that we have some of what we want and it will pay to follow the patterns by which we got it, at least if we want more of *that*. This is why, except to the philosophical skeptic, proposing to vet claims to knowledge by appeal to the ways we get such knowledge as science gives does not simply jettison the pursuit of norms, but supposes that much of science as practised embodies the relevant norms. That is, the several sciences embody such norms as conduce to obtaining the kinds of knowledge at which they respectively aim. (And that the norms in play at any given time are revisable does not mean that at any given time there are not norms.)

The relevant norms for moral knowledge, however, would have to be the ones owing to which moral knowledge delivers what is wanted from *it*. We want moral knowledge in order to know how to live. This is what beliefs embodied in actually practised morality or the simplified theoretical constructions of normative moral theory tell us: the necessity, importance, or superior value of, for example, human dignity, eternal salvation, the greatest happiness, harmony with nature, the preservation of natural hierarchies, proper respect for ancestors, nonviolence and universal compassion, or more or less coherent combinations of these or others. If the going moral norms (what we think we know morally, theoretically or on the hoof) *successfully* produce what is wanted in their respective forms of life, the question nonetheless remains open: is this a form of life we should want? This version of naturalized moral epistemology seems to have no way to supply the kind of normativity involved in people's living as they really ought to live. And if moral inquiry in either its philosophical or nonacademic versions is to retain its *normative* identity as an inquiry into what is *really* right or good, into how human beings get right how they *ought* to live rather than how they variously in fact do, it seems that moral inquiry must be something other than a purely scientific investigation.

This is not to deny that empirical findings of a scientific sort might fulfill a part of the empirical burden of moral philosophy. Insofar as moral epistemology needs, as it does, to understand what people know in understanding how to live *as they in fact do morally*, to that extent the parallel holds. Scientific studies of several types, for example, might well help us understand how people come to master the moral concepts in use, recognize the patterns of behavior their extant morality requires or suppresses, and cultivate the perceptions and feeling responses that enable people to bring expression and action into morally appropriate play, both in fulfilling moral demands or ideals as well as in understanding the terms of deserting or defying them. A very important part of moral epistemology is the investigation of the actual conditions of moral competence of various kinds. Naturalized moral epistemology should be eager to reap the benefits of whatever scientific studies of individual capacities or group processes successfully explain how we are able to share a way of life and to learn how to live within it (which does not always consist in living in accordance with it).[12] But this robustly empirical study, ripe with potential for scientific contributions, leaves us one question short of philosophical ethics. The missing question is: no matter how successfully some group of people sustain a way of life they happen to live, is the way they live how they *ought* to live? A naturalized moral epistemology that has been absorbed into scientific studies might give us the best accounts we can have of how they do it, without yet touching in what sense they should.

Just here, though, there is more than one way to understand the normativity problem. It might seem as if the kind of knowledge that comes in with asking whether a given moral way of life is *really* how to live cannot be any kind of empirical knowledge, and so must either be

---

12 One collection that takes up a variety of issues surrounding the meanings of naturalism and the relevance of empirical studies to moral philosophy is Larry May, Marilyn Friedman, and Andy Clark, eds., *Mind and Morals: Essays on Ethics and Cognitive Science* (Cambridge: MIT Press, 1996).

knowledge of something nonempirical ("transcendent moral reality," "non-natural properties"), or nonempirical knowledge of something ("pure practical reason," "the logic of moral language"). But these moves to transcendence or to knowledge *a priori* throw in the towel on naturalized epistemology for morality. Alternately, we might hold that aside from what we know about how to get around in a "local moral world," there is no kind of moral knowledge left over to have. This idea, however, can be taken in more than one way. It can be taken to say that there is nothing that could be an answer to that "normative question."[13] Or, on the contrary, it could be a starter for naturalizing moral epistemology. There is no knowledge "over and above," but there are further uses of the *same* kinds of naturally acquired moral knowledge we already have, together with whatever else about the world we think we know, to assess our and others' moral beliefs and our or others' ways of arriving at them.

3. Naturalizing Moral Knowledge

In line with this idea, now try a different naturalizing model, one that does not so much "extend" the naturalizing of science to ethics as take up the structural analogy for ethics.

NME2: The epistemology of moral knowledge tells us under what conditions we have real knowledge of how we ought to live.

Moral epistemology must have a normative dimension, its inquiries must distinguish conditions under which we have genuine knowledge of how we ought to live from those under which we have something else (beliefs about how to live that are not warranted).

---

13 The phrase "the normative question" is the centerpiece of Christine Korsgaard's *The Sources of Normativity* (Cambridge: Cambridge University Press, 1996).

> Moral knowledge is one kind of knowledge about the world (rather than about a transcendent or non-natural realm).
>
> So, there is no kind of purely nonempirical knowledge that could validate moral knowledge.
>
> Moral knowledge is knowledge about what understandings of how to live are "valid" (true/right/acceptable/deserving of authority.)
>
> There is no kind of knowledge that can assess the moral validity of a way of life that does not include moral knowledge, no knowledge of the validity of values that does not include evaluative knowledge.
>
> *So, there is no kind of knowledge that without moral knowledge can be used to establish the validity of moral knowledge.*
>
> So, the account of how we have real knowledge of how we ought to live becomes another application of moral knowledge. That is, we will use our best (presumptively genuine but always in principle fallible and revisable) moral and other knowledge of how to live to explain how we can come to such a thing as knowledge of how to live.

If we take seriously this approximation to a prototype for naturalizing moral knowledge, other facets of naturalized moral epistemology have to configure compatibly with it.

A naturalized moral epistemology will be holistic. But if we take (NME2) seriously, we need to rethink what kind of holism about knowledge it is plausible to endorse. "The" web of belief is a powerful image that retains the pleasing picture of knowledge as all of one piece, even as it jettisons the older architectural metaphor of a single structure with *fixed* foundations. But what is the status of the idea that knowledge *is* all of one piece? Surely an *a priori* conviction of the necessity of the unity of knowledge does not comport with a naturalized epistemology. Furthermore, (NME2) incorporates a commitment to natural moral knowledge. But if moral knowledge introduces a kind of normativity and forms of normative question open to natural investigation that some other types of natural knowledge cannot answer or explain, then it seems that moral knowledge (and perhaps other types of evaluative, practical, and craft knowledge) is a distinct type of knowledge, and we should not suppose that methods of discovery or patterns of validation are simply identical to or continuous with ones that obtain in other contexts. Finally, the image of "science" is apt to play a mystifying role in these discussions: is there a unified theoretical web of "science"? The "unity of science" represents a regulative ideal invested with philosophical hopes (akin, interestingly, to the reduction programs whose failure Quine remarks in introducing of the idea of naturalizing epistemology), not the known reality of a web of seamlessly interconnected theory, or even methods entirely homologous (much less uniform) in detail.

So it seems we have not enough reason to affirm a single web of belief, and some reasons not to. I suggest that a naturalized moral epistemology should opt for a *contextual holism* about knowledge. Instead of the view that every belief in the web is linked by some connections to all others, contextual holism would affirm only what we know: every belief is linked in some network of beliefs to indefinitely many others, including to normative standards that may be context-specific.[14] How and to what extent "webs" of belief overlap or intermesh is itself *open to inquiry*. Whether the "web" idea with its pleasing connotations of lithe transparency, springy flexibility, and tensile strength is apt for imaging the organization of our knowledges is *to be explored*. There is something after all very "unpragmatic," in its way, about Quine's web: it pictures a tissue of belief holistically hovering outside diverse action-repertoires, practices, relations, techniques and institutions that are involved in making available and vetting the status of beliefs. Open-ended contextual holism neither seals "morality" and "science" off from each other as separate language games nor pre-emptively unifies moral and scientific belief into a single field.

---

14 Wittgenstein's fitful but insightful treatment of the grammar of knowledge is one standard locus for this view in *On Certainty*, ed. G.E.M. Anscombe and G. H. von Wright, trans. Denis Paul and G.E.M. Anscombe, (New York: Harper & Row, 1972). See also Michael Williams, *Unnatural Doubts: Epistemological Realism and the Basis of Skepticism* (Cambridge, Mass.: Basil Blackwell, 1991), which rejects a global view of knowledge.

Of course, one approach to naturalism in ethics tries to preserve the autonomy of morality precisely by getting it off the secure path of science, lest it be "secured" (as in NME1) by the disappearance of ethics as a normative inquiry.[15] This can be done by making morality something natural that is other than knowledge. In this category come noncognitivist and expressivist views. I sympathize with this move in that I think it a distortion to picture morality as only, essentially, or even primarily a matter of knowledge. This slights the complex economy of feelings and the expressive and directive aspects of our moral practice and discourse. But I consider ethics as pursuing an understanding of morality, which provides *understandings* of ourselves as bearers of responsibilities in the service of values.

Instead, I reject two equations. One is the identification of "natural" or "empirical" knowledge exclusively with what can be known from within the world about the ways the world in fact is. The other is the equation of knowledge about how the world in fact is with scientific knowledge of the world. We sometimes know from within the world how the world might or could be *for* us, that is, how the world could

---

15 See Stephen Darwall, Allan Gibbard, Peter Railton, "Toward *Fin de siècle* Ethics: Some Trends," *Philosophical Review* 101 (1992): 115-89, for an anatomy of some contemporary metaethics organized by the issue of "placing" ethics with respect to "empirical science as the paradigm of synthetic knowledge." (The authors attribute the terminology of placing to Simon Blackburn.) In a footnote, they demur from the view that "objective knowledge" has a definite meaning and deny that it amounts to "knowledge as attained in the empirical sciences," leaving room for alternative conceptions of objectivity, as well as the corrective impact of an alternative conception of ethical objectivity upon understanding of objectivity in mathematics and science (see p. 126, n. 29). But the authors' admonitory remark that "Such 'placement' would enable us to see how much of morality remains in order" shows their own investment in the tribunal of science. In contrast, see John McDowell's "Two Sorts of Naturalism," which chastises "neo-Humean naturalism" in favor of a reality that encompasses our "second," moral natures, in *Virtues and Reasons: Philippa Foot and Moral Theory*, ed. Rosalind Hursthouse, Gavin Lawrence, and Warren Quinn (Oxford: Oxford University Press, 1995). But see also essays on Humean epistemology and naturalism in Annette Baier's *Moral Prejudices: Essays on Ethics* (Cambridge: Harvard University Press, 1995). There are varied alternatives to scientific naturalism.

be *better or worse* for us in some ways. Indeed, our knowing this is a condition for our understanding many ideas basic to morality, such as cruelty, suffering, and humiliation, or dignity, gratitude, and trust, and for identifying the states and relations these ideas represent. It is also true that much of our understanding of how the world in fact is and could be is available not only through commonsense knowledge, but through refined and methodic inquiries that are not scientific, or are of the more dubiously scientific sorts. Humanistic and critical disciplines, like history, philosophy, critical social theory, historical and critical studies of scientific practice, institutional genealogies, literature, literary studies, cultural studies, and semiotics, as well as in those scientifically lower-ranking social sciences and their still lower ranking parts, such as social psychology, sociological theory, ethnography, and their like, illuminate ways people live and how these ways are understood by those who live them. In sum, for moral knowledge and its improvement we must always use some of what we know about the world, and some of what we know that bears most crucially on moral knowledge and its refinement is not scientific knowledge. For a suitably generous naturalism, we and our experiences of the world and each other are in the world; how our world is, could be, and would be better or worse are among the things we can know from within our world about it.

In casting off global holism and scientifically regimented naturalism, I have pulled out the main struts of a "scientism" that can prop up some visions of naturalizing epistemology. Scientism is not (any) science, but an ideological vision of the cultural role and human significance of scientific knowledges. "Scientism" is a vision of a mythicized entity "science" as the ultimate source of valid answers to anything worth knowing and the tribunal of what could possibly be taken seriously as a question. Scientism is really a full-blown normative view; it is an ethics and a politics, not exclusively of knowledge, but inevitably of culture, authority, and society. That, however, is not something wrong with it. What's wrong with it is its spurious regimentation of scientific practices into mythic "science," and it's *a priori* imposition of incontestable and pre-emptive closure on our pursuits of understanding. What renders scientism ideological is its obscuring the variety, complexity, and fallibility of scientific practice, its claiming strictly universal (and necessary?) dominion in the realm of knowledge, and its borrowing the mantle of "scientific objectivity" when it is itself not science. Scientific inquiries don't need scientism. And naturalized epistemology should avoid the embarrassing irony of putting "science" in the place of an incontestable and universal epistemic tribunal, which was exactly what classical epistemology is usually understood to have hoped itself to be. It will be necessary to repeat: I am not criticizing scientific inquiries or saying that scientific method is an ideology. It is scientism, not science, that has no place in a fallibilist and naturalized approach to epistemology.

Freed from confining and reductive pictures of knowledge, it becomes easier to acknowledge what is essential to a naturalist and naturalized knowledge of morality. Moral knowledge needs all the reliable and useful empirical information of any type that it – or rather we – can get. Part of the point of seeing morality naturalistically is to dig into the idea that there is no prior restriction on what we could come to know about ourselves in our world that might not have implications for our beliefs about how to live. By the same token, moral knowledge is as open-ended, revisable, and ultimately fallible as any other kinds of natural knowledge. Here, as elsewhere, we use what we know, and accept that we are likely at any time to be wrong about something. And we must rest on some presumptive knowledge in order to examine where knowledge itself comes from, while this very examination may reveal that what we thought was knowledge was not what it appeared. A naturalized epistemology needs to be free-wheeling and fallibilist, which is to say *open* to the best and most contextually useful fruits of all inquiries and experiences. And the naturalized epistemology of morality, in particular, seeks an understanding of moral knowledge that is necessarily both epistemically and morally reflexive.

4. Normative Questions

What now of that "normative question," not a question of simply explaining the causes, organization, and effects of any individuals' or communities' moral behavior, but a question of establishing whether we *must* or *should* do what our going morality demands? This is a question about morality's *authority*, not merely its de facto power but its *rightful dominion* over us. It is easy to start thinking that "the normative question" is one big jackpot question about "all" morality that arises from some reflective standpoint outside of or beyond morality. It can seem as if this is a sort of super-question that requires a sort of super-answer, that is, an answer to the question "Is it *really* right (obligatory, good, etc.)?" that is of a different order from answers to those garden variety questions of "must I really ...?" and "would it really be wrong to ...?" or "how much does it really matter if I ...?" that arise about different matters and at different levels of generality in people's lives. I suspect that the idea that there is a separate, external question about morality's authority is rooted deeply in non-naturalist, and perhaps supernaturalist, thinking about morality that yearns for its validation by something "higher," be that God, human nature, the natural law, pure practical reason, or perhaps "science." Even theories of ethics that understand it as a human construction, like a procedure, or a contract, or a discursive situation, still often think that the construction that could answer the normative question must be an *ideal* construction. This is the idea that nothing any group of people is doing at a place at a time is – indeed, could possibly be – our touchstone in ethics when we ask whether a way to live *really* has authority.

But there cannot be *just one* normative question. For one has to stand on some part of morality to pose a normative query about some other; and there is always at least the possibility (although it is not inevitable) that the moral judgment on which one stood for those purposes at that time might come in question at some other. "The" normative question is not one question, but a kind of question that recurs applied to different matters or reapplied to earlier answers. And there is no way for it to be posed "outside" some moral assumptions or other.

The situation is no different for moral theorists. As naturalists, we do not hesitate to look at the facts about the formation of moral beliefs. The fact is that what and how we can think about morality depends on what we have learned in the context of our places within particular ways of life, questions within them, and perhaps comparisons between them and other ways more or less comparable. In *fact*, then, "reflection," in moral philosophy or outside it, is *on* or *of*, or better *from*, some bits of (putative) moral knowledge, some already familiar forms of moral reasoning, some extant norms of responsibility, that allow us to know that it is *morality*, what is right and good, that we are thinking about here. Moreover, a large mass of critical work in the late twentieth century maps the deliverances of "reflection" in moral philosophy onto specific locations in a given social field: moral theorizing "reflects" characteristic roles, expectations, and life-experiences or the absence of experiences that track race, education, national culture, religious heritage and practice, economic status, gender, age, sexuality, physical ability and other factors that account for different social worlds or very different experiences within the same social world.[16]

Actual moral ideas, practices, norms, patterns of reasoning, and paradigmatic judgments are in fact always in play in moral philosophy at the outset. The philosopher no more asks after the moral authority of "morality" from outside of it than does anyone reflecting on moral demands when the garden variety questions work their way to the surface out of confusion, temptation, or ennui. The moral philosopher may be more relentless, more systematic, and more logically acute in pursuing normative questions. She may invent in thought startlingly simple or idealized or schematic moral views the social realization of which may or may not be determinate, available, or habitable in reality; this, too, may have its uses. But in all cases of moral reflection, she starts where we all do: we start *from here*, for some "we," and some "here."

In moral theorizing, as at other times, we resort in all cases to what Christine Korsgaard calls "reflective endorsement."[17] If we are able to endorse morality once we understand what about us and world, especially our actual social world, grounds and enables the morality we

---

16 See Walker, *Moral Understandings*, especially chaps. 1-3 for a critique of epistemic placelessness and lack of reflexivity in moral theorizing, as well as structural and historical analysis of the emergence of the "theoretical-juridical model" of compact theory. See also chaps. 1 and 3 for examination of the feminist critique of gender and other bias in moral theorizing.

17 Korsgaard's initially naturalistic treatment of "reflective endorsement" as the way to answer the normative question unfolds into an argument for the universality and necessity of our valuing our humanity as a condition for acting on reasons, hence bringing back in a bit of the old *a priori* when it comes to securing morality. This view makes for interesting comparison with the naturalized version of reflective endorsement of actual ways of living. See Korsgaard, *The Sources of Normativity*, Lectures 2 and 3.

have, or if we can endorse a change based on the comparison between what we have and what we might, based on these same understandings, then this justifies the extant or revised morality's authority, its "normativity." Reflection can thus produce or sustain, as it can defeat or chasten, confidence in the claims morality makes on us. But we can only test our moral views by *finding them good or not* upon reflective examination. So the normative question requires the application of some morally normative standards or judgments in the vetting of others.

What results when some of our moral practices, judgments, or concepts pass moral review is that our confidence in aspects of ways we live is confirmed or perhaps enlivened; when they fail it is weakened or destroyed. But it is not as if there are our moral beliefs and our (always in part moral) reasons for them, and then there is our "confidence" in them, the way a cherry sits on a sundae. "Confidence" is not something we might have or not have about those standards we hold as moral ones. When we hold some ways we in fact live as "how to live," i.e., the right or better founded or more enlightened ways, this way of holding certain standards marks them as morally authoritative ones. When confidence wanes or is damaged, we are inclined to wonder whether the standards we have held as moral ones are in fact standards of some other kind (for example, etiquette or mores) or whether we have held the wrong moral standards. So, too, confidence does not replace knowing what is right or good; it is confidence *in* our knowing at least some of, or approximately, what is right or good. Our standards and judgments (or some specially central or important ones of them) being, literally *for all we know*, valid constitutes the *moral authority of morality*, whatever other powers of de facto social authority and inertial social practice hold the standards and supporting practices in place.[18]

---

18 Compare Bernard Williams's somewhat elusive appeals to "confidence" in Bernard Williams, *Ethics and the Limits of Philosophy* (Cambridge: Harvard University Press, 1985), 170-3. See also J.E.J. Altham, "Reflection and confidence," in *World, Mind, and Ethics: Essays on the Ethical Philosophy of Bernard Williams*, ed. J.E.J. Altham and Ross Harrison (New York: Cambridge University Press, 1995) and Williams, "Replies," in the same volume. While Williams seems to consider confidence an alternative to knowledge, I see our confidence as a kind of trust in what we know.

Naturalized epistemology of science needs to investigate belief-producing cognitive, social, and institutional processes with an eye to uncovering whether or not they are conducive to the kinds of truth the sciences seek, and in doing so uses with confidence what it seems most reasonable to think we already know.[19] Moral epistemology, whether practiced systematically by philosophers or in the event by any thoughtful agent, needs to investigate belief-producing cognitive, social, and institutional processes with an eye to uncovering whether or not they are conducive to the kinds of worth upon which a moral form of life rests its authority or in terms of which its authority is understood. But "worth" here is a dummy expression for some form of value or necessity that will not be identifiable independently of some standards of moral judgment already in hand. Indeed, we cannot so much as characterize what our or someone else's form of moral life is without importing some understandings of what to identify as the moral parts, and in what sort of evaluative language to identify them. Wherever we invoke some moral concepts, standards, and judgments to test whether some others "really" have the authority they purport, the ones we invoke are invested with our confidence in their representing what we (already) reasonably understand to matter morally. This does not prevent the very commitments in which we have reposed confidence from becoming objects of critical reflection in their turn.

An open-minded and empirically robust naturalism about morality readily discovers that morality is not socially modular: moral understandings are (indeed must be) effected through social arrangements, while social arrangements include moral practices as working parts. Our concepts and principles are given meaning by the practices they in turn make sense of. For this reason there is not nor could there have been a "pure core" of moral knowledge completely extricable from some actual social world or other.[20] That is why moral knowledge requires extensive empirical inquiry and intensive reflexivity

---

19 See Kornblith, "A Conservative Approach to Social Epistemology," 102ff.

20 See Walker, *Moral Understandings*, chaps. 2, 3, and 9 on the genealogy and implications of the "pure core" idea.

about both the moral and non-moral conditions under which we believe we know how to live.

A central mode of examination of our moral understandings is "transparency testing," which involves both moral and epistemic aspects.[21] We need to ask whether we in fact know how it is we *do* live in our moral-social worlds. In fact, in most societies, "we" do not all live the same lives, and "we" often fail to understand or do not try to understand how the places our moral-social worlds provide for us are the conditions for the very different places of others of us. Our intermeshed moral and social understandings may be incomplete, self-serving, distorting, or rigged; they may render the lives of some of us morally invisible, incoherent, or diminished. The moral values we "share" may be ones we do not equally freely endorse or enjoy. We need to discover whether what are represented as morally authoritative understandings are ones whose authority is or is not really earned by their being shown answerable to well-founded fact and critically tested moral standards. We need to explore whether practices that purport to embody values, standards, and judgments "we" share and in which "we" trust are really driven and reproduced by coercion, deception, manipulation, or violence directed at some of us by others. Where transparency testing of our actual lifeways does not sustain confidence that "we" know either how we do live or how to live, the understandings in play lose their *moral* authority. Then we really are left with mere customs, habits, or mores; with ways some people in fact live that are no longer credible as "how to live." But to discover whether authority is warranted and confidence is in point, we must bring to bear a lot of, and the most relevant and reliable, information we have about morality and society. This is especially so in moral theo-

---

21 The idea of "transparency" as an ideal of moral views or social orders appears in Williams, *Ethics and the Limits of Philosophy*, 101-10, and Korsgaard, *Sources of Normativity*, 17. Although she does not use the phrase, I have profited most from Annette Baier's application of what she calls a "minimal condition of adequacy" that a moral view "not have to condemn the conditions needed for its own thriving," that it not fail to acknowledge or deny acknowledgment to that which is a condition of its working as it does. See Baier, *Moral Prejudices*, 96.

rizing and moral epistemology, where we are promised a high degree of sophisticated scrutiny of the tenability of moral conceptions.[22]

5.   What Do "We" Know Best?

I have argued against a purely scientific naturalism, or a scientifically insupportable "scientism," lest we claim prematurely or irresponsibly for scientific theories or findings a relevance to morality that they do not have, or that we do not know they have. A different danger for naturalists, and perhaps a greater, is that preoccupation with science as our best empirical knowledge can turn our attention away from other kinds of inquiry that bear deeply and directly on our understandings of how we live and how to live. Between the Scylla of scientific naturalism about morality and the Charybdis of a transcendent moral reality accessible to "pure" reflection lies a great deal we can and already do know about our social worlds and moral theories and traditions that is crucial for testing our moral understandings. Above, I mentioned humanistic disciplines, critical studies, and the methodologically less rigorous parts of social and political theory and sciences as important resources for moral reflection, that is, for reflection on actual forms of life that claim moral authority for those who live them (and perhaps beyond). Some contemporary philosophical theorizing itself, empirically attentive and reflexively critical about its empirical burdens and moral commitments, offers moral reflection and moral theory materials it cannot honestly proceed without.

I am going to use here, very briefly, a single example of such empirically enriched but normatively motivated work that sharply focuses a point about the kinds of things moral philosophy needs to examine and who is likely to want to find them out. Charles W. Mills's *The Racial Contract* constructs a deliberately stylized theoretical model to

----

22 The thorough intermeshing of moral and epistemic considerations in the reciprocal relationship between understanding who we are, how we live, and how to live, might be a very rich case of what Richmond Campbell calls "fact-value holism." See Campbell, *Illusions of Paradox*, Chapter 7.

foreground both "the most important political system of recent global history – the system of domination by which white people have historically ruled over and, in certain important ways, continue to rule over nonwhite people"; the invisibility of this system and the issues it raises in mainstream ethics and political philosophy; the obscurity to, or outright denial of, this system by most white people; *and* the intimate relations among these.[23] Specifically, Mills argues that the tradition of social contract theory, still a hugely influential tributary of modern Euro-American moral and political theory, cannot be understood in its normative implications and historical reference without seeing the broad and deep Racial Contract – a set of interlocking political, moral, and epistemological assumptions and their effects – that underwrites it.[24] Mills, in effect, proposes that if contractarian models are honored devices in philosophy for exposing the logic of liberal political legitimacy, we ought to consider their potential for diagnosing the logic of politically legitimated racism in liberal polities. More broadly, Mills asks us to try examining the apparent contradiction of modern European moral philosophy as such: "an antipatriarchalist Enlightenment liberalism, with its proclamations of equal rights, autonomy, and freedom of all men, thus took place simultaneously with the massacre, expropriation, and subjection to hereditary slavery of men at least apparently human" (64).

In what he describes as a "naturalized" ethical account, Mills makes use of the large and expanding body of historical, demographic, anthropological, and critical studies of race, colonialism, modern European history, economic development, and exploitation of non-

---

23 Charles W. Mills, *The Racial Contract* (Ithaca: Cornell University Press, 1997), 1.

24 Among the facets of the Racial Contract Mills connects with the massive and grim historical record are: a "partitioned social ontology" and juridical elaboration of persons and racial subpersons (14); a racial polity that is obligated to the privilege of necessarily white citizens at the expense of nonwhites (12); a racialized geography that placed most human beings in a irremediable state of nature (13), their lives uncounted (49-50) and their lands unpeopled (49); an "epistemology of ignorance" that precludes understanding of social and political realities (18), produces "moral cognitive distortions" (95) and disqualifies cognition or cultural production of non-Europeans (44).

European lands and peoples. He also pays critical attention to aspects of philosophy's own history and to specific texts that have been passed over silently or left out of sight in perpetuating a particular version of a canonical history of philosophy. Mills's project is not a grand unified explanatory theory but a morally and epistemically strategic intervention, a "rhetorical trope and theoretical method" (6) for reorganizing perceptions of fact and by doing so posing questions about what theories and professional discourses of moral and political philosophy have seemed interested or uninterested in knowing about our world. If one looks where he does determinedly enough, it becomes a good deal harder to believe certain things or not to think about others. It becomes harder to think that Kant and other modern European thinkers created visions of an ideal moral polity and merely failed, due to lamentable but local prejudice, to imagine certain people within it. Mills makes a compelling case by direct textual and inductive historical evidence that it was integral to the construction of that ideal polity that certain people be imagined outside it. One is dignified not only by what one is, but by what, or rather whom, one is not.[25]

An ostensibly "universalist" tradition of ethical thinking about "man," "human nature," and "humanity" in Western philosophy, from ancient to contemporary times, has in fact consistently been understood and intended *not* to apply to the majority of humankind, female and nonwhite. Yet is seems to depend on who moral theorists are, and on to whom they give their accounts and are accountable, whether

---

25 For a primer of short and disturbing selections that exhibit the modern construction of race within Enlightenment terms by Enlightenment thinkers, see Emmanuel Chukwudi Eze, ed., *Race and the Enlightenment: A Reader* (Cambridge, Mass: Blackwell, 1997). Two sobering historical studies that document the enormous energy and evasion needed by Europeans to avoid the simplest path of taking Africans or indigenous people as *simply* other human beings who lived differently, even exotically differently, from Europeans are Olive Dickason's study of early North American colonization in the Northeast, *The Myth of the Savage: And the Beginnings of French Colonialism in the Americas* (Edmonton: University of Alberta Press, 1984, 1987), and Winthrop D. Jordan's *White Over Black: American Attitudes Toward the Negro, 1550-1812* (Chapel Hill: University of North Carolina Press, 1968).

they will question the significance of this. The ostensible universalism of most contemporary moral philosophy and the bowdlerized universalist presentation of its history conceals the actual history in which the enunciation of "universal" truths has not only coexisted with but has served persisting social practices of dividing, excluding, stratifying, subordinating, degrading, and dehumanizing the larger part of humankind. Most moral philosophers continue to import assumptions about the uniformity of moral intuitions, standard conditions of responsibility, or the universal recognizability of "common humanity," in a way that disguises the ways moral perceptions are characteristically formed in societies in which social *and moral* differentiation is nearly universally the rule.[26] Do we know whether our systems of moral philosophy even now are free of conceptual features or substantive assumptions that continue the actual tradition and the understandings it has in fact required? Do we routinely and methodically make sure that we use what we know to find out? Do "we" really know more about the evolution of social co-operation than about recent histories and ongoing dynamics of social subordination or imperialism? Or do these questions not seem important enough, or philosophical enough, for "us" to address? It depends on who we are.

In fact, it is overwhelmingly women who have explored the sexism of ethical theory; people of color, ethnically marginalized people, or indigenous people who have insisted that we know about racism or colonialism; gay, lesbian, and transsexual theorists who ask us to review the moral intuitions of a hetero-normative cultural universe critically. Not all of "us" know what others do, and not all of us try to, or care to.

---

26 The importance for moral philosophy of recognizing, not ignoring or obscuring, the pervasive fact of differentiated social-moral positions in human societies is a main theme of *Moral Understandings*. I have elsewhere examined several philosophers' arguments that presuppose, while purporting to prove, that recognizing the "common humanity" of other human beings is in some sense unavoidable. Sadly, it has been and continues to be avoided in numerous forms more often than not by human beings. See Margaret Urban Walker, "Ineluctable Feelings and Moral Recognition," in *Midwest Studies in Philosophy*, vol. 22, *The Philosophy of Emotions*, ed. Peter A. French and Howard K. Wettstein (Notre Dame: University of Notre Dame Press, 1998).

Louise Antony says naturalizing knowledge "requires us to give up the idea that our own epistemic practice is transparent to us...."[27] So too for our moral practice, and the epistemic practice, moral philosophy, that seeks to know it, from within it. In moral epistemology, we cannot but ask ourselves what we know best about science, morality, and social life, and how we know it. Yet here it is epistemically and morally urgent that we open the question that Moore would never have asked: who are "we"? And how, in point of fact, do we know that?[28]

27 Louise M. Antony, "Quine as Feminist," in *A Mind of One's Own: Feminist Essays on Reason and Objectivity*, ed. Louise M. Antony and Charlotte Witt (Boulder, Colo.: Westview Press, 1993), 202.

28 I thank John Greco, Richmond Campbell, and Bruce Hunter for their helpful comments on an earlier draft. An opportunity to present a shorter version of this paper in a symposium on naturalized moral epistemology at the Canadian Philosophical Association in Edmonton, May, 2000, helped me to rethink the final form of this essay. I thank the CPA for this invitation.

CANADIAN JOURNAL OF PHILOSOPHY
Supplementary Volume 26

Naturalized Epistemology, Morality, and the Real World

LOUISE M. ANTONY

"Our impartiality is kept for abstract merit and demerit, which none
of us ever saw." – George Eliot, *Middlemarch*, book 4, chap. 40, 1871.

Naturalized epistemology, as I understand it, is the practice of treating
knowledge – human or otherwise – as a natural phenomenon, suscep-
tible of investigation by the methods of empirical science. A naturalized approach to the study of knowledge differs saliently from more
traditional forms of epistemology in taking the existence of knowledge
for granted. Naturalized epistemologists do not concern themselves
with skeptical challenges. Nor are naturalized epistemologists much
concerned with questions about what counts as "knowledge," properly
speaking. They do not worry if a bird's natively specified program for
star-based navigation is "justified" for the bird, nor if the sub-personal
data structures and algorithms posited by cognitive psychologists can
be properly counted as "beliefs." The naturalized epistemologist is
interested in the explanation of anything that even *appears* to be a
cognitive achievement, whether or not it passes muster as "knowledge"
in some preferred sense.

This indifference to what some philosophers regard as the defining
issues of epistemology has provoked the charge that naturalized epistemology is not really epistemology at all. According to these critics,
the problem of skepticism and the analysis of knowledge are part and
parcel of epistemology's *normative* charge: to specify the conditions for
good knowing. But, they claim, naturalized epistemology offers only
descriptions of cognitive processes, replacing normative accounts of the
relation between evidence and theory with genetic, causal accounts.

As Kim puts the complaint, "Epistemology is to go out of the business of justification" (Kim 1994, 40).

Given the nature of this objection to naturalized epistemology in general, it might seem doubly misguided to urge that we take a naturalized approach to *moral* epistemology. If a naturalized approach to knowledge in general means eschewing the notion of justification in favor of the notion of causation, what more could a naturalized *moral* epistemology tell us than how we come to hold our moral beliefs? Interesting as that question may be in its own right, it's not the one we look to a moral epistemology to answer: *justification* of moral beliefs is what it's all about. Nonetheless, my aim in this essay is to explore some of the consequences of taking a naturalistic approach to moral knowledge. I think that naturalized epistemology has some extremely interesting and edifying things to tell us about *epistemic* norms, and I think its lessons have close analogues in the moral realm.

In the first part of the paper, I'll try to answer the critics who think that a fully naturalized epistemology leaves no room for the normative. I'll then explain what a naturalized approach has to tell us about the epistemic norm of objectivity, and why I think a similar approach yields insight into right and wrong. In both cases, I'll argue, the naturalistic perspective counsels us to attend to the actual conditions under which human beings do things – how they seek to know and how they strive to act rightly. We'll see then that the adoption of a naturalistic methodology not only permits the endorsement of norms, but offers normative guidance for knowing and acting within the real-world constraints that define the human epistemic and moral condition.

Naturalism – the Descriptive and the Normative

Naturalized epistemology is often characterized in terms of what Hilary Kornblith has called "the replacement thesis," viz., the thesis that traditional epistemology ought to be abandoned in favor of empirical psychology (Kornblith 1994, 4). It is this radical thesis that most disturbs critics of naturalized epistemology, for it seems to them to either conflate the question of how we *ought* to arrive at our beliefs with the question of how we *do* arrive at our beliefs, or else to ignore the question altogether. Naturalized epistemology thus conceived is held to entail not only a flat-out rejection of the normative aims of traditional epistemology (Kim 1994, 40), but also the repudiation of all *a priori* elements in the study of knowledge (Haack 1993, 119-20). And indeed, very few contemporary epistemologists are willing to defend naturalism in this form: even those who identify themselves as proponents of a naturalized approach to knowledge hasten to qualify their commitment. These epistemologists prefer to defend some weaker form of naturalism – one that holds that traditional epistemology is not to be replaced, but only to be somehow constrained or informed by the empirical study of epistemic processes. Thus Kornblith offers for our consideration a weakened version of the replacement thesis: "psychology and epistemology provide two different avenues for arriving at the same place" (Kornblith 1994, 7). If this thesis, rather than the strong replacement thesis, is true, then, Kornblith tells us, there is no danger of traditional epistemology's being replaced by or eliminated in favor of a wholly descriptive, wholly *a posteriori* science: "If the [weak replacement] thesis is true, the psychology of belief acquisition and epistemology are two different fields, which ask different but equally legitimate questions and have different methodologies." Susan Haack says that she wants to defend a "modestly naturalistic position" according to which traditional apriorism will take its place as "the philosophical component of a joint enterprise with the sciences of cognition" (Haack 1993, 118).

Of course, these "weak" and "modest" forms of naturalized epistemology have all the defects of liberal compromise over radical clarity: they forge a false consensus by making the proposal so vague no one can disagree with it, meanwhile doing very little to alter the status quo. What's the alternative to "naturalism," thus construed? The view that empirical psychology has *nothing* to offer the epistemologist? Who wants to be stuck saying *that*? *Nobody* wants to be naively aprioristic, any more than anyone wants to be crudely scientistic.[1]

---

1 See, for example, Susan Haack: "mine is, in a sense, a naturalistic epistemology: it is not wholly *a priori*, since it relies on empirical assumptions about human beings' cognitive capacities and limitations, and so acknowledges the contributory relevance to epistemology of natural-scientific studies of cognition. But this modest naturalism is very different from the much more radical, scientistic approaches which also go by the title, "naturalistic epistemology." (Haack 1993, 4).

There's a more forthright way, I think, to answer the concerns about the elimination of norms within a naturalized framework, and that is to challenge the conception of empirical enquiry presupposed by those who are scandalized by the "strong" version of naturalized epistemology. There are two points in particular that are wrong. First, it's assumed that a strongly naturalized epistemology can contain no normativity because science is a purely descriptive enterprise. Indeed, some critics consider that the whole point of naturalization, as Quine conceives it, is to eliminate the normative in favor of the descriptive. The second assumption is that a strongly naturalized epistemology may make no appeal to the *a priori*. The idea here is that Quine's attack on positivistic reductionist epistemology is essentially an attack on the notion of analyticity, which is itself essentially an attack on the *a priori*.

Now I do not deny that there is textual evidence from Quine's writings in favor of both these assumptions, especially the second. There's counter-evidence, too, to be found, for example, in *The Web of Belief*, in which Quine (with Joe Ullian) both describes and makes a stab at justifying what he himself calls the "virtues" of a hypothesis (Quine and Ullian 1978). But I do not think that the central issue here is or ought to be an exegetical one. As I see it, the core of the call for naturalization, which is simultaneously the core of the attack on the analytic/synthetic distinction, is a challenge to the notion that there is a *distinction* between types of knowledge-seeking, between types that do and types that do not depend upon empirical evidence. Let me explain the difference I think this makes to our assessment of the prospects for a normative naturalized epistemology.

As I interpret Quine's critique of positivism, the problem was not simply that positivistic epistemology relied on an indefensible distinction between the analytic and the synthetic. Rather, I think Quine saw positivism as failing by its own lights in the project of "vindicating" scientific practice. Carnap (at least on Quine's reading of him) offered "rational reconstruction" as a solution to a problem in *normative epistemology*: viz., if it is experience and experience alone that justifies belief, how can we justify belief in a science that contains both *a priori* elements and references to unobservable entities and processes? Carnap's solution was to a) segregate the *a priori* elements of theories from the empirical elements, b) explain the *a priori* elements as "conventional," and then c) display the empirical elements as arranged in a hierarchy of dependence on sensory data, where the structure of the hierarchy is determined by the conventions that generate the *a priori* elements. Quine's objection to this story was simple: it isn't true. There is no way to segregate *a priori* from *a posteriori* elements, the *a priori* cannot in any case be explained by reference to convention, and the dependence of theory on data is not unidirectional. Since it's a minimal condition on a justification that the grounds cited in the justification must be correct, the positivists' attempt to justify scientific practice by means of rational reconstruction must be counted a failure.

An important difference between my reading of Quine (which, remember, I recommend for its internal cogency rather than for its textual aptness) and that of the anti-naturalist critics is that they have him rejecting the whole idea of normative epistemology, whereas I have him rejecting *one particular approach* to normative epistemology. The approach he favors, I'm suggesting, is an approach that is constrained by the facts about our actual epistemic practice, in just the way any empirical inquiry is constrained by the facts about its subject matter. This does not entail eschewing all reference to norms; it does entail an openness to the question of what our norms are and what they ought to be.

Another way to look at it: the suggestion that there cannot be an *empirical* approach to a normative issue begs the central question against Quine, which is whether there is a sharp distinction between the descriptive and the normative. I take the blurring of this traditional boundary to be one of the many consequences of Quine's dismantling of the positivists' epistemological package. Within epistemology, the rejection of the analytic/synthetic distinction[2] is tantamount to a rejection of the normative/descriptive distinction, since it was supposed to be our tacitly conventional acceptance of the analytic framework principles that explained the normative force of logic – obviously this strategy cannot work if the framework principles cannot be articulated out in the first place. Moreover, the rejection of foundationalism means

---

2 I should say that I am speaking of the analytic/synthetic distinction in its epistemological form. There may still be a basis for an *empirical* reconstruction of a form of analytic/synthetic distinction, *if* there turn out to be any such things as "linguistic rules." See Antony (1987).

that there can be no part of a theory immune from revision; once the rejection of the analytic/synthetic distinction puts all claims on a par, *all* claims become fair game for empirical reconsideration. Recall that Quine does not say that linguistic convention *plays no role* in determining the conditions under which our theories are true or false; he says rather that there are no *limiting cases* of sentences true *by convention alone*. I believe something similar can and ought to be said about the normative: it is not that there is no normativity involved in our characterization of the world; it is rather that there are no limiting cases of purely normative claims that make no descriptive demands on the world at all.

What does it mean, after all, to say that normative claims differ in kind from descriptive claims? To me, it means that there is no domain of fact that makes normative claims true or false – it means the denial of normative realism. (It is no accident that the positivists were non-cognitivists about both logic and ethics.) My view, on the contrary, is that logic and other principles of reasoning do characterize features – highly general ones – of our world. In this I concur emphatically with Richard Boyd, who sees naturalized epistemology as integrally connected to realism, not only in the scientific domain, but in the moral domain as well. (Boyd 1995). He argues that the best defense of moral realism against traditional objections is to show, drawing from post-Quinean work in realist philosophy of science, that "moral beliefs and methods are much more like our current conception of scientific beliefs and methods" than the objector presumes (Boyd 1995, 299).

Yet another way to put the point: critics of naturalized epistemology charge that the naturalized approach begs one of the central questions of normative epistemology by taking the existence of knowledge for granted. My naturalized epistemologist counters that the traditional, *aprioristic* epistemologist begs an equally central question of normative epistemology by taking our knowledge of *norms* for granted. The traditional epistemologist may respond that there can be no question of knowing epistemic norms, since these are *a priori*. But such a response only raises a further question for the naturalized epistemology, viz., how do you explain the *a priori*, anyway? And this brings us to the second of what I identified as the mistaken assumptions of traditional epistemologists – their assumption about the status of the *a priori* within a naturalized framework. My reading does not have Quine rejecting categorically the possibility of *a priori* knowledge – it has him, instead, offering the outlines of an empirical *justification* of (at least some of) the *a priori* elements in our epistemic practice. Indeed, it seems to me that naturalized epistemology is the only non-theological strategy that has a chance of even explaining, much less rationalizing, *a priori* knowledge in general, whether it's knowledge of norms or anything else. Here's the sort of story that a naturalized epistemologist can tell: *a priori* principles are an integral part of human epistemic strategies. Our *access* to these principles is explained in terms of our ability to reflect on and theorize about these strategies. Our commitment to these principles is *warranted* by the success of the practices – like the scientific realist's explanation of the success of theories generally, we propose to explain the success of practices that rely on certain epistemic principles in terms of the truth (or approximate truth) of those principles. In short, the story that the naturalized epistemologist can tell about *a priori* knowledge not only leaves room for norms, but provides the first clue about what it might be like to have a rational justification for the acceptance of norms.[3]

---

3 Contrast the positivists' account of *a priori* knowledge in terms of *conventions*. Quine, of course, famously challenged the part of this account that was supposed to explain warrant, but when you think about it, you can see that it can't really explain access, either. We cannot really have *privileged access* to conventions, since what the convention is, and whether it is in force depends as much upon other people's intentions and behavior as on mine. Even if we allow that I can reliably introspect my own intentions, I can't introspect yours, and knowledge of what other people are doing cannot require empirical experience.

   Richmond Campbell has objected that this account doesn't really preserve the *a priori*, since it leaves so-called *a priori* beliefs in need of empirical warrant. But I don't think this is so. If we assume, as I am, a broadly reliabilist epistemology – needed, anyway, I think, on a naturalistic approach, then we can count the beliefs and practices traditionally classified as *a priori* as warranted so long as they are generated by a reliable process. It's the existence of a reliable etiology that warrants them – we needn't wait for a theoretical understanding of that etiology.

Approaching Norms Empirically

I've argued that much of the criticism of naturalized epistemology stems from a suspicion that the approach leaves no room for the normative or for the *a priori*, but that such concerns are ungrounded. It may be, however, that in allaying these concerns, I've only awakened others. I see these concerns as falling into two groups. The first is what I'll call the *liberal* worry (to continue the political trope): it is the worry that a naturalized approach to normative questions forecloses the possibility of *reform*, that such an approach makes it impossible to assume a *critical* stance toward the norms that human beings are discovered to obey. If these are the norms that we in fact endorse, would it not be illegitimately *aprioristic* to recommend others instead? Doesn't the naturalized approach mean agreeing that fifty million Frenchmen can't be wrong?

No. It's a mistake to think that a naturalized approach to the study of knowledge cannot issue in normative judgments. It may be that some defenders of a naturalized epistemology feel duty-bound to canonize current scientific practices, whatever they may be, on the bare grounds that this is what we do here, but this attitude is not mandated. Instead, as I see it, naturalized epistemology is concerned with explaining the success of human epistemic practice – but only to the extent that it actually *is* successful. A serious empirical study of the strategies that we actually employ in everyday reasoning can provide powerful evidence of the need for reform. The now famous work of psychologists like Kahneman, Tversky, Slovic, Nisbett, and Ross shows that in certain predictable situations, human beings who rely entirely on intuition and reflexive judgment reliably fall prey to a variety of "cognitive illusions" – we fail to take account of background probabilities, we assign overly high probabilities to salient possibilities, we systematically neglect certain logical options, and so forth.[4] Although such foibles are clearly part of human epistemic life, there is no reason, from a naturalized perspective, to endorse them, and there is every reason to criticize and reform them.

------

4 For a summary of the relevant work, see Stich (1990) and Stein (1996).

The critical process I envision here is no different from the one described by many philosophers and historians of science with respect to the development of a variety of scientific taxonomies, particularly biological ones. (And insofar as this is true, it supports my contention that there is no sharp division between normative and descriptive study.) Classifications of animals or natural phenomena often undergo revision in light of empirical discoveries of deep similarities and differences among animals classified apart or together: whales used to be thought of as fish (or so the story goes), but a more adequate biology tells us they are not fish, but mammals. So does a naturalized epistemology tell us that some judgments and inferences we thought to be sound are in fact fallacious.

But there's a second set of critics, whom we might call the *conservatives*. Their concern is not that naturalized epistemology will forebear from making critical recommendations; quite the contrary. The conservatives are worried that a naturalized approach will end up *overthrowing* cherished epistemic norms. After all, these critics may say, nothing in the naturalized picture is safe from critique: what counts as knowledge, what counts as a good epistemic norm – these and all other foundational questions become matters of the overall goodness of an empirical theory. Norms, on this view, are not self-warranting. They must receive *instrumental* justification: they're good if, and only to the extent that, they foster our epistemic goals, where these "goals" are identified, in turn, by *aposteriori* investigation of our actual cognitive activity, and not by conceptual analysis or other "first philosophy."

It's tempting to dismiss these concerns as alarmist. How real, after all, is the danger? What traditional epistemologist would want to say that the epistemic norms he or she endorses do *not* facilitate our epistemic goals? And what epistemic goals could a naturalized epistemologist come up with that a traditional epistemologist would eschew? But I think the conservatives have a point, one that becomes apparent if we look at a different kind of example. The cases mentioned above, in which we discover that human beings routinely engage in fallacious patterns of thinking, are all ones in which traditional epistemic norms are presumed and upheld. But if the naturalized approach is taken fully seriously, it must be admitted that there is a real possibility that traditional norms may instead be called into question.

I have argued, for example, that work in linguistics and cognitive psychology strongly supports the view that our most mundane and fundamental cognitive achievements – acquiring language, recognizing faces, understanding the behavior of our fellow human beings – depend upon our possessing strong native biases of various sorts. Some of these may be simply innate preferences for certain kinds of stimuli – human speech sounds, for example – over others. In other cases, they may amount to theories of particular domains. According to one intriguing theory of autism, propounded by psychologists Uta Frith and Simon Baron-Cohen, the disorder is caused by the absence of a "theory of other minds," an understanding, innate in normal humans, of such things as the meaning of various human vocal and facial expressions (Frith 1989; Baron-Cohen 1995). These findings cohere with and support the more general point made by Quine and others that human theories in general are vastly underdetermined by sensory evidence, to the extent that we must bring *to* the task of theorizing an array of tools for paring down the set of hypotheses consistent with our paltry bodies of data, or else flounder forever. All in all, I contend, these considerations show there to be something wrong with a norm of objectivity where this is conceived as perfect impartiality: it is not simply that human beings are not *capable* of genuine impartiality (though they probably are not); it is rather that, for creatures of our sort, the implementation of perfect impartiality would be an epistemological disaster.

The Bias Paradox and Epistemic Agency

I see this point – the importance of being partial – as providing considerable help to feminist epistemologists concerned to expose the pernicious effects of an *ideology* of objectivity – "Dragnet Epistemology," I've called it – that operates, *de facto*, to legitimize the opinions of the powerful, and to discredit (often as "biased") the viewpoints of subalterns. Once we can show that the features cited as evidence of partisanship in dissident voices are not only present in the mainstream voices taken as paradigms of "objectivity," but are, in any case, features that are endemic to *good* epistemic practice, we can show that there are no *formal* grounds for dismissing the dissonant voices, and, if we are dealing with people of good will, we can refocus critical attention back to its proper focal point – to the *substance* of the dissident's claims (Antony 1993, 185-225).

Another point of contact between naturalized epistemology and feminist epistemology on the subject of epistemic norms is apparent in feminist work that challenges idealizations within epistemology that abstract away from the material and social circumstances of human knowing. Feminist epistemologists have shown a great deal of interest in models of "situated knowing" – models that admit the variety of ways in which the human ability to know may depend upon our being placed in hospitable circumstances. The burgeoning interest in "social epistemology" seems to me to be directly attributable to feminist insistence on the *epistemic* importance – for real, embodied human knowers – of social interaction, of social support, and of trust in others. I have argued that a properly naturalized approach to the social dimensions of knowing shows that we not only do but must assign probative value to various "markers" of epistemic authority. This point, again, is crucial for the feminist project of challenging the adequacy of the processes that construct expertise, a challenge which, once again, attacks a norm of "objectivity" that counsels sublime obliviousness to such factors as the social position of the theorist.

But if I am right that naturalized and feminist epistemological work converge in their respective critiques of a norm of objectivity, this only means that they must face the conservative challenge together. The conservative demands at this point to know how far we are prepared to go in endorsing bias. Do we envision science as nothing more than the play of partisan forces? Do we mean to be saying that everyone should just take things the way they're inclined to, and make no effort to achieve a modicum of disinterestedness? What's to prevent science from turning into mere wishful thinking? Or political advocacy? Is that really what we want? Do we not want to condemn *prejudice*?

Herein lies an irony, at least for feminists. The fact of the matter is that the conservatives have a point – and a point that has particular urgency for us. We are, or should be, the last people in the world to advocate for more partisanship in, for example, science. We are the ones who have been arguing for decades that male hegemony over science has not only deprived women of intellectual opportunities and material, technological benefits, but that it has *distorted science itself* – that we know *less* than we would if science had not been developed exclusively through a male perspective. We have, in other words, criticized science for *being biased*. This does not sit easily with an epistemological position that insists that bias is not really such a bad thing at all.

This is the problem that I have elsewhere called "the bias paradox:" the problem that progressive complaints about the role of class, gender or other bias in scientific research tend to be self-undermining when combined with critiques of the norm of impartiality (Antony 1993). What's really needed, to solve the bias paradox and to answer the conservative critic, is some principled way of distinguishing the good biases from the bad biases. When I first wrote about this problem, I argued that what naturalized epistemology had gotten us into, naturalized epistemology could get us out of – that is, the same naturalized approach that disarmed any *general* attack on bias, could supply a principle for making the needed invidious distinctions. The principle I had in mind was this: the good biases are the ones – like the innate tendency to develop stereotypes of local flora and fauna – that facilitate the construction of theories that are *true,* whereas the bad biases are the ones – like racial stereotypes – that lead us in the opposite direction, or else take us nowhere at all.

Karen Jones, however, has argued that this approach to the bias paradox is unsatisfactory because it leaves the norm of truth too disconnected from the other norms that constitute our conception of good epistemic practice (Jones 1998, and personal correspondence). It is not only the norm of impartiality that seems now to be only contingently connected with truth-tracking; the problem arises for rationality, as well. To make truth a sort of "master virtue" as I do suggests that the norm of rationality is *only* instrumentally justified, that it might be legitimately abandoned in any case where some other strategy for forming beliefs leads more reliably to the truth. But the idea that rationality is simply one trick we have available in a grab bag of epistemic instruments makes hash of the very notion of epistemic *agency*. Commitment to rationality involves, among other things, a norm that bids us make our reasons transparent to ourselves as we reason – arguably that is what reasoning *is.*[5] To view ourselves as devices that simply undergo different forms of "registration" – with this reasoning thing being one form among others – is, arguably, to give up a conception of knowing as an *activity* at all. Thus, the problem Jones is raising can be represented this way: how do we integrate a normative conception of epistemic agency, according to which we ought to deliberate strictly on the basis of considerations we can discern to be evidentially relevant, with a naturalized understanding of ourselves as creatures whose finitude entails that we cannot get by epistemically without shortcuts and tricks of all kinds, many of which would not survive scrutiny by traditional epistemological lights.

This is the challenge – the conservative challenge *redux*, if you will – that I want to take up in the remainder of this paper. But before I do, I want to complicate the matter in one more way, by turning, finally to the question of *ethical* norms. I have already said, briefly, why I think a naturalized epistemology promises the best possible defense of moral realism; what I want to suggest now is that the details of the human moral situation raise the same kinds of challenge to the ethical norm of impartiality as the human epistemic situation, and that a naturalized moral epistemology therefore faces an analogue to Jones's problem. Consideration of the two sets of problems together will, I hope, be doubly illuminating.

Here is the problem in the moral domain, stated baldly: given the facts of our embodied human lives, the constraints of impartialist moral theory seem impossible to satisfy. I do not mean just that our spirits are willing but our flesh is weak – that is, I do not mean to be calling attention to the fact that we often do not do what we think we ought to

---

5 For a probing discussion of the assumption – standard in the epistemology literature – that justification requires some kind of transparency condition, see Henderson and Horgan (2000a). Henderson and Horgan argue persuasively that justification cannot be made fully transparent because of in-principle limits on computational size in human cognition and discuss the consequences of this fact for traditional conceptions of epistemology. They also endorse, however, my contention that intuitions requiring transparency must somehow be accommodated if we are to retain the core of our pretheoretic notions of knowledge and justification.

do. I mean, rather, that the demands of any moral theory that bids us take a disinterested and fully general view of the moral issues that confront us are demands that creatures who are embodied as we are cannot meet and still be moral agents. The situation, as I see it, is pretty precisely parallel to the epistemic case: just as our ability to gain knowledge of our world, given the constraints of our physical finitude, depends upon our *not* being epistemically indifferent to all the logically available options, so too does our ability to relate morally to each other – to exercise a moral quality of concern for other people – depends on our not in fact according the same kind and amount of moral concern to all others at all times.

And, as in the epistemological case, this theme is one that has been emphasized by both mainstream ethical theorists critical of impartialist traditions, and by feminist ethicists. Within the mainstream, there is, for example, Bernard Williams, who points out that a friend who pays a sick call to another friend is not acting properly *as a friend* if the visit is motivated by a sense of *moral duty* – whether this is determined by a maxim check against the categorical imperative, or a quick calculation of the effect of such a visit on the well-being of the human population as a whole (Williams 1982). The proper feelings of friendship, if present, preclude such considerations. A proper friend simply *wants* to cheer up a suffering friend – it is the suffering of that particular friend that prompts the visit, not the Moral Law or the Principle of Utility, and anyone who appealed to either of the latter to explain her motives would be thought monstrous. (I heard Williams lecture on this theme when I was a student in London. One of my British friends confided to me after the talk that his – my friend's – parents, with whom he had a cold and unsatisfying relationship, had told him that they had decided to have him in response to a post-war appeal to help re-populate the country.)

Feminist ethical theorists have sounded the same theme – that the perspective of "care" – a particularist, empathetic and pragmatic approach to moral decision-making – has been neglected in favor of impartialist, formalistic approaches (Gilligan 1982; Trebilcot 1984). Theorists like Sara Ruddick believe that this sort of perspective – what she calls "maternal thinking" – has been neglected largely because it is the perspective that develops naturally from the kinds of nurturing activities for which women have been, historically, almost exclusively responsible (Ruddick 1989).

The element of these critiques that I want to underline is this point: that there is moral *value* in certain kinds of partiality. It is morally admirable for a friend to be motivated simply and directly by the needs of that particular friend, or for a lover to side with a lover in a dispute, or for a mother to have faith in the innocence of a child charged with a crime. We call such attitudes "loyal." (From an impartialist perspective, it is puzzling how loyalty could be a virtue: if your lover is in the right, then you should side with her for *that* reason – if she's in the wrong, then you shouldn't side with her at all. There seems to be no scope for loyalty, per se.)

One final parallel: just as I believe it is politically important to explode the false ideology of Dragnet Epistemology by pointing out the role of various kinds of bias in good epistemic practice, so too, I think, it is politically important to remind ourselves of the value we actually set on certain kinds of partiality when the "fairness" of practices such as affirmative action are called into question. The idea of a meritocracy, I find, is an easy sell: most of the people I talk to about this – certainly most of my students – are eager to affirm their commitment to the principle that "all that should matter" is qualifications. On the other hand, I've yet to find anyone who thinks there's anything wrong with, say, putting in a good word with their boss for the son of a friend who needs a summer job. (The whole concept of "networking," after all, is premised on the idea that *connections* count – and I've heard of very few people who have a *moral* problem with networking.) Now various things can and will be said to justify these departures from pure meritocratic procedure – it's impractical to think you can find the absolutely best qualified person, lots of people are qualified enough so it's OK to use personal connections as tie-breakers – whatever. But once it's been acknowledged that meritocratic principles may be trumped, it becomes an open question whether considerations of racial and gender equity can trump them too.

Finally, a naturalized moral epistemology faces the same conservative challenge, complete with the same ironic twist: how are we supposed to account for the moral value of partiality, without throwing justice out the window? How do I give value to my child's well-being in an appropriately partial way, while staying mindful of the needs of other children that happen not to be mine? How do I negotiate conflicts between loyalty to friends and commitment to abstract principles of either a moral or an epistemic kind? These are real-world moral problems, and they are problems that traditional moral theory gives us very little help in answering. For my money, they're the kinds of problems that are really at the core of issues in "professional ethics," but they are barely touched by the currently popular curricula. Specialized ethical codes – I'm familiar with such codes in the areas of scientific research ethics, and collegiate athletics – tend to articulate principles so general and so obvious that no one would disagree with them. For this reason, they serve to foster the official fiction that the only threats to the integrity of research or to the preservation of sportsmanship are those few miscreants – the proverbial "rotten apples" – who are either too ignorant to know right from wrong, or too venal to care.

Alongside the apprehended necessity of frequent, public reiteration of one's commitment to lofty principles, there co-exists a public awareness that the codes and declarations are not to be taken too seriously in practice – an understanding that these documents are not meant to actually constrain anyone by ruling out practices that otherwise recommend themselves. The Mission Statement of the University of North Carolina announces that we, as members of a public university, are bound to:

> provide high-quality undergraduate instruction to students within a community engaged in original inquiry and creative expression, while committed to intellectual freedom, to personal integrity and justice, and to those values that foster enlightened leadership for the State and the nation [and to] address, as appropriate, regional, national, and international needs. (http://www.unc.edu/about/mission.html)

And yet anyone who appeals to this statement to argue for or against some actual policy – say, conditioning contracts for licensed products to companies' guarantees of fair labor practices, or aggressively promoting academically empty "web courses" – will be dismissed by the people in charge as a naive crank, an uncompromising idealist who can't come to grips with the demands of the real world. (I speak from experience.)

But while I am, of course, insinuating that I'm right and they're wrong in the particular cases I mention, I do not mean to suggest, by citing these cases, that the main problem here is hypocrisy. I do think there is a great deal of hypocrisy in this world; I've certainly contributed my fair share. But I do not think that the moral problems of the real world can be solved simply by our sticking more scrupulously to our principles, any more than the epistemological problems of the real world can be solved by our sticking more scrupulously to the norm of objectivity. It is too simple, much of the time, to condemn the advocates of "realism" and "pragmatism" as liars or cowards. The advocates of "realism" and "pragmatism" are on to something: they know that mission-statement principles are just not the whole story about how we ought to act. And if we are to forestall the kind of nihilistic cynicism that dismisses such principles altogether, we very much need a complete story – a more nuanced and complicated story that attends at an earlier stage to the real-life dilemmas that confront us daily.

Without getting too grand about it, I'd like to say that Hannah Arendt's assessment is right: most of the evil we face is *banal*. Consider C. S. Lewis's characterization of a fall from grace: Mark is a public relations officer at a large corporation and has been asked to fabricate an event for a press release:

> This was the first thing Mark had been asked to do which he himself, before he did it, clearly knew to be criminal. But the moment of his consent almost escaped his notice; certainly , there was no struggle, no sense of turning a corner. There may have been a time in the world's history when such moments fully revealed their gravity, with witches prophesying on a blasted heath or visible Rubicons to be crossed. But, for him, it all slipped past in a chatter of laughter, of that intimate laughter between fellow professionals, which of all earthly powers is strongest to make men do very bad things before they are yet, individually, very bad men. (Lewis 1996, 130)

The evil that most of us do stems from small missteps taken in non-propitious circumstances or rather in steps that *are* missteps for being made in non-propitious circumstances. It's because the missteps can so closely resemble the steps that in other circumstances seem morally right – cowardice or bonhomie? favoritism or loyalty? capitulation or compromise? community or chauvinism? – that we badly need a *realistic* moral epistemology. And this is what I think a *naturalized* moral epistemology might offer us.

Saving Agency

But now we have to confront what the conservative challenge *redux*. If we do take a naturalized approach to this situation, and modify our conception of morally permissible behavior by a recognition of our *de facto* moral judgments, which apparently condone a great deal that our stated principles appear to condemn, we must ask what sense we are to make of our own moral *agency*. How are we to represent to ourselves the reasons according to which such "tolerated" behavior is deemed morally permissible or even morally good, if our moral agency is partly constituted by our binding ourselves to the norms that these problematic moral judgments belie?

Once again, the picture that seems to be presented by the naturalized approach has our agency "dissolving" into an agent-less dynamical system that simply responds to a variety of forces: a principle here, a personal attachment there.[6] But this picture is repugnant. Impartial moral principles – for example – are not just "soft constraints" to be optimized alongside lots of others. Nor are we passive moral registers, mere devices for the detection of the good and the right. No – we are moral *agents*, which means that we represent our moral situations to ourselves and deliberate about how to proceed. At least this is how it appears to us, and if it turns out not to be true, it will mean, probably, that we have lost moral value itself.

So this is the problem that naturalized moral epistemology must solve, analogous to the one that naturalized epistemology in general must solve: find the norms that save the appearances, where the appearances include our sense of our selves as active knowers and moral actors. Or rather, what I should say, is that *any* epistemology must solve these problems, and, if any can, my bet is that it will be a naturalized one.

---

6 This is not to speak against connectionist theories of the *acquisition* of moral knowledge (see, for example, Paul Churchland's proposal in Churchland 1989). I have other things to say against such theories, but these other things have to do with the shortcomings of connectionist theories in general, and not with problems for applying connectinism to moral learning in particular.

Unfortunately, I'm not quite out of space, so I will have to say something about how I think the problem may be solved, and why I think a naturalized approach has the particular resources needed to do it. Let me just mention and set aside two general approaches within a naturalized framework that I do *not* endorse. One might think, first of all, that we can solve the problem by taking *utility* as a "master value," analogous to truth in the non-moral epistemic realm. I reject this approach for two reasons: a) I don't think utilitarianism is true (that's the main one) and b) I want truth to be the "master value" everywhere – this is still epistemology, after all, just epistemology in a restricted domain. The second approach that might recommend itself is to advocate a kind of "moral division of labor" (Amelie Rorty has suggested this to me in conversation); this would be analogous to various forms of "social empiricism," like those suggested by Helen Longino, Lynne Hankinson Nelson, and Miriam Solomon (Longino 1990; Nelson 1990; Solomon 1994). My problem with all such socialized solutions is this: if the social aspect of the proposal is doing any work, it's doing it by deflating or denying the kind of individual agency that I've made it a desideratum for a theory to preserve.

So what *should* we do? The first step, I suggest, is to mine the purely epistemic literature for parallels. So let's look briefly at the debate about human rationality, where the character of the problems looked to be "reformist" in nature, and see what lessons we might derive that might be applied in the more troubling epistemic cases and in those moral cases where an important norm is apparently called into question.

Kahneman and Tversky and others have demonstrated that the judgments ordinary people make in certain circumstances do not conform to principles of "best reasoning" – they will completely ignore base rates, for example, or will violate the priniciple of conjunction (the probability of 'p & q' cannot exceed the probability of 'p'). What can we conclude from such findings? Before indulging in wholesale self-deprecation, let's note two facts: First, notice that *endorsement* of the violated principles is also forthcoming under certain other circumstances. My evidence here is largely anecdotal, but many subjects (I speak again from experience – as a subject) will endorse the violated principles when they are presented abstractly – I've never seen anyone try to deny the conjunction principle, for example – and many can be brought to see that they have made mistakes. Second, note that the principles are extractable from human epistemic practice – they must be, since it is human beings who have discovered them. I do not mean to be glib about this: the point is that the principles were not just found in a book labeled "follow me if you want to live" – they were abstracted from reflective judgments of probability and validity, or inferred from principles so abstracted, where the process of inference itself provides further evidence of human commitment to the practice.

If we take the evidence for human beings' commitment *to* various principles of rationality and set it beside the evidence that they often violate these principles, the picture that emerges suggests that we are looking at a competence/performance phenomenon – that logic and probability theory are part of human epistemic competence, which, in interaction with other systems like memory and perception, produce sometimes imperfect performance. The trick then becomes getting an *accurate* delineation of the environmental circumstances in which the interacting mechanisms produce error. This may be hard to do – sets of circumstances may have features in common that are not obvious, and others that look similar may turn out to be crucially different. The work of psychologist Stephen Ceci and others shows that human "intelligence" is a much more complex phenomenon than either psychometrical or philosophical models presume (Ceci 1996). People's skill at deploying many cognitive abilities that might reasonably be assumed to context-independent has been shown to vary markedly from setting to setting. Murtagh (1985), for example, showed that the majority of supermarket shoppers instructed to optimize volume for price, without aid of either posted unit pricing or calculator, were able to make the correct choices. When the same subjects were later given the MIT test of mental arithmetic – a measurement, presumably of the subject's skill at performing the very mental operations the they had just employed – there was found to be no relation between test performance and shopping accuracy.

On this picture, deviations from norms evident in actual human behavior are still analyzed as errors: logic and probability theory are right, and our judgments are wrong, and the only question is, how did we goof? Typically, the answer will advert to some feature of our psychology or our circumstances that *limits* or *interferes with* the good judgment embodied in our epistemic competence. The analogue in the moral case would be the situation in which some deeply endorsed value should be implicated, but is not, due to the "interference" of some other faculty. Emotion and affection, of course, have been held by many philosophers (and many ordinary people, by the way – it's not right to lay this all at the hands of Enlightenment intellectuals) to be the main culprits. But this result will be deeply unsatisfying to the critics of impartialist and rationalistic moral theory: these critics do not think it's correct to view affective attachments and feelings as *amoral*, much less as *anti- moral*. At the very least, they want it to work out that many instances of partiality are morally *laudable*. And I think that's right.

The more precise analogue may lie, then, not in the cases where people are properly viewed as committing an error, but in cases where an apparently irrational decision-method turns out to work better than the method suggested by classical principles. Many such cases are described by Gerd Gigerenzer and Daniel Goldstein: they note, for example, the widespread reliability, across a number of domains, of a strategy he calls the "recognition heuristic": when asked which American city is larger, San Diego or San Antonio, 62 percent of U.S. college students in the study gave the correct answer (San Diego), as compared with 100 percent of their German counterparts. Gigerenzer's explanation of this discrepancy is that the German students, who know much less about medium-sized American cities than U.S. students, have likely never even heard of San Antonio, and chose the one city of the pair that they recognize. Since it is, in fact, more likely that a foreign city you recognize will be larger than one that you don't, reliance on the rule of thumb that bids you go with the one you recognize will serve pretty well (Goldstein and Gigerenzer 1999, 43).

The recognition heuristic, obviously, is not going to be completely reliable – it depends for its success on a variety of contingent conditions. The users of the heuristic must, for example, know a little, but not too much about the target domain. In this case, the U.S. students cannot use the recognition heuristic because, paradoxically, they know too much about U.S. geography. Because they are familiar with too many U.S. cities, recognition will not serve properly as a filter. On the other hand, if the German students had known nothing about U.S. geography, or if they had been able to recognize only the names of three or four U.S. cities, their recognition filter would have been too crude. Gigerenzer calls such heuristic strategies, which depend for their reliability on contingent but stable features of the environment, "ecologically valid." Lest you think that such strategems could have only limited value in real-world decision-making, consider this result, reported in Borges et al. (1999): stock portfolios constructed by polling 360 Chicago pedestrians about which stocks they *recognized* significantly outperformed portfolios constructed either randomly or by the advice of financial experts.

Here's another example of an ecologically valid heuristic: In a study of ER diagnosis procedures, it was found that a simple dichotomous choice test (or "classification and regression tree" – CART) that looked at a maximum of three factors did better at classifying patients as high- or low-risk for heart attack than a classical multiple-regression model that took account of nineteen known risk factors (Gigerenzer 2000; Gigerenzer and Goldstein 1999, 91). Why is this so? An analysis of the contribution of each of the factors to the explanation of variance reveals that the first factor – minimum systolic blood pressure over a specific time interval – explains a whopping percentage of the variance. After that, the drop-off for the other two factors incorporated into the test is extreme, and after the third factor, all the remaining factors contribute almost nothing.[7] In situations with this structure, a model that takes account of the neglibile factors is actually more likely to mis-predict in new cases than a model that neglects them. (New motto: Neglect the negligible.) As Gigerenzer points out, the more information a model is required to account for, the less robust it is – the less likely it is to work well in new cases. The problem, intuitively, is that the more information we get about a limited set of cases, the more idiosyncratic our data may become (Gigerenzer 2000). This point is, I think, identical to the point that philosophers of science have been making, at least since Quine, about the trade-off between simplicity of hypothesis and empirical adequacy (Quine and Ullian 1978).

What do these cases show? They might be taken to show that the norms embodied in classical statistical methods are wrong – after all, statistics is meant to be a guide to the best ways to draw conclusions on the basis of limited information. But I think this conclusion would

---

7 These data, from Breiman et al. (1993), were reported in Gigerenzer (2000). See also Gigerenzer (1999, 91).

be unwarranted. The cases do show that the utility of the models generated by classical principles are limited by empirical factors, not only by psychological factors that make using the models difficult for human beings – we now have electronic prostheses that obviate those problems – but also by facts about the distribution of information. The more successful strategies in these cases are not, therefore, irrational, and no longer appear to be so once we take the circumstantial facts of our epistemic situation into account. What the existence of ecologically valid strategies shows is not that the norms employed by the classical models are wrong or invalid, but rather that the circumstances of ecology make certain shortcuts better routes to the end goal of predictive validity than the classical computations.

But the availability of an explanation in classical terms of the successfulness of these strategies shows that the norms have not been flouted at all – rather, what's been shown is that the best way to conform to certain norms of (in this case) probability estimation is *not to compute directly in terms of the norm*. This is the lesson that heuristics teach us across the board: aiming directly at what you want is not always the best way to get it. Utilitarians have long recognized this in arguing for the distinction between taking the principle of utility as a constitutive norm, and treating it as a decision procedure.

The worry about reliance on instrumentally justified heuristics was that we risked a loss of transparency that would threaten our epistemic agency. These examples show us, though, that even if a certain nontransparency is recommended in *practice*, the transparency is restored at the meta-level, where the norms return to form part of the explanation of the heuristic's success. This points out two important facts about norms that will apply in the moral case: first, norms can play an explanatory role even when the norms are not explicitly invoked in the procedures whose success they explain. Second, the fact that norms can play such an explanatory role tells us something about the *value* of the norm itself. Let me say a little more about this point.

A naturalized approach counsels us to seek accounts of the value of our norms – unlike *aprioristic* epistemology, it tells us not to take norms for granted. We need to ask how the adoption of certain norms contributes or would contribute to the goals toward which those norms are oriented. In some cases, it may turn out that the value of a norm is purely instrumental. It might well be argued, for example, that epistemic objectivity, at least considered as a practical norm to be employed in everyday reasoning, has just this character – the removal of partiality or bias is valuable only insofar as it functions to remove *idiosyncracy*, and idiosyncracy is problematic only insofar as it leads us away from the truth. To the extent that biases represent stable contingencies of the domain under investigation, it will be inefficient, relative to our immediate epistemic goals, to try to reason without them. More pertinently, nothing of epistemic value is lost if we indulge "biases" of the right sorts – this is, indeed, what justifies our taking a rather cavalier attitude toward departures from objectivity in many everyday cases.

At the same time, a look at the role of norms can also explain why objectivity cannot be so blithely cast aside as a *regulative* norm. Our broadest and most general epistemic goals involve seeking a kind of epistemic flexibility, an independence from any particular circumstance. We are creatures whose questions and concerns far outstrip the epistemic challenges endemic to our ancestral environments, and so we cannot rely as heavily as less ambitious creatures do on being situated in epistemically propitious circumstances. The abandonment of a commitment to objectivity – construed now as a background imperative to assess the contribution of one's situation to one's ability to know – would mean putting ourselves at epistemic risk in novel circumstances, as well as relinquishing epistemic projects, like science, not tied to our immediate animal needs.[8]

In either case, the norm of objectivity is justified instrumentally – it is a good norm, given its contribution to our epistemic goal of seeking useful or meaningful truth. But there is a different kind of justification that a norm can be given. Consider what I said earlier about the role of *rationality* in our epistemic practice. Certain aspects of rational practice – reasoning according to the laws of logic, for example – are certainly instrumentally justifiable, since they facilitate truth-tracking. But rationality in all its guises has another function as well: an *expressive* function. Rationality, as I said earlier, is a norm that bids us make our

---

8 See Henderson and Horgan (2000b) for a discussion of this point: the value of, as they put it "practicing safe epistemology."

reasons transparent to ourselves as we reason. Since it is the active and self-conscious consideration of reasons that makes one an epistemic agent, the norm of rationality can be said to express our conception of what it is to be an epistemic agent; and to endorse the norm is to express one's commitment to the value of such agency. The difference this makes to our attitude toward the norm is important. Whereas our commitment to objectivity is conditional – we should follow the norm unless and until it fails to get us the kinds of truths we want – our commitment to rationality is absolute. Well, not quite absolute: to be committed to rationality is to be a certain kind of knower – an active and self-conscious seeker of knowledge. It must be acknowledged that it is not impossible for a human being to relinquish their commitment to rationality, and hence not impossible for a human being to cease to be an active and self-conscious knower. I thus cannot say that there are no conditions under which a human could cease to value rationality; I can claim only that it is deeply regrettable if it happens. Epistemic agency, I contend, is a profoundly valuable thing: a mind is a terrible thing to waste. So the loss of the norm of rationality would mean, in and of itself, the loss of something of value.[9]

Situating Impartiality

It is the norm of rationality in the epistemic realm that provides, I think, a way of understanding the norm of impartiality in the moral realm; that is, impartiality in the moral realm should be understood as having a crucial expressive function, as well as whatever instrumental justification one may discover for it. Many feminist critics of impartialist moral theories would agree that the norm of impartiality serves an expressive function and, indeed, have argued that what it expresses is a pathological disregard for the human importance of contingencies and circumstances. Perhaps this is indeed one of the functions of this norm in the minds of some theorists, and, if so, surely provides no

---

9 I didn't say whether this value is epistemic, or moral, or aesthetic or what. I just can't decide. What do you think?

justification for retaining the norm. If this were the whole story, in fact, it would provide strong reason to reject the norm, as some have argued we should.[10] But I think the norm of impartiality expresses something else, and something that strikes me as extremely valuable and important: I see it as an expression of our commitment to the equal moral value of every human agent. Commitment to this norm appears to me to signal the same kind of extension – or, if you don't mind, *transcendence* – of our instinctive animal sympathies (the sort of things to which evolutionary psychologists would like to reduce the entirety of our moral sensibility) as science and other self-conscious epistemic practices represent with respect to our evolved epistemic instincts. To treat another being morally is to go beyond sympathetic reaction or instinctive response; it is to appreciate the morally valuable characteristics that the being possesses, and to treat these characteristics *as reasons* for making a moral response. Moral impartiality is the recognition that these characteristics are present in many, many more beings than the ones to whom we happen to have personal connection; commitment to this norm, then, is commitment to the moral point of view.

But what about the problems that impartialist moral theories seem to have when we apply them to real-world situations; the sorts of problems that have led feminist critics and others to advocate the abandonment of impartiality as a moral norm? I think the epistemic cases I've surveyed suggest an adequate and satisfying way of resolving these problems without giving up on moral impartiality. The way a commitment to this norm may result in a pathological disregard for the human importance of contingencies and circumstances is through neglect of the ecological features of the human situation in which our moral commitment to the equal value of all persons must be expressed. Such neglect is what makes

---

10 The idea that objectivity encodes male pathology is developed in different ways by Evelyn Fox Keller (Keller 1985) and Catherine MacKinnon (MacKinnon 1989). Richard Rorty thinks that a commitment to objectivity reflects a pathological *metaphysics* and thinks it should be rejected on those grounds.

impartialist theories inapplicable in any immediate way to the real-world – as ultimately irrelevant to human practice as epistemic models that take no account of actual human computational capacities and actual ecological location.

What's needed, I contend, is an ecological model of human moral activity that respects the expressive norm of impartiality without neglecting the circumstantial features of human life within which that norm must be pursued. Such an account, I suggest, would be able to explain a great deal about partiality: it would tell us, first of all, when partiality should be tolerated, and indeed when it should be actively cultivated (this would satisfy those critics who maintain that some forms of partiality have positive moral value), just as a general naturalized epistemology should tell us when heuristics should be employed and when they will likely lead us astray. But secondly, such an account can embody our commitment to the norm of moral impartiality in the way it prescribes the evaluation and regulation of our broader principles and institutions. In other words, the account does not treat human affectional connections as a species of moral "error," but it does not repudiate the value of impartiality, either. Let me conclude by sketching the sort of account I have in mind.

My naturalized account of moral partiality is inspired by Barbara Herman's reconstruction of Kant's treatment of property and of sexuality in the *Rechtslehre* (Herman 1993). According to Herman, both these things are, on the face of it, morally problematic within the terms of Kant's moral theory. In the case of property, the problem is that it is unclear what could give one person a right against another to prevent that person's use of some mere stuff. The mere fact that I want or even need certain stuff could not, in Kant's terms, justify my coercing some other person to prevent their using it. Sexuality is morally problematic, because the pursuit of sexual satisfaction appears to Kant to inherently involve the use of some other person as a mere means – to involve "objectification" in Kant's technical sense. Kant could, of course, have concluded that there simply are no such things as property rights, or that sexual intercourse is just morally forbidden, but he did not. He recognized that, given the conditions of human embodiment, rational agents of our sort cannot pursue our legitimate ends without (a) rights of exclusive use of at least minimal amounts of material stuff, and (b) sexual expression.[11] He therefore had to come up with a way of justifying these things.

His solution, Herman explains, is to appeal to what she calls the "morally creative" (Herman 1993, 53) function of social institutions. Civil society can create mechanisms by which property rights are defined, and through the threat or use of state power, effectively protected. It is the existence of these mechanisms that actually transforms mere inanimate stuff into stuff that belongs to someone – in this way the mechanisms literally create property. The mechanisms and the institution of property they define are then transcendentally justified: since it is a condition of our exercise of our rational agency that we have exclusive control of stuff, we are rationally obliged to consent to be bound by the rules and obligations created within such a society, and so the entire civil framework is rendered legitimate.

The story about sexuality is similar. Here the relevant institution is the institution of marriage: because the problem is that individuals who are acting out of sexual passion will view and treat each other simply as objects, rather than as persons, it becomes the job of the civil institution of marriage to create a legal framework within which sexual partners do not risk the loss of their own personhood by engaging in sexual intercourse, nor jeopardize their partner's. By articulating a specific set of rights and duties for each member of a sexual partnership, the institution of marriage transforms private individuals into new kinds of beings – "husbands" and "wives," Kant would call them. (Herman takes pain to emphasize that we can endorse Kant's overall strategy here without endorsing the specific details of the institutions he imagines – there is no reason why we could not, for example, construct a marriage-institution that permits many other forms of union than traditional heterosexual monogamy.)

---

11 I am not clear from Herman's discussion whether Kant accepts the human necessity of sexual activity as a matter of biological necessity – either because it is necessary for reproduction, or because it would be physically frustrating for the average individual to have to abstain – or because he believes that sexual expression is a positive and legitimate aspect of the life of a rational being embodied in the way human beings are embodied. This doesn't matter for my point.

What I want to borrow from these accounts is the idea that when the particularities of our embodiment necessitate certain forms of action and interaction among us, as conditions of the development of our rational agency, their necessity can generate a moral requirement, and hence a justification for, the creation of social institutions within which such action can take place. It is the background of respect for autonomy, together with an understanding of the specific requirements of human, embodied existence, that justifies the creation of human social arrangements within which it becomes morally permissible to act in certain ways – ways that would otherwise be prohibited. This, I think, gives us an excellent way of understanding the role of partiality in our own moral lives.

Given our physical, biological and psychological natures as human beings, each of us needs, for at least some periods of our lives, a certain amount of highly focused concern in order to develop properly as autonomous agents. To begin with, we are a highly neotanous species, virtually helpless for a good two years, and extremely vulnerable for many years afterward. During this time, we are dependent on others for our very lives. Moreover, our emotional, cognitive, and moral development is highly dependent on proper social interaction: we know that at extremes of isolation children fail to develop language, and in some cases of severe abuse, become unable to experience sympathy.

But the material requirements for the satisfaction of these needs are set by other facts about human nature. For example, the labor necessary to care for an infant is often physically demanding, boring, disgusting, or all those things at once; moreover, the needs of an infant are non-negotiable and frequently require the caregiver to postpone or give up the satisfaction of their own needs. Parents, therefore, stand in psychological need of something powerfully motivating to take on such a daunting task, and are, fortunately, often provided with it – parental love.[12] Parental love is intense, non-rational, and highly focused – and it is a feeling – or disposition, actually – that one individual cannot feel for an arbitrarily large number of others. Moreover, the development

---

12 For a wonderfully nuanced discussion of parental, as well as other forms of love, see Harry Frankfurt's "Mysteries of Love" (unpublished manuscript).

and preservation of parental love requires that parents spend an extended and connected amount of time with the same child – the necessary feelings do not simply spring into being as occasion demands. All this means that, as a matter of practical necessity, parents are going to have to be *partial* to their own children if they are going to provide their children with the physical and emotional perquisites of normal human development. Parental love depends upon – both causally and constitutively – a parent's according their own child moral priority above other individuals in the world of their own concerns.

Obviously, there are many other human relationships – romances, friendships, group affiliations – with similar structures. Indeed, I'd contend, all of the cases in which we are inclined to assign some kind of positive moral value to partiality are ones in which the partiality is inherent in a structure of feeling and disposition that constitutes some form of sustaining human relationship. So we have the first piece of my neo-Kantian, naturalistic account of partiality: we can see that certain forms of relationship are both necessary for human beings to become and exist as autonomous rational agents, and these relationships require partiality among the parties. This much will give us a justification for endorsing social institutions – if we can discover any – that can create a moral background for the pursuit of such relationships.

What could such institutions be? Herman, in her discussion of Kant's theories of property and marriage, points out that Kant requires and expects the design of the relevant institutions to be constrained by considerations of justice. It is, after all, respect for the autonomy of each individual agent that is ultimately rationalizing the creation of the institution in the first place. Thus, in the case of property, it would not be permissible to grant ownership of everything to just one individual. (It seems equally apparent that it would be wrong to set up marriage in a way that gave one partner legal sovereignty over the other, but Kant apparently did not object to this then-standard feature of legal marriage.) So it's appropriate to consider how we might design the institutions that will create morally permissible partiality so as to eliminate the morally problematic features that partiality would otherwise carry with it.

I said above that I thought that our commitment to *impartiality* reflected our commitment to the equal moral value of all persons. But I've also argued that if we want any individual human person to flourish, we should ensure that that person is provided with an appropriate amount and level of exclusive concern – of loving care, in short. These points together highlight the moral danger of leaving the distribution of partiality in a "state of nature." In such conditions, it becomes a matter of luck for each individual whether they receive the loving care that they need to flourish, but leaving a matter of such fundamental importance to luck is inconsistent with a full regard for the equal moral worth of every individual. What we need, then, is a set of institutions that collectively do two things: first, provide institutional support and safeguard for the necessary forms of affectional relations, like filial relations, but second, do what can be done to ensure that the benefits of participation in such relations are equitably distributed. At the very least, this means that we must ensure economic justice. No individual child, for example, may be allowed to do without the material benefits that accrue from having loving parents looking out for their well-being, and no individual child must be permitted to gain substantial unearned material advantages over others deriving from the partiality of the privileged child's parents.

We may also appeal to the background requirements on the legitimacy of partiality to make the needed distinctions between various kinds of discriminatory policies. Thus, as many progressive theorists have urged, there may be justification for separatist institutions or preferential policies when and to the extent that such institutions and policies are needed to redress the effects of past practices that compromised the autonomy of individuals in certain groups.[13]

My intention here for a "transcendental" justification of our institutionalizing various kinds of particularistic connections is that we can address the legitimate demands of impartiality in the moral realm by creating a certain sort of moral environment – a well-ordered environment within which we can, to an appreciable extent, indulge our partialist modes of moral activity and decision-making, without moral risk, and indeed, with confidence that we are furthering important

---

13 See Wasserstrom (1977) for a slightly different, but fully compatible way of arguing for the justifiability of practices like affirmative action. For a more recent discussion of strategies for justifying affirmative action, see Anderson (2000).

moral goals. The situation, as I envision it, is analogous to the epistemic situation in which we can self-consciously appreciate the features of our epistemic ecology that warrant our relying on heuristics, hunches, instincts, and so forth, even when these appear to embody irrational strategies. My transcendental justification of partiality should then offer some guidance as well about the kinds of everyday moral dilemmas that confront us, and for which grand, unqualified, impartialist moral principles proffer little concrete advice. The basic idea is that the difference between, say, loyalty and favoritism, or between compromise and capitulation, may lie not in the inherent quality of the act, but rather in the moral structure of the social background against which the act is performed. Helping your best friend's daughter get a summer job may be justifiable, even laudatory, in a world in which access to quality employment is equitably distributed throughout the society, so that everyone's best friend's daughter has a roughly equal chance of having beneficial connections. In a world in which such opportunities are restricted to members of a small group, the same action would be morally suspect, possibly even reprehensible.

I've argued that a naturalized approach to moral epistemology is possible – naturalizing does not entail the elimination of normativity – and, moreover, salutary. Taking seriously the actual moral judgments human beings make, we learn a great deal about the limits of *a priori* moral theorizing. Taking seriously the conditions set by our particular embodiment on the exercise of our moral faculties and the expression of our moral principles, we can achieve a reconciliation between the defenders and the critics of impartialist moral theory, and gain insight into the moral problems that confront us in the real world.

References

Anderson, Elizabeth. 2000. "From Normative to Empirical Sociology in the Affirmative Action Debate: Bowen and Bok's *The Shape of the River.*" *Journal of Legal Education* (forthcoming).

Antony, Louise. 1987. "Naturalized Epistemology and the Study of Language." In *Naturalistic Epistemology: A Symposium of Two Decades.* Ed. Abner Shimony and Debra Nails, 235-57. Dordrecht: Reidel.

———. 1993. "Quine as Feminist: The Radical Import of Naturalized Epistemology." In *A Mind of One's Own: Feminist Essays on Reason and Objectivity*, 185-225. Ed. Louise Antony and Charlotte Witt. Boulder, Co.: Westview.

Baron-Cohen, Simon. 1995. *Mindblindness: An Essay on Autism and Theory of Mind.* Cambridge: MIT Press.

Borges, Bernhard, Daniel G. Goldstein, Andreas Ortmann, and Gerd Gigerenzer. 1999. "Can Ignorance Beat the Stock Market?" In *Simple Heuristics That Make Us Smart.* Ed. Gerd Gigerenzer, Peter M. Todd, and the ABC Research Group. New York: Oxford University Press.

Boyd, Richard. 1995. "How to Be a Moral Realist." In *Contemporary Materialism: A Reader.* Ed. Paul K. Moser and J.D. Trout, 297-356. London: Routledge. (Previously published in *Essays on Moral Realism*, ed. G. Sayre-McCord, 181-228. Ithaca: Cornell University Press, 1989.)

Breiman, L., J. H. Friedman, R. A. Olshen, and C. J. Stone. 1993. *Classification and Regression Trees.* New York: Chapman & Hall.

Ceci, Stephen. 1996. *On Intelligence: A Bioecological Treatise on Intellectual Development.* Cambridge: Harvard University Press.

Churchland, Paul. 1989. *A Neurocomputational Perspective: The Nature of Mind and the Structure of Science.* Cambridge: MIT Press.

Frith, Uta. 1989. *Autism: Explaining the Enigma.* Oxford: Blackwell.

Haack, Susan. 1993. *Evidence and Inquiry.* Oxford: Blackwell.

Henderson, David, and Terry Horgan. 2000a. "Iceberg Epistemology." *Philosophy and Phenomenological Research* (forthcoming).

———. 2000b. "Practicing Safe Epistemology." *Philosophical Studies* (forthcoming).

Herman, Barbara. 1993. "Can It Be Worth Thinking About Kant on Sex and Marriage?" In *A Mind of One's Own: Feminist Essays on Reason and Objectivity*, 49-67. Ed. Louise Antony and Charlotte Witt. Boulder, Co.: Westview.

Gigerenzer, Gerd. 2000. "Unbounded Rationality: the Adaptive Toolbox." Presentation to the Cognitive Science Group at the University of North Carolina, Chapel Hill, April 2000.

Gigerenzer, Gerd, and Daniel G. Goldstein. 1999. "Betting on One Good Reason: The Take the Best Heuristic." In *Simple Heuristics That Make Us Smart*. Ed. Gerd Gigerenzer, Peter M. Todd, and the ABC Research Group. New York: Oxford University Press.

Gilligan, Carol. 1982. *In a Different Voice: Psychological Theory and Women's Development*. Cambridge: Harvard University Press, 1982.

Goldstein, Daniel G., and Gerd Gigerenzer. 1999. "The Recognition Heuristic: How Ignorance Makes Us Smart." In *Simple Heuristics That Make Us Smart*. Ed. Gerd Gigerenzer, Peter M. Todd, and the ABC Research Group. New York: Oxford University Press.

Jones, Karen. 1998. "Feminism, Values, and Epistemology: Comments on Sally Haslanger and Louise Antony." APA Central Division Meetings, May 7, 1998.

Keller, Evelyn Fox. 1985. *Reflections on Gender and Science*. New Haven: Yale University Press.

Kim, Jaegwon. 1994. "What Is 'Naturalized Epistemology'?" In *Naturalized Epistemology*, 2d ed. Ed. Hilary Kornblith, 33-55. Cambridge: MIT Press. (Previously published in *Philosophical Perspectives*, 2, ed. James E. Tomberlin. Atascadero, Ca.: Ridgeview, 1988.)

Kornblith, Hilary. 1994. "Introduction: What Is Naturalistic Epistemology?" In *Naturalized Epistemology*, 2d ed. Ed. Hilary Kornblith, 1-14. Cambridge: MIT Press.

Lewis, C.S. 1996. *That Hideous Strength*. New York: Scribner Paperback Fiction.

Longino, Helen. 1990. *Science as Social Knowledge: Values and Objectivity in Scientific Inquiry*. Princeton: Princeton University Press.

MacKinnon, Catherine. 1989. *Towards a Feminist Theory of the State*. Cambridge: Harvard University Press.

Moser, Paul K., and J.D. Trout. 1995. *Contemporary Materialism: A Reader*. London: Routledge.

Murtagh, M. 1985. "The Practice of Arithmetic by American Grocery Shoppers." *Anthropology and Education Quarterly* 16: 186-92.

Nelson, Lynne Hankinson. 1990. *Who Knows: From Quine to a Feminist Empiricism*. Philadelphia: Temple University Press.

Quine, W.V., and J.S. Ullian. 1978. *The Web of Belief,* 2d ed., New York: Random House.

Rorty, Richard. 1991. "Solidarity or Objectivity?" In Richard Rorty, *Objectivity, Relativism and Truth: Philosophical Papers,* vol. 1. Cambridge: Cambridge University Press.

Ruddick, Sara. 1989. *Maternal Thinking: Toward a Politics of Peace.* Boston: Beacon Press.

Solomon, Miriam. 1994. "Social Empiricism," *Noûs,* 28: 325-43.

Stich, Stephen. 1990. *The Fragmentation of Reason.* Cambridge: MIT Press.

Stein, Edward. 1996. *Without Good Reason: The Rationality Debate in Philosophy and Cognitive Science.* Oxford: Clarendon.

Trebilcot, Joyce, ed. 1984. *Mothering: Essays in Feminist Theory.* Totowa, N.J.: Rowman & Allanheld.

Wasserstrom, Richard. 1977. "Racism, Sexism, and Preferential Treatment: An Approach to the Topics." *UCLA Law Review,* 581-622.

Williams, Bernard. 1982. *Moral Luck.* Cambridge: Cambridge University Press.

CANADIAN JOURNAL OF PHILOSOPHY
Supplementary Volume 26

Moral Naturalism and the Normative Question

SUSAN E. BABBITT

Moral naturalism, as I use the term here,[1] is the view that there are moral facts in the natural world – facts that are both natural and normative – and that moral claims are true or false in virtue of their corresponding or not to these natural facts. Moral naturalists argue that, since moral claims are about natural facts, we can establish the truth about moral claims through empirical investigation. Moral knowledge, on this view, is a form of empirical knowledge.

One objection to this metaethical view is that even if moral naturalists are correct in their claims about truth, they cannot answer the question of normativity. Jean Hampton, for instance, argues that it is not enough to explain the conduct's wrongness by showing it to be a property that necessarily supervenes on natural properties.[2] For nothing in this analysis explains the relationship between these properties and *us*. The question is why should people *care* about these properties. Christine Korsgaard claims that moral realists take the normative question to be one about truth and knowledge.[3] But the normative question

---

1 In another use of the term, moral naturalism is the view that, given a naturalistic understanding of the world, there are no moral facts and that consequently moral claims have no truth-value. Although the two views are directly opposed to each other on the cognitive status of moral claims, they both aim at understanding "moral" from a naturalistic perspective.

2 Jean Hampton, *The Authority of Reason* (Cambridge: Cambridge University Press, 1998), 50.

3 Christine Korsgaard, *The Sources of Normativity* (Cambridge: Cambridge University Press, 1996), 30-48.

arises because of our capacity to reflect upon the truth and decide about its *importance*. Our freedom consists in our capacity to distance ourselves from processes of belief formation and to ask ourselves whether we really ought to believe or act when we know we have reason to do so. Korsgaard suggests that moral naturalists just have confidence that once we know that something is good, we will care about pursuing it, but they cannot explain why.

I will argue that moral naturalism can explain why we have a motive to act morally once we have a reason to do so. That is, I will argue that moral naturalism can explain why we care about acting morally once we have adequately understood the rightness or wrongness of a choice. Korsgaard argues that it is the reflective character of consciousness that gives us the problem of the normative – the fact that unlike other animals we can fix our attention on ourselves and become aware of our intentions, desires, beliefs and attitudes and how they are formed. We feel compelled to act morally, Korsgaard argues, because our endorsement of moral reasons is an expression of ourselves and to not act morally is to destroy ourselves. I argue below that there is something importantly right about Korsgaard's suggestion, but that naturalistic realism better explains the nature of the connection between self-conception and the identification of moral reasons in important cases.

The Normative Question and Realism

Korsgaard points out that the normative question arises because moral concepts do not just describe. They make claims upon us. They say that we must. They oblige us to do something. When we seek excellence, the force that value exerts upon us is attractive; when we are obligated, it is compulsive. Beauty, knowledge and meaning are also normative but in ethics the question of the normative is more urgent. For what morality commands, obliges or recommends is sometimes *hard*. This is why we seek foundations for ethics.

To explain moral concepts is not to answer the problem of normativity (14, 16). The normative question is a first-person question that arises for the agent who must do what morality says. We want to know what *obliges* me to act morally when I understand what morality requires, not what explains why I do. For instance, I may accept an evolutionary explanation for how I came to have moral concepts and principles. Perhaps I think that evolutionary processes explain why I feel obliged to act morally. But recognizing such an explanation, when I feel such obligation, will not itself give me a reason to risk my life or the lives of others that I love.

One answer to the question of normativity is the Hobbesian one: obligation derives from the command of someone who has legitimate authority over the moral agent and can make laws for her. Normativity springs from a legislative will. The problem with the Hobbesian account is that if we derive normativity from gratitude or contract, as suggested, we then have to explain why that consideration is normative, where its authority comes from (28).

The realist answer is, according to Korsgaard, that moral claims are normative if they are true and true if there are intrinsically normative entities or facts that they correctly describe. Realists try to explain normativity by arguing that values or reasons really exist, or by arguing against the various sorts of scepticism about them (40). These realists, like G.E. Moore, just end the debate by declaring that such facts are reasons for acting. Korsgaard argues that this does not answer the question because the question is not whether we have reasons but why, once we know we have reasons, we care about them. Why do we care so much about moral reasons, once we recognize them, that we risk our lives or the lives of others?

Naturalists, of course, are not necessarily committed to intrinsically normative entities in the world. Nagel, for instance, thinks we only have to determine whether certain natural interests, like our interest in having pleasure and avoiding pain, have the normative character that they appear to us to have. Such naturalists argue that we don't need to look for the normative *object* but rather that we should look more objectively at the apparently normative claims that present themselves in experience. The problem is not whether there exist peculiar normative entities in the world but whether reasons exist, or whether there are truths about what we have reason to do.

Naturalists of this sort avoid the problem of queer entities, but they do not answer the normative question. For even if we accept such arguments, all the realist can say, according to Korsgaard, is that moral claims can be true. But the fact that it is true that I ought to face death to save someone else does not explain why I might be motivated to do so. Arguments about truth and knowledge, according to Korsgaard, do not explain why people care about acting morally, why they feel obliged to act morally. Beauty attracts us but why are we compelled by obligation? What explains the hold upon us of obligation?

Hampton, like Korsgaard, distinguishes between two sorts of reasons: (a) *Explanatory reasons* or "reasons why" are useful in explanation, but they do not purport to be good or justifying reasons. For instance, I may act out of stress, but the fact that I am stressed does not justify my action. (b) *Directive reasons*, or "reasons to," generate directive reason to act, choose or believe. They motivate me. Of course, directive reasons can be explanatory reasons when the agent acts because he recognizes that he has such reasons. But explanatory reasons are not always directive, particularly in the hard cases in ethics. To have a directive to do *x* is to have a consideration, which matters enough to me, in the specific circumstances, to undertake to do *x*.

Hampton refers to this problem as that of moral properties' *directive authority* over us: It is not enough to explain the conduct's wrongness by showing it to be a property that necessarily supervenes on natural properties. For nothing in this analysis explains the relationship between these properties and *us*. We can understand that wrongness supervenes, but why should *believing* it lead one to act morally, to feel compelled to do so?

Practical Identity

Korsgaard's proposal is that we care about moral claims because the process of reflective endorsement, according to which we fix our attention on ourselves and become aware of our intentions, desires, beliefs and attitudes and how they are formed, depends upon self-conception. An agent acting for reasons is aware of herself causing her own action. But to be aware of ourselves as a cause, we have to be aware of patterns. We cannot see ourselves as acting, as opposed to reacting or being pushed, unless we conceive of ourselves generally in a certain way and conceive of the action as a certain sort.

Korsgaard suggests that we might think of reasons in *exactly* the same way that we think of causes. Reasons, like causes, are what *make happen*. What the power of causes and the normativity of reasons have in common is that they are forms of necessitation. A cause makes its effect happen, and a reason for action or belief necessitates a person to act or believe as it directs. Our ordinary notions of causation involve ideas of power, of one thing *effecting* another, and ideas of universality, of something being effected in a regular or law like way. Our ordinary notions of reason involve ideas of normativity or of obligating someone to act or believe, and of being obligated ourselves.

In agency we are aware of ourselves *as* causes. I, as a subject, *make happen* that which occurs. Hume argued that we cannot identify causes and distinguish them from constant conjunction without regularity. If we did not experience patterns of specific sorts – what he called regularities in nature – we would not possess expectations on the basis of which some things *cause* other things, as opposed to just following after them or being constantly conjoined. Korsgaard points out that when we recognize ourselves as causes we do so on the basis of expectations involving general characterizations of ourselves and our actions. Without regularity we would not be aware of ourselves as selves causing the action; rather, we would, analogously with the problem of constant conjunction, be aware of separate, disjointed events. If I am to constitute *myself* as the cause of an action, then I have to be able to distinguish between *my* causing the action and some desire or impulse that is "in me" causing my body to act. Korsgaard suggests that as an agent I cannot just be the *location* of a causally effective desire. Instead, I must be the agent who acts *on* the desire. Thus, if I endorse acting in a certain way now, I must endorse acting in the same way in every relevantly similar occasion.

This is not just a point about the generalization of all language and thought. It is true, as Korsgaard recognizes, that we always have to describe desires in a certain way as a *sort* of desire. It does not make sense to talk about some *wholly* particular desire. Indeed, we don't encounter any entity as wholly particular. If we recognize an entity, we recognize it as a kind. But the generalization of desires does not, in itself, commit someone to acting the same way in relevantly similar circumstances. When we recognize a desire as a sort, we do so in terms of a relationship to that desire and on the basis of a conception of ourselves as a sort of person. Korsgaard's point is that just as the special relation between cause and effect cannot be established in the absence of law and regularity, so the special relation between agent and action, the necessitation that makes that relation different from an event's merely taking place in my body, cannot be established without at least a claim to universality. Without the conception of a sort of self, acting within a sort of pattern, there is just a series of disjointed events, not *actions*. I need to identify generalizable patterns of behaviour in order to see my action as something that *I* do in particular. In order to see my actions as brought about rather than just happening for some reason whatever, there needs to be some set of relations according to which that action effects an end of a relevant sort. Regularity establishes my ability to see myself as having a choice in the first place, as having a will. For the act is chosen, as opposed to just happening, when it is chosen in spite of relevant alternatives. Regularity establishes my ability to have the kind of *self-conscious* causality that *is* a rational will.

In identifying and endorsing considerations as reasons, the agent therefore makes a judgment about explanatory role. For actions and events have many causes. But when we identify causes as *effecting* the action in question, we attribute to some causes a special explanatory role. When we ask about what *causes* an event, we are asking about what explains that event in the relevant way in the circumstances, about what allows us to understand the event. So, for instance, we wouldn't say that Smith's going to buy cigarettes explains his death on the highway, even though he would not have died if he had not gone out to buy cigarettes. Jones's drunk driving better explains Smith's death because it is the sort of action that is relevant to understanding highway deaths.[4] Although Smith's going out to buy cigarettes is a reason he died, Jones's drunk-driving in this case is explanatory and Smith's smoking is not because of what each contributes to a direction of understanding. The rationale is that we can pursue our concern about car crashes if we know more about drunkenness and inattention, whereas knowledge about the errands that lead people to be in the wrong place at the wrong time does not help.

When we look for explanations we look for causes that play a particular explanatory role relative to what needs to be understood.

---

4 I owe this example and the point to R. W. Miller, *Fact and Method* (Princeton: Princeton University Press, 1987), 93-4.

The patterns of regularity – within which some reasons are explanatory and others are not – constitute an investigative program, which generates certain cognitive needs. According to Philip Kitcher, rational decisions are those that issue from a process that has high expectations of cognitive progress, for we have to have expectations of success to generate certain directions of evaluation.[5] Causes become explanatory ones when they explain what needs to be understood. In agency, in acting self-consciously *as* the cause of our action, we take the explanatory role of some impulses, as regards determinate ends, to constitute the status of such impulses as reasons. And this depends upon a generalizable understanding of the agent, the circumstances and the objectives of the action in question. In discussions of explanation, it is generally acknowledged that the explanatory status of certain causes as those that necessitate an event depends heavily upon facts about the particular circumstances and how they are characterized.

According to Korsgaard, we have to act in a way that is generalizable in order to be human agents at all: "I cannot regard myself as an active self, as *willing* an end, unless *what I will* is to pursue my end in spite of temptation" (231). And to conceive my action as something I do in spite of alternatives, I have to characterize the action as of a general sort of action by a sort of person. To see myself as effecting an action, I need to see my choice as having a particular explanatory role relative to some end. If it is *I* that am choosing – if it is a self that chooses as opposed to a desire that just happens somehow – then there has to be a sense in which what I do now is done specifically *by me* and that it could have been done otherwise or resisted at another time. This presupposes generality. For it assumes a general conception of what I now do according to which other particular choices and actions at other times can constitute relevantly similar ones. Endorsement of an impulse as a reason *for me to do something* is dependent upon unity presupposed in conception of oneself *as* a self. For an impulse explains an end *for* the self to the extent that that end is relevant, in some sense, to the pursuit and realization of such unity. The *must* involved in moral

---

5 Philip Kitcher, *The Advancement of Science* (New York: Oxford University Press, 1993), e.g., 193.

claims, according to Korsgaard, is explained by the unity required to be a self, for it is an explanation relative to the achievement of that unity.

Korsgaard takes her view to resolve a problem in Kant. She notes that it is commonly accepted that the Kantian view leaves unclear the scope of universal laws. Thus, she suggests that the scope of laws depends upon practical identity, i.e., upon the identity under which we act – e.g., as member of a community, a citizen, as member of a Kingdom of Ends (xiv). We give consent to the law by identifying with a certain self-conception, and that also explains the law's hold on us. Going against such a law flagrantly enough is like destroying yourself. Practical identity explains the content of laws according to which considerations constitute reasons for someone.

Korsgaard's claim about practical identity is interesting. Some will object that the role of practical identity in Korsgaard's account relativizes reasons. Thomas Nagel, for instance, thinks that on this view morality will support any kind of action as long as people think of themselves in the right way.[6] In response to Korsgaard, he argues that it is trivializing of moral actions to say that people act on the basis of their self-conception. If I sacrifice my life so that others do not die, to say that I do so because otherwise I could not live with myself, undermines the significance of my moral choice in Nagel's view (206). Of course, if someone prefers the lives of others to her own, this says something about her self-conception. But, in Nagel's view, to explain the grip of those reasons in terms of the self-conception is to get things backward and to cheapen the motive. The real explanation is whatever it is that *makes it* impossible for someone to live with herself if she prefers her life to the lives of others. And to decide this, one has to think about whether what has made her want to do something is really a reason to do it. Answering this question requires that one think about the world, not just about oneself. The answer may partly determine one's self-conception, but it will not derive from it.

According to Nagel, freedom consists not, as Kant says, in the will, in our *deciding* to believe or to act. Rather, he says that freedom consists in identifying influences and compulsions, in understanding why

---

6 "Universality and the Reflective Self," in *The Sources of Normativity*, 200-9.

certain impulses have explanatory importance. When I know why it appears to me that I should act or believe in a certain way, I am better able to control influences upon me. According to Nagel, when we reflect upon whether what appears to be the case is *really* the case, we have to think about what the world would have to be like in order for things to appear the way they do. We have to think about the world of which we are a part rather than about ourselves and who we feel ourselves to be (205-6).

But when we think about the world of which we are a part, we do so on the basis of expectations generated, in part, by who we take ourselves to be. According to Nagel, freedom consists in identifying influences, which requires looking at the world. But, as Korsgaard suggests, how we conceive of ourselves constitutes grounds for giving importance to influences, or even identifying them *as* influences in the first place. To the extent that self-conception is involved in thinking about the world, it is not relativistic to suggest that moral deliberation, *while* involving reasons derived from looking at the world, is also deeply dependent upon self-conception.

Barbara Herman, for instance, suggests that philosophers often tend to misrepresent the relationship between "objectivist" views of morality – depending upon principles – and those based in sentiments or human nature. She argues that the idea that moral commitment, based upon rules and principles, is fundamentally at odds with particular, personal commitments, based upon sentiment, involves a confusion about the relation between motives and object.[7] Worries about personal commitment and morality are often explained by failure to see *how* rules enter a moral agent's motivational commitments. There is a tendency to think that rules introduce content by identifying right and wrong actions; this makes it look as if what I am trying to do is instantiate a rule when I act upon it. The agent is seen as attached to the rules as a source of authoritative guidance. What is missing from this picture is that moral rules are internalized. We learn them without knowing that we are learning or being able to recite them from memory. Herman

---

7 Barbara Herman, *The Practice of Moral Judgment* (Cambridge: Harvard University Press, 1993), 23-44.

says that when they are learned in the right way, they are a constitutive part of a person's self-concept. When we learn rules, we know how to go on. According to Herman, "if [rules] have the status in the life of a moral agent that I suggest, the relation of motives to moral rules will not take the form of trying to obey them (or bringing about the condition of their satisfaction). Moral action can be an arena for self-expression" (26).

This makes the role of duty more like that of a compassionate person: "A compassionate person (one to whom it is a good that he is moved by feelings of compassion) does not act in order to be compassionate or to do the compassionate thing. His actions are expressions of his compassion" (28). A person who acts out of duty does not act in order to be dutiful; rather, she acts in a certain way for the sake of the act and that action is an expression of her commitment to the values that define duty. The suggestion is that arguments about the relationship between morality and identity-commitments disregard the fact that moral rules are internalized and are part of who we are, so that one's commitment to morality is also constitutive of one's sense of self.

I return to this notion of rules below. The point here is that the role of self-conception in defining moral content need not be relativizing, as Nagel suggests. It need not be in opposition to some sorts of realism because we learn about the world *as* we acquire a certain self-conception.

Seeing Oneself *As*

One part of Nagel's critique of Korsgaard does represent a challenge, although Nagel does not develop his criticism in the way that I now suggest. In objecting to the defining role of practical identity in Korsgaard's account, Nagel says that "depending upon how we conceive of ourselves as reflective beings, the law may be egoistic, nationalistic, truly universal or just plain wanton" (204). If I am creative enough in conceiving of myself, I can make almost anything morally obliging. Now Korsgaard can respond to such an objection by pointing out that the sorts of generalizations involved in moral deliberation depend upon collaboration. We cannot generalize *by ourselves*, as individuals, because our being able to generalize successfully requires some recognition and response from other members of the relevant community. I may be able to invent a story for myself about the moral value of being egoistic or nationalistic, but I cannot control the recognition or the response to this story by others. To the extent that my interpretation of events depends upon expectations generated by such responses, I may fail to be able to apply or rely upon the story I've made up. What generalizations we can *act* upon depends, to some extent, upon the actions and expectations of others. It depends upon (social and moral) community.

But if a *society* is egoistic, nationalistic or involves other limiting, distorting conceptions of how to be human, an individual's socially derived self-conception could well become generalizable in the moral sense that Korsgaard describes. That is, the patterns according to which people develop expectations about right and wrong, according to which people characterize themselves and their actions in certain ways, can represent tendencies that are egoistic, nationalistic, etc., if the society involves such tendencies. Moreover, they are normalized as such. They come to seem natural, normal, human. Claudia Card, for instance, describes the difficulty of identifying the practice of rape as *inhuman*.[8] Inhuman practices can evolve and become accepted as part of the social fabric so that it is the *victim* of rape who is taken to have transgressed moral norms. Card points out that identifying the institution of rape as inhuman has been more than an intellectual effort; it has been a difficult, lengthy, political effort aimed not at identification only but at changing attitudes, responses, patterns of interpersonal relations. It has been an effort aimed at changing practices *in order* that rape become able to be properly identified as wrong.

Rape had to become seen *as* something specifically wrong. It had to become generalizable as having particular properties of wrongness for the purpose of theorizing about it *as* wrong. This meant identifying it in certain ways intellectually but also *treating* it as such in practice, and adjusting other beliefs in order to do so. The notion of generalizability, of classifying entities as *sorts* or *kinds*, is fundamental in the philosophy

---

8 *The Unnatural Lottery: Character and Moral Luck* (Philadelphia: Temple University Press, 1996), chap. 5.

of science because without such a notion successive theories would differ in subject matter: The notion of kinds makes it possible to talk about a common subject matter when there exist different understandings of the particular instances. Were it not for the presence of such clusters of properties, maintaining themselves as a unity of properties, inductive inference would not be possible. For the presence of any properties would provide evidence for the presence of any other properties.

But *kinds* are dependent upon practices, even on a realist view of scientific investigation. We come to divide up the world one way rather than another *as* we investigate the world and in the process of applying our theories and considering them in the light of empirical evidence. Philip Kitcher points out that how we divide up the natural world depends upon what we are trying to understand, which is not to say that kinds are just made up, or merely socially constructed.[9]

There has not been as much discussion about judgments of kinds in self or social understanding. When we generalize about ourselves and see ourselves *as* sorts of persons, we also do so, as Korsgaard suggests, within patterns of action and reaction, and in relation to goals. And we rely upon our generalizations to make inductive inferences about cause and effect, about what constitutes *acting* in relation to goals as opposed to reacting or being arbitrarily pushed.

Robin Dillon argues that individuals are sometimes unable to see themselves as certain *sorts* of person precisely because of the social situation in which others recognize them in a certain way. In her analysis of self-respect in "Self-Respect: Emotional, Moral, Political,"[10] Dillon discusses the example of Anne, a successful professional. Anne *knows* that she deserves to take pride in her accomplishments and that she lives self-acceptably, but she continually feels that people who praise her are just being nice and that it is just a matter of time until her mediocrity is exposed (232). Anne knows she has worth, but she cannot bring herself to see her accomplishments *as* being of that sort. She thinks

---

9 See Philip Kitcher, "Species," in *The Units of Evolution*, ed. Marc Ereshefsky (Cambridge: MIT Press, 1992), 317-42.

10 Robin S. Dillon, "Self-Respect: Moral, Emotional, Political," *Ethics* 107 (1997): 226-49.

of them as flukes. She recognizes her accomplishments as accomplishments, but she does not take them to be relevantly similar to things that are of human worth. Anne's failure to unify her accomplishments as things *of real worth* is expressed in her inferences. Intellectually, she can say to herself that her accomplishments are of worth. But when she makes generalizations about her experiences, she doesn't consider her accomplishments to be *of the same sort* as things of real worth.

In this case, Anne believes intellectually something that is true, namely, that she is competent and respected. But Anne possesses a sense of self as a result of her social situation according to which it is *surprising* that people respect her for her intellect. That is, Anne's experience of regularities in her society has led her to possess expectations according to which the respect that she receives is unusual. So when people praise her or she achieves a goal, it is surprising and in need of explanation, and she looks for an explanation that in fact ends up undermining her belief in her own self-worth. As Korsgaard points out, we have to conceive of ourselves within patterns of regularities in order to see ourselves as actors, in order to recognize ourselves as the cause of our actions. In order to see our actions as *making happen* as opposed to just happening arbitrarily we have to conceive of ourselves in a certain way in relation to those actions. And in Anne's case, there is no pattern of regularities according to which it is she as a worthy, competent human being that *makes happen* the successes in question. According to her experience of regularities, the successes are flukes.

What's interesting about this example, though, is that, while it is partly Anne's self-conception that explains her difficulties in deliberation, it is also self-conception that allows Anne to *discover* what sort of thing those difficulties are. Dillon describes the situation of Anne as one in which Anne's beliefs – namely, in her human worth – are at odds with her expectations. She believes that she is worthy, but she expects, given her experience, that she is unworthy and that her successes are just flukes. Thus, Anne experiences a discrepancy between her beliefs and her feelings. Now it could have been the case that when Anne experiences her successes as flukes, she gives up her belief that she is competent. That is, her self-conception could have provided grounds for revising her beliefs about her worth. Instead, Dillon suggests that Anne takes the discrepancy between her beliefs and her feelings to provide *reason* to pursue a *different* self-conception.

Anne gives to the discrepancy a certain importance. She attributes to that discrepancy an explanatory role according to which it constitutes a *reason* for pursuing a different sense of self, perhaps even, as Dillon suggests, a different community. Anne is ashamed of the discrepancy because she thinks she ought not to think of successes as flukes. We seek a certain unity when we try to resolve discrepancies. If my expectations about you fail, I may just adjust my beliefs and hence my expectations about you. But I may, alternatively, look for an explanation for why your actions were surprising. I may even go to some trouble to find the explanation, giving up other important beliefs as I do so. Whether I adjust my beliefs or pursue an explanation for the failure of my expectations depends upon the strength of my expectations and their relation to other important beliefs. It also depends upon a direction of thought and action. For instance, Anne takes the discrepancy between her beliefs and her feelings to provide a *reason* for shame and a *reason* to pursue a more adequate sense of self. But she might have taken the discrepancies to mean that she really is mediocre. The importance she gives to discrepancies depends also upon expectations for herself as a person. It depends upon the kind of person she *aims* to become and the understanding she needs to acquire in order to realize such a self.

Ann expects her expectations about herself to be different than they are and her expectations *about* her expectations are well enough supported by some beliefs and experiences that she endorses them as reasons. Such second-order expectations presuppose a sense of self which is not yet fully articulatable by Anne, but which is well enough supported by some patterns of experience to be *directive.*

It has been popular recently to discredit the idea of a normatively unifying sense of self.[11] Many feminist theorists have argued against

---

11 For an overview of feminist positions on the self, see "Introduction," *Feminists Rethink the Self,* ed. Diana Meyers (Boulder, Co.: Westview, 1997), 1-11. Feminists have generally rejected the *homo economicus* view of the "free and rational chooser and actor whose desires and ranked in a coherent order." See Cheshire Calhoun, "Standing for Something," *Journal of Philosophy* 92, no. 5 (1995): 235-61, for arguments against wholeness, intactness views of integrity.

notions of a "unified self" in favour of a fragmented self.[12] But the "fragmented self" is one in which some discrepancies are more important than others, and in which discrepancies – between beliefs and feelings, say – take on a certain importance. In Anne's case, we could say that she maintains a "fragmented self." But Anne need not do so. She could very well resolve the discrepancy by settling for a conception of herself as mediocre. Anne lives with discrepancy because she believes that she ought not to resolve that discrepancy in terms of one sort of unity, namely, one in which she is characterized to herself as mediocre; instead, she should resolve it, if she can resolve it at all, in favour of another sort of unity of self, namely, one in which she sees herself as morally and humanly worthy. Anne lives with discrepancy because she *presumes* a specific sense of unity of self, even if she may not know exactly what it will be like. Her rejecting one sense of identity as inadequate depends upon her presumption of the possibility of another more adequate sense of unity.

Dillon's suggestion is that self-respect is a "normatively interpretive perception of self and worth" (241).[13] It is the sense of self that one *ought* to have as a person and also a sense of unity on the basis of which one can evaluate one's actual sense of unity. It is seeing oneself *as* a certain sort of person within a process in which one seeks also to become that sort. Thus, in some cases the sense of self that is presumed in giving importance to events and experiences is one of which an individual is in pursuit, though not explicitly. It is one *requiring* support and articulation; it cannot therefore constitute grounds for the articulation and evaluation of other goals.

---

12 See, e.g, Judith Butler, *Gender Trouble: Feminism and the Subversion of Identity* (New York: Routledge, 1990); Maria Lugones, "On the Logic of Feminist Pluralism," in *Feminist Ethics,* ed. Claudia Card (Lawrence: University Press of Kansas, 1991), 35-44;

13 I discuss Dillon's argument in more detail in *Artless Integrity: On Moral Imagination, Agency and Stories* (Lanham, MD: Rowman & Littlefield, 2000), chap. 2.

Consider also the following example from Mab Segrest's auto-biographical *My Moma's Dead Squirrel*:

> As racial conflict increased in Alabama in the 1960s, I also knew deep inside me that what I heard people saying about Black people had somehow to do with me. This knowledge crystallizes around one image: I am thirteen, lying beneath some bushes across from the public high school that was to have been integrated that morning. It is ringed with two hundred Alabama Highway Patrol troopers at two-yard intervals, their hips slung with pistols. Inside the terrible circle are twelve Black children, the only students allowed in. There is a stir in the crowd as two of the children walk across the breezeway where I usually play. I have a tremendous flash of empathy, of identification, with their vulnerability and their aloneness within that circle of force. Their separation is mine. And I know from now on that everything people have told me is "right" has to be reexamined. I am on my own.[14]

Segrest does derive moral reasons in this case from her self-conception. A consideration – her relatedness to children within the "circle of force" – becomes a reason to act. She endorses a consideration as a reason because of the importance she gives to her identification with the black children. But Segrest's identification with the black children provides her with reason for questioning *everything* she has ever been told is right, indeed everything she sees as having informed her identity so far. Thus, she says she *feels* that she is now on her own, presumably because her expectations for herself in general are no longer supported by evident patterns of social regularity. She endorses as a reason for action a judgment of likeness where she had not judged likeness before. As a result she loses the stability provided by previous relevant judgments of similarity and difference.

Now according to Korsgaard, I care about moral reasons because my recognition of such reasons is an expression of unity of self, which I seek to preserve. But in this case Segrest cares enough about her feeling of identification – with the black children – to seek some other conception of unity of self than that which she understands herself to possess. Like Anne, in Dillon's example, Segrest is motivated by

---

14 Mab Segrest, *My Mama's Dead Squirrel: Lesbian Essays on Southern Culture* (Ithaca: Firebrand Books, 1985), 20.

judgments of importance, by expectations *about* the expectations generated by a community of relations and responses.

According to Korsgaard, and Hume, we see things as necessary or not on the basis of expectations generated by experience of regularity. But Segrest describes an experience in which her expectations fail and in which as a result she questions her conception of the sort of regularity generating those expectations, in particular of their moral value. Segrest wonders whether what she expects to be right, given her experience, is *really* right. As already mentioned, we might think of freedom as the capacity to reflect upon whether what I believe I really *ought* to believe. In this case, Segrest's freedom involves capacity to reflect upon the patterns of social regularity that support such reflective endorsement. The sense in which Segrest *feels* identified with the Black children is not how she expected to feel identified with them, and instead of deciding that she ought not to feel the way she does, she decides that she ought not to have expected to feel otherwise. She gives importance to what she does feel and is motivated to question her expectations about this importance.

Of course, we might dismiss Segrest as irrational. To endorse a feeling as a reason when a feeling is in conflict with regular patterns of beliefs and expectations could be considered aberrational, something someone would do under stress or coercion. Such endorsement might be similar to cases in which people act on whims, phobias or obsessions. In such cases, people endorse considerations as reasons, but they do so without good reason. They do so without, it seems, considering the relation between the impulse in question and relevant social patterns and relations, generating goals.

The problem is that we don't always treat such examples as irrational. There are cases in which people act as Segrest does – giving importance in ways that are out of sync with expectations – and they do so irrationally. But we also sometimes admire people who deliberate in this way. Segrest describes the incident as one involving reasons and she describes it as if readers will recognize it as one involving reasons. It is intuitively plausible that she has good reasons. It is intuitively plausible that in endorsing a consideration – of likeness – she is supported by experience of regularity, even though they are not the regularities already bestowing stability on her identity.

To take another example: In Miriam Tlali's *Between Two Worlds*, Muriel is a Black woman in apartheid South Africa who possesses a relatively good job in a radio store.[15] The title of the novel – *Between Two Worlds* – suggests that there are both two ways of life and two systems of meaningfulness bestowing importance on ways of life: "The Republic of South Africa is a country divided into two worlds. The one, a white world – rich, comfortable, for all practical purposes organized – a world in fear, armed to the teeth. The other, a black world; poor, pathetically neglected and disorganized – voiceless, oppressed, restless, confused and unarmed, a world in transition, irrevocably weaned from all tribal ties" (11). Yet Muriel's experience, as she describes it, is not of *two* different worlds, at least not when it comes to two worlds of moral meaningfulness.

Muriel knows, for instance, that she herself cannot expect certain forms of treatment towards herself because she is black. She cannot, for instance, expect to be respected:

> I have come to realise that the more you are ready to give the less you are likely to receive.... But here I am referring to respect.... You respect a 'white' person because he is a fellow human being and what do you get?
>
> You always get brushed off, that is, if you do not land in the street or in gaol. After that, you get some 'respect' but it is of a grudging sort – always bordering on hatred. And always you will be tolerated rather than accepted; because you are an indispensable nuisance.
>
> It goes something like this. You are standing next to a smartly-dressed white lady perhaps near a counter, both waiting to be served. She inadvertently drops something which you quickly rush to pick up and hand to her. She in turn grabs it from your hands without even thanking you. She may perhaps even give you a scornful look. You see, according to her, you picked up the article because it was your duty to do so and she does not have to be grateful to you. If you were daring enough you might perhaps ask her why she does not thank you, and very likely she would throw in your face, 'My girl, you must remember that I am white and you are black!'. You suddenly realise that you should never have picked up the article. That if you had not, you would have spared yourself all the degradation, aggravation and humiliation, and that would serve as a lesson you would never forget, you tell yourself. But sooner or later, you find yourself 'respecting' again and extending your hand to help because you

---

15 Miriam Tlali, *Between Two Worlds (Muriel at Metropolitan)* (White Plains, NY: Longman African Writers Series, 1987, 2d ed., 1995).

realise that it does not help to be bitter. You laugh at yourself and you shrug your shoulders. It is because you have been taught by your Christian mother to respect all humans. You slowly learn that not all Christian mothers teach respect; some teach that respect must be shown only after looking at the colour of the skin" (62-3).

We can explain conflicts here in terms of social regularities. Institutionalized racism explains why Muriel is expected to pick up the glove and why it is that she should not expect to be thanked. And her expectation that this is wrong is explained, she says, by her Christian mother's influence.

But what explains Muriel's strong expectations about the wrongness of the situation in general? There are supposed to be two systems of meaningfulness – two different worlds. But Muriel describes the situation as if there is only one. For while it is clear that the white woman in the passage understands respect one way and Muriel another, the point of the discussion is that the white woman's understanding of respect is inadequate. The point of the passage is that what some people call "respect" is not *really* respect. Thus, the suggestion is that in fact there is *one* sense of respect, but that there are some people who have been *mistaken* about what it means to respect others.

If there are two worlds, it becomes possible to say that some things that we might otherwise think wrong are not really wrong. For what is wrong in one world is not wrong in the other. So, for instance, Muriel can see the reasoning behind Douglas's proposal that they – Muriel and Douglas – steal from the store. Douglas reminds Muriel – "you'll never achieve anything sitting at that lousy desk and being underpaid" (83) – and we know Muriel knows this is true. But Muriel resists for reasons that are not clear to her: "I did not know what to say. I tried to look for any flaws in the scheme, but it all seemed to be a perfect crime which could not fail" (85). If there are two worlds, it is easy to rationalize stealing because one can think that, while stealing is usually wrong, in this world of systemic racism, the "poor, pathetically neglected and disorganized – voiceless, oppressed, restless, confused and unarmed" world, we cannot rely upon the usual standards for what is right and wrong, and we might think that because the situation is abnormal in this way, what we usually think wrong is not really wrong.

Yet Muriel thinks it is wrong to steal from the store, although she is not sure why. It is not clear in the case of Muriel what regularities define the self that gives content to Muriel's moral expectations. We might think that it is her religious background, as she suggests in explaining her expectations about respect. But in Muriel's story, what seems strongest in her account of her religious upbringing are the already disappointed expectations: "As an infant, you are christened in church, brought up in a Christian home and you acquire some education.... But the truth begins to stare you in the face. Life is not what it should be. After marriage, you do *not* live happily ever after. You shudder at the thought of bringing into this world children to be in the same unnatural plight as yourself, your parents and your grandparents before you – passing on a heritage of serfdom from one generation to another. You are not human. Everything is a mockery" (126).

In order for the truth that "life is not what it should be" to stare her in the face, to convince her that "everything is a mockery," Muriel must have pretty strong and clear expectations about what life *should* be like. Now one may say that Muriel can draw conclusions from history and literature. She may know about what life has been like for others and draw conclusions for herself from judgments of sameness. But in order to do this she has to think that such information applies to her, that she is *relevantly* similar to those people in other times and places. Like Segrest, she judges some similarities to be more important than others. But when she does so she also rejects *other* similarities which she might also have had reason to think important. How does she see herself *as* relevantly similar to people somewhere else with particular expectations, and relevantly different from Douglas and Adam with whom she shares traditions and history?

To the extent that practical identity grounds deliberation, it is not clear that the unity of self that defines us *as agents*, as making happen, is best explained by experience of regularities. The sets of expectations motivating Muriel – those about what her colleagues expect her to be, and those of her Christian mother's training – are set in a conflicting relation to each other. And Muriel makes a judgment about the adequacy of that relation. Muriel, like Anne, relies upon a second-order sense of order and unity, according to which the regularities informing her actual self-conception can be taken to be *ir*regular. She relies upon expectations, grounded in a normative unity of self, *about* the expectations that define her actual self. While it seems right, as Korsgaard suggests, that our conceptions of ourselves depend upon social patterns and background belief structures, in practice we often take some particular patterns to have special importance as regards our self-conception, and they may not be the most evident patterns, or evident at all. Muriel's strong expectation that her general situation is "unnatural" depends upon expectations about what *is* natural, about what *ought* to be natural. Moreover, it depends upon a conception of herself as belonging to that realm. Muriel's expectations for *real* human treatment are informed by some human experience somewhere. But it is not clear why, given her situation, upbringing and current community, she should identify herself so strongly with those tendencies, and not with others. In generalizing about herself and her actions, Muriel makes a judgment about *relevant* similarities that is not evidently rooted in her experience of the regularities characterizing either of the two worlds in which she lives.

Naturalism and Unreduced Causal Notions

In Richard Boyd's account of moral naturalism, there are two features that go hand in hand.[16] The first feature of moral naturalism is that whether or not we are right or wrong is a matter of empirical investigation. There are no principles for defining right and wrong that can be justified in advance of empirical investigation. We have to go out and investigate the world. The other side of the coin, according to Boyd, is that we expect to be causally affected by the world in investigation and we rely upon such causal influences in unifying our experience, that is, in judging one instance to be relevantly similar to another. Alex Rosenberg argues that Boyd is just mistaken in claiming such an important role for unreduced causal notions.[17] I suggest, however, that this aspect of naturalistic realism can help explain why we feel compelled to act upon moral truths once we have fully grasped them.

---

16 "How to be a Moral Realist," in *Essays on Moral Realism,* ed. G. Sayre-McCord (Ithaca: Cornell University Press, 1988), 181-228.

17 Alex Rosenberg, "A Field Guide to Recent Species of Naturalism," *British Journal for the Philosophy of Science* 47, no. 1 (1996): 1-30, n. 3.

I have suggested elsewhere that one of the particularly interesting results of naturalistic realist accounts of knowledge is the role in knowledge claims of what we might describe as "subjective" dimensions of experience: Attitudes, interests, even feelings and emotions explain increased understanding when such subjective experiences are as they are because the world is as it is – in other words, when they result from causal interaction with actual structures of the (physical and social) world.[18]

Boyd points out that philosophical accounts of explanation have depended upon a Humean definition of causation. According to Hume, causation is defined in terms of our expectations about regularities in nature. We experience one sort of thing being followed by another sort of thing, and we come to expect the second sort of thing whenever we experience the first. The positivists relied upon a Humean definition of causation when they developed the deductive-nomological account of explanation, for the notion of law likeness taken to characterize laws of nature depends also upon experience of regularities in nature.[19] But Humean definitions of causation in terms of experience of regularities in nature famously fail to account for our identification of *relevant* regularities. When we take two experiences to be similar, to constitute a regularity, we make a judgment about the greater significance of some similarities between the two experiences than others: Two experiences of fire, for instance, are similar, above all, in terms of their tendency to burn, which is already a causal notion. In other respects – shape, colour, for instance – they are quite different. Thus, it looks as though our judgments about similarities in nature, upon which our recognition of

---

18 See, e.g., Peter Railton, "Marx and the Objectivity of Science," *PSA* 2 (1984): 813-25, rpt. in *The Philosophy of Science*, ed. R. Boyd, P. Gaspar and J.D. Trout (Cambridge: MIT Press, 1991), 763-73. I have discussed this aspect of naturalistic realism in *Impossible Dreams: Rationality, Integrity and Moral Imagination* (Boulder, Co.: Westview, 1996), chap. 6.

19 See, e.g., R.N. Boyd "Observations, Explanatory Power and Simplicity: Toward a Non-Humean Account," in *Observation, Experiment and Hypothesis in Modern Physical Science*, ed. P. Achinstein and O. Hannaway (Cambridge: MIT Press, 1985), 47-94.

causal powers is supposed to depend, already presuppose recognition of causal powers.

This is what the critique of the Humean notion of causation implies (367). We rely upon our experience of causal relations to distinguish between actual causal relations, involving necessity, and mere constant conjunction. And we give a certain importance to those relations involving necessity. It seems true that we develop expectations on the basis of experience of regularities. But we already make a distinction between relations involving necessity and those of mere conjunction when we take some regularities to be relevant ones, and others to be unimportant. According to the naturalistic realist view, to give an account of a law or regularity in nature, is to "give an account (presumably partial) of the causal factors, mechanisms, processes, and the like that bring about the regularity of the phenomena described in the law" (369).

The idea is that Hume was mistaken to think we make judgments about causal relations because of our experience of regularities in nature; instead, it is because we experience causal relations that we are able to properly identify regularities. The traditional philosophical picture of explanation is that when some theory E explains some phenomenon p, it is just the explanatory power of E that is demonstrated. But Boyd points out that neither scientific usage nor scientific practice conforms to this picture. What usually happens instead is that the explanatory success of E is taken to provide evidence for some more general theory. Indeed, we would not ordinarily speak of the explanatory power of E being manifested at all; instead, E's being able to explain p "would ordinarily be taken to indicate the explanatory power of those other, more general theories and to provide evidential support for them" (370).

Philip Kitcher makes something like this point in a discussion of justification in *Abusing Science*: Darwin's theory was justified by repeated demonstrations that the theory provided the resources for telling appropriate sorts of stories about phenomena that stood in need of explanation.[20] Darwin's theory raised many particular questions that needed to be answered – about how variation occurs, for instance. And

---

20 *Abusing Science: The Case Against Creationism* (Cambridge: MIT Press, 1984), 45-54.

his theory was successful to the extent that the general, broader theory provided the resources to explain such phenomena, or to point in the direction of their explanation.

The particular importance of Boyd's account for present purposes is that it establishes a link between discussions about the nature of causation in the philosophy of science and questions about how we develop the expectations on the basis of which we interpret social, personal and emotional experiences. We might think that we develop expectations – about people, customs, behaviour, and so on – because of our experience of social regularities.[21] We come to expect certain responses – from others and from ourselves – as a result of our experience of social institutions and on the basis of what Searle calls "dramatic scenarios," or the stories constituting our background (134-5). We attribute meaningfulness and make judgments of importance on the basis of expectations acquired as a result of social and theoretical traditions.

But sometimes we have strong expectations *about* our expectations about how things ought to be, as in the examples discussed above. And it is sometimes the case that we do not appropriately identify our real interests and goals until we act on such expectations. I have argued elsewhere that popular pictures of individual and social rationality sometimes get the means/end picture backwards, at least for important cases.[22] The philosophical picture, roughly, is that I act rationally when I give importance to my desires, interests and preferences in light of carefully considered ends. Sometimes, however, people need to be able to give importance to particular desires, interests and preferences in order to *discover* their real ends. This is particularly the case in situations of long-standing systemic injustice, in which social and theoretical traditions have resulted in seriously diminished expectations for the human flourishing of some social members.

----

21 John Searle develops this sort of account in *The Construction of Social Reality* (New York: Free Press, 1995).

22 In *Impossible Dreams: Rationality, Integrity and Moral Imagination* (Boulder, Co.: Westview, 1996).

Boyd's view explains the significance in deliberation of expectations people sometimes have about what it means to be human, expectations they may not explicitly acknowledge. As part of the natural world, acting in specific ways, we acquire understanding of the world and its relations, and, in doing so, we acquire interests, attitudes, expectations. But in some cases, the theory we possess and can make explicit to ourselves is not adequate for the realization of important expectations. We may possess interests or expectations as a result of engagement with the world and not be capable of theorizing such interests, of properly understanding their significance and importance, and their relation to other interests. In such cases, we may be compelled to act in certain directions by the *need* to better understand such expectations and interests. David Velleman, for instance, has suggested that goals are sometimes emergent from experience, that practical deliberation is sometimes dependent upon goals that emerge from practical traditions that are a result of our being and behaving in certain ways, not necessarily of carefully thought out life-plans.[23] Boyd's notion of "epistemic access" explains how we might be compelled by the understanding such goals demand. We develop goals as a result of action and engagement, and we are compelled to act in certain ways by such goals, in part as a result of the further questions raised. We are compelled by demand for explanatory unity.[24] We develop expectations and goals as a result of practical pursuits, and then seek the explanatory unity that allows us to better act upon them. The success of explanations *as* we pursue them accounts for our giving importance to some ways of unifying the world over others.

The naturalistic realist view reverses the explanatory relation between experience of uniformity and the development of expectations: We don't experience uniformity and then as a result of such experience, give importance to expectations; instead, we experience certain

---

23 Velleman, J. David. "The Possibility of Practical Reason," *Ethics* 106 (1996): 694-726.

24 The "explanatory burden" created by certain actions and commitments is explained in *Artless Integrity: On Moral Imagination, Agency and Stories* (Lanham, MD: Rowman & Littlefield, 2000).

relations as important, thereby developing expectations, and then we seek the appropriate sense of uniformity to be able to further understand and act upon such importance. That is, we experience certain relations – including explanatory relations between impulses and ends – as important. Moreover, we do this even though the ends in question may not be able to be properly theorized by us as important. We are then compelled by the demand for explanatory unity to act and to interpret in certain directions, a demand which is also partly constitutive of practical identity.

It is important to recognize that a "normatively interpretive" sense of unity, such as is described by Dillon, need not be a sense of unity that dictates, that defines. A normatively interpretive sense of unity can be one that is itself constrained by explanatory need depending upon a process of development. As regards the definition of kinds in nature, there is on the naturalistic view a process of accommodation between conceptual and classificatory practices and causal structures, and the actual success of accommodation is necessary for successful induction and explanation.[25] Thus, the unity of kinds is not a matter of specific sets of properties, or of some specification of necessary and sufficient conditions for reference. Instead, Boyd suggests that in the process of accommodation, which is a historical process, the fact that a category actually does refer to an entity in the world, that it makes possible successful generalizations and explanation, contributes to the naturalness, or the reality of that category. In his view, "The historicity of the individuation criterion for the definitional property cluster reflects the explanatory or inductive significance (for the relevant branches of theoretical or practical inquiry) of the historical development of the property cluster and of the causal factors which produce it, and considerations of explanatory and inductive significance determine the appropriate standards of individuation for the property cluster itself" (144).

It could be that, similarly, the role of successful induction and explanation in accommodation of conceptual and classificatory practices helps explain the sort of importance given to some perceptions of

---

25 R. N. Boyd, "Homeostasis, Species and Higher Taxa," in *Species: New Interdisciplinary Essays*, ed. Robert A. Wilson (Cambridge: MIT Press, 1999), 141.

similarity in the process of individual deliberation and action.[26] Anne, for instance, perhaps cannot fully articulate the sense of human worth according to which her expectations for herself are inadequate. But she gives importance to the possibility of such a conception, and it is probable that she will be able to make sense of such a notion if she continues to apply it. Anne's judgment of importance becomes endorseable because it does in fact play an explanatory role as regards goals that are emergent in Anne's actual personal development. According to Boyd, the individuation criterion is a process of accommodation between categorization practices and actual causal structures, which result in successful explanation and induction. We might think that self and moral understanding also involve processes of accommodation in which the way we see ourselves plays a role in our attempts to explain and make sense of experiences and relations. In cases in which we actually are successful, our normatively interpretive categories become more real, more natural – although perhaps imprecise – and thus more motivating.

This gives to practical identity a role, not in constituting the content of moral obligation, but rather as a vehicle for identifying the greater explanatory power of some moral principles and concepts over others. For practical identity is, as Korsgaard suggests, an activity of unification, in the process of acting and deliberating relative to ends. However, if our ends are sometimes emergent from mechanisms of activity and deliberation, we have reason to see ourselves one way rather than another because of the constraints of explanatory unity: Some ways of generalizing about ourselves and our ends allow us to become better aware of those ends, and what we need to understand to realize them. Anne, for instance, aims for human worth – a goal that in her particular case may not be completely articulatable because of lack of conceptual resources. Such a goal, however, emerges from her life experiences and acquires moral content in this way. As she individuates herself *as* worthy in some sense, she gains understanding of that goal and is able

---

26 I have discussed the naturalistic conception of individuation and its implications for integrity in *Artless Integrity: On Moral Imagination, Agency and Stories* (Lanham, MD: Rowman & Littlefield, 2000), chap. 3.

to give it more explicit content, including moral content. Her success in gaining such understanding – what Boyd calls "epistemic access" – provides partial justification for expectations and beliefs not evidently rooted in experience of social regularities.

Consider further the example of Segrest, cited earlier. Segrest describes a situation in which she feels compelled to re-examine *all* her beliefs about what is right. We understand that she feels compelled in this way because she has recognized, as a result of her feeling of empathy with the black children, that her social expectations, based upon practical, theoretical *and moral* traditions, are wrong. And Segrest's decision is hard. She knows that such a commitment carries a cost for her. She loses an important sense of security. As she says, she is on her own.

Nagel suggests that what is important in cases of moral obligation is that which makes it impossible for me to live with myself if I do not act in a certain way. In other words, what is important are the facts that explain the impossibility, not that I feel about myself in a certain way. Thus, we may say about Segrest that her compulsion to re-examine her moral beliefs is explained by the fact that she does indeed share something important with the black children, that she has in fact been prevented by social expectations from recognizing her shared humanity with black children and that her recognition of communality is indeed significant to her personal development.

But what explains Segrest's apprehension of these facts in particular and what explains her judgment about the importance of such facts? Her apprehension of the facts can be explained naturalistically. She engages with the world and, as a result of complex patterns of causal interaction with the physical and social world, she acquires beliefs about her social world and relations including some that she cannot explicitly articulate – tacit beliefs. The facts apprehended are non-moral facts about the physical and social world. But Korsgaard's criticism is that naturalists cannot explain why we care about such facts, once apprehended. Why does the fact that it is true that Segrest shares humanity with the black children mean that she should value and act upon such commonality?

On the naturalistic view, the importance of such facts can be explained in terms of their role in the presumption and pursuit of a certain sense of unity promoting "epistemic access." Moreover, such a role explains moral significance because, in particular cases, such as the example of Segrest, the unity presumed and pursued has explanatory power as regards being *better* as a human being. Korsgaard is right about the compulsion we feel toward maintaining a certain sort of unity of self. In her view, we endorse considerations as reasons when they play an explanatory role as regards our ends. But sometimes the explanatory role of considerations is in relation to ends which are moral ends and which may not yet be explicitly recognized as such. In Segrest's case, the significance that she attributes to the facts apprehended can be accounted for in terms of explanatory role related to a way of being. But this is not simply means/ends reasoning even if it is instrumental reasoning in some sense, for there is an interesting question about why the end involved is an important one. It is not the way of being which currently comprises her "practical identity" because what she pursues, as she describes, is at the cost of that identity.

Korsgaard's claim about the definitional role of practical identity is attractive, for one thing, because it removes the difficulty of one sort of externalism.[27] It is hard to defend the idea that we might have reasons to do something independent of our inclinations. That is, it is hard to explain how some considerations can be reasons for someone in and of themselves. As she points out, there is a strong sense in which we feel compelled to act morally, in the hard cases, because *not* to do so would be *worse* than death. So in some sense we act so as not to destroy ourselves, or be destroyed. But the notion of practical identity by itself cannot explain how we are sometimes compelled, morally, for the sake of identity, to act in ways that seriously disrupt actual unity of self, in ways that put our sense of ourselves, as community members, at risk. Korsgaard's view does not explain why, as in the example of Segrest, we sometimes feel obliged, by something very much like integrity, to put ourselves in a position in which we may *not* be able to defend our actions or choices to the moral community. We may not even be able to defend them to ourselves at the time.

---

27 By "externalism" here I mean the view that reasons are independent of inclinations, although I recognize that more plausible versions of externalism are consistent with the contingency of reasons upon inclinations. My own view is externalist on some moral naturalist understandings of externalism but for reasons I cannot discuss here I resist this terminology.

Consider the following passage from J. M. Coetzee's recent novel *Disgrace*.[28] A disgraced professor, who describes himself as selfish, takes on the responsibility of delivering the corpses of dead dogs to the dump. He does it himself, at some sacrifice, so that the corpses don't have to sit there for long periods of time and so that they are not mistreated by the people whose job it is to feed garbage into the incinerators. He wonders why he is so committed to dead dogs. It is not just to help Bev, who runs the animal clinic, for he would be helping her just as much if he left the corpses at the dump on Sunday night rather than first bringing them home and taking them again on Monday: "For himself then. For his idea of the world, a world in which men do not use shovels to beat corpses into a more convenient shape for processing.... Curious that a man as selfish as he should be offering himself to the service of dead dogs. There must be other more productive ways of giving oneself to the world, or to an idea of the world.... But there are other people to do these things – the animal welfare thing, the social rehabilitation thing, even the Byron thing. He saves the honour of corpses because there is no one else to do it. That is what he is becoming: stupid, daft, wrongheaded" (146-7).

The compulsion cannot be explained instrumentally, for the ends to be achieved are not identifiable. They are ends the proper articulation of which still needs to be discovered. In Coetzee's passage, the professor feels "stupid, daft, wrongheaded" and yet he is compelled by an idea, which is "for himself." What might explain the explanatory importance of that idea, as regards moral ends – in this case a notion of honour – is something like the "epistemic access" that Boyd appeals to to explain judgments of importance in scientific cases. In the story, the professor feels compelled to act in a certain way for the sake of honour. Thus, he gives importance to his impulse to act in relation to an end, which is moral. But he does not identify the end, except vaguely. And he does not see it as important in terms of his other values – Byron, Beth, his image of himself, for instance. He recognizes that the idea that is expressed by his action, whatever it is, is important for him, on whatever sense of himself turns out to be appropriate. And he is

---

28 J. M. Coetzee, *Disgrace* (London: Vintage, 1999).

compelled by that recognition, by that actual experience of explanatory (causal) relationship.

Drawing upon Boyd's conception of individuation, normativity is explained, not primarily by practical identity itself, but instead by the sometimes tacit understanding we acquire of our human needs and goals, and the compulsion to pursue such understanding through specific sorts of action. Contrary to Korsgaard, access to truths *is* sometimes important in explaining why we *care* about certain truths. For when we have access to truths about human needs and capacities, we have reason to care in particular about other truths upon which the realization of such needs and capacities depends. We sometimes have access to truths about needs and capacities without being able to make such truths explicit to ourselves. Segrest had access to truths about similarity between herself and the black children. Such truths had explanatory importance as regards other ends, in this case moral. But she does not act *for* those ends. For she does not explicitly identify such ends. Instead, she acts for the unity of self and explanation that the importance of her perception demands. And she feels compelled to act in certain directions in order to achieve such unity, and the understanding and possibilities it promotes.

It is possible that the unity of self that motivates us to act morally is defined in terms of the explanatory resources required for the realization of cognitive and personal goals apprehended as a result of action within and for the sake of social and moral community. The apprehension of such goals, as Nagel suggests, is explained by our thinking about ourselves in the world. The moral significance of such ends, in cases in which there is such significance, is explained by their explanatory role as regards moral possibilities. That is, in cases in which we feel obliged to act morally, at a cost, the explanation for such obligation is the causal relationship between the endorsement of certain considerations as reasons and the enhancement of moral perception or moral being, even if we do not recognize such moral significance at the time. Thus, normativity is not explained by the existence of intrinsically normative entities in the world, entities that compel us to act in and of themselves, a view that Korsgaard dismisses. Rather, normativity is explained by our dependence, as knowers, upon an appropriate unifying perspective in order to acquire a full and adequate grasp of relevant truths, some of which have to do with becoming better persons in a better world, morally. It is a property, not of entities themselves, but of relations between judgments of importance – of beliefs, concepts, impulses – and possibilities for the action required to survive as the person we take ourselves to be, or as the person we *might* take ourselves to be if we are successful in claiming such importance.

The significance of an impulse in rational deliberation, for instance, depends upon its role in explaining certain ends – which may not be explicit – and the understanding required to realize these ends. We give importance to impulses in deliberation when we recognize such impulses in their causal (explanatory) role relative to significant ends. Such normativity is not intrinsic in precisely the way Mackie described. We feel compelled to act on impulses endorsed as important in this way, because we depend upon a specific sense of unity of self in order to maintain, to properly interpret and to act upon relevant expectations. Moreover, we experience such compulsion as a result of participation in a process of development as a result of which we are influenced *as persons* and from which specific goals emerge.

Boyd's view suggests as an addition to Korsgaard the idea that the unity upon which moral deliberation depends is itself dependent upon our discovery of relevant facts about the world, facts, for example, about actions and understanding required for self-realization of a specified sort. As part of the natural world, affected and indeed transformed as persons by causal interaction with natural and social forces, we sometimes apprehend such facts without conscious awareness. Moreover, we sometimes apprehend their explanatory significance as regards other possibilities for existence, as might be the case in Coetzee's example. To act upon such recognition, we have to be able to attribute importance, which depends, among other things, as Korsgaard suggests, upon self-conception. The need for adequate self-conception sometimes compels us to act in ways that increase our moral understanding, but the self-conception that we need, and our understanding of it, is explained by our apprehension of relevant facts about the world in which we exist.

Nagel says that Korsgaard's answer to the question of normativity is an example of the "perennially tempting mistake of seeking to explain an entire domain of thought in terms of something outside that domain, which is simply less fundamental than what is inside" (205). In his view, the explanation for why a belief or action is justified "must be completable, if it is completable at all, within the realm of relevant reasons themselves" (205). For instance, all we can do when we have to decide whether a belief that appears to be right really is right is to think about how the world would have to be in order to explain why it appears as it does (205-6). But when we think about how the world is and how we are within the world, we make judgments about what *sorts* of entities and events are involved. We unify our experience. And we unify ourselves. What the naturalist view can explain better than Korsgaard's suggestion is how we sometimes come to unify our experience, and to attribute importance to it, in ways that conflict with our more stable background beliefs, and with the expectations derived from experience of evident regularities. It explains our endorsement of considerations the explanatory role of which is in relation to moral ends not yet fully articulatable. But to the extent that practical identity is also a unification process involving reasons, reference to practical identity need not take us outside the domain of the problem, as Nagel suggests that Korsgaard's reliance upon practical identity does.

This brings us back to the notion of rules and the supposed opposition between acting according to duty – that is, being obliged – and acting out of virtue in the pursuit of excellence. There is supposed to be a question about why we act morally when we consider that duty compels us. The emphasis on virtue is taken by some to better answer the question, "why be moral?" than emphasis on Kantian notions of duty because virtue is attractive. Excellence *attracts* whereas duty *compels*. But as Herman suggests, this opposition is misleading when we consider how the rules of duty come to be meaningful. We come to give importance to moral rules, Herman suggests, as we act upon them, and as those rules become expressions of ourselves. We have an idea of moral rules as *dictating* actions. According to the traditional picture, we acknowledge the rules and then we try to comply. But this involves the positivist-type assumption that rules are justified *a priori*, and then applied to empirical results – the conceptual/empirical contrast. In practice, as philosophers of science have argued, we rely upon the explanatory power of rules and concepts relative to specific cognitive and practical ends *during the process of investigation* to justify rules and principles. As Herman says, we internalize rules even before we recognize that they are rules, and when we act upon them we are acting out of a sense of wholeness, of character. To the extent that that wholeness is itself also a project, obligation is *also* attractive: The explanatory role according to which rules become internalized by us as we act upon them is also in relation to beauty, for it is dependent upon our capacity to identify the sense of wholeness that attracts.

The idea of a whole *can* be empowering when what is brought together by that whole makes it possible to understand something else, and to engage with what has been understood, or intuited. Kathleen Okruhlik says that if one studies the history of science, it is hard not to be moved by the power of unification: "Kepler united the heavens and the earth for the first time. Newton brought together tides, pendula, apples, planets and comets. Phenomena that were previously disparate became unified, and an incredible increase of knowledge was the result."[29] When Kepler brought together heaven and earth, other questions and answers became possible, something was discovered. And what was discovered was empowering. But Okruhlik's point is more general. She says we experience the power and beauty of unity all the time: "Many of those 'clicks' in the early issues of *Ms.* were the sounds made by unifying conceptions falling into place. Sometimes a single concept like the 'eroticization of subordination' makes many disconnected experiences fall into place and become understandable."[30]

There is a kind of empowerment in bringing things together that can be explained by the relation between practical identity and the pursuit of understanding. Korsgaard argues that naturalists have been mistaken to make normativity a question about knowledge and truth. For the problem is about why we *care* about such truths, why they move us to action. Naturalism answers this question by explaining the sense of unity that we depend upon in making sense of the world and ourselves. To the extent that such unity is presupposed in moral understanding, we feel compelled to act upon such understanding. We pursue certain sorts of unity for the sake of understanding, and some sorts of understanding – of ourselves as *sorts* of persons performing *sorts* of action – are necessary in order even to act, and to take relevant control.

---

29 Paper given at the Annual meeting of the Canadian Society for Women in Philosophy, Dalhousie University, Halifax, Nova Scotia, Sept. 28, 1997, 20.

30 Ibid., 21.

As in Kitcher's example of Darwin, we justify a generalizable conception of ourselves by employing such a notion in explanation. And we identify what *needs* to be explained – what is surprising – as we pursue such a conception in action. As Okruhlik says, there is beauty in such unification, and the power it creates. For certain kinds of stories only become able to be developed when a certain control becomes possible, and what has not been possible before, and becomes possible, can be beautiful in its incipience.

Conclusion

One important result of Boyd's naturalistic, causal account of the individuation of entities is that the unity of natural kinds involves a predictable degree of vagueness. The unity is not precise, but it is unity nonetheless. It has been important in recent discussions about the nature of the self to emphasize fragmentation and disruption. This has been partly due to the recognition of the profound role of social institutions – sometimes systemically unjust – in forming an individual's sense of self and worth. We need to ask, though, why it makes sense to talk about *self*-transformation or *self*-knowledge in such situations, and not just of a series of conjoined changes or insights. Korsgaard is right that practical identity explains the importance we give to certain impulses. But in important examples, individuals are driven to give explanatory importance to impulses in relation to human and moral ends that are not, and cannot easily be, endorsed by one's social and moral community. I have argued that the sense of compulsion rooted in practical identity is sometimes dependent upon access to truths, moral and non-moral. The importance of a certain sort of practical identity, especially in cases in which real *human* identity has been eroded and thinking about it has become confused, is explained by a naturalistic conception of the individuation of selves and experiences upon which both moral and non-moral deliberation depend.[31]

---

31 I am grateful to the editors, Richmond Campbell and Bruce Hunter, for encouraging me to write on this topic. I have particularly benefited from Rich Campbell's thoughtful, thorough and persistent comments.

CANADIAN JOURNAL OF PHILOSOPHY
Supplementary Volume 26

Statements of Fact:
Whose? Where? When?

LORRAINE CODE

The phrase "statements of fact" has a clear, unequivocal ring. It speaks of a stable place untouchable by contests in epistemology and in more secular places, around questions of constructivism, subjectivism, and the politics of knowledge. It offers fixity, a locus of constancy in a shifting landscape where traditional certainties have ceased to hold, maintains a vantage point outside the fray, where knowledge-seekers can continue to believe in some degree of "correspondence" between items of knowledge and events in the world. Within the social institutions and practices where knowledge is an issue, it designates a secure starting place for deliberation, a way of ensuring that processes of decision-making remain cognizant of the "realities" they have to address.

In the institutions of knowledge production and knowledgeable practice that generate the examples I appeal to in this essay – medicine and law – "statements of fact" appear to comprise an incontestable core around which interpretive strategies may indeed have to be enlisted, but which itself functions as a kind of interpretation-exempt zone.[1] There are good reasons for its retaining that status, for resisting the instabilities and sheer whimsicalities that would follow from dislodging it. If doctors could not rely on statements of fact about

---

1 This point recalls Wittgenstein's claim: "It may be that *all enquiry on our part* is set so as to exempt certain propositions from doubt, if they are ever formulated. They lie apart from the route travelled by enquiry." Ludwig Wittgenstein, *On Certainty*, ed. G.E.M. Anscombe & G.H. von Wright; trans. Denis Paul & G.E.M. Anscombe (Oxford: Basil Blackwell, 1969), #88 (italics in original).

thermometer readings, lawyers or judges on statements of fact about fingerprint evidence, then bases for treatment or judgement would be so shaky as to destroy confidence not only in the knowledge that purports to inform medical and legal agency, but in the social fabric of which these institutions comprise central threads. These examples come, by design, from places where basic empirical observation yields the evidence on which knowledgeable practice is based. And indeed in scientific-technological societies, the reliability of everyday empirical knowledge about the simple behaviours of people and things counts virtually as an "absolute presupposition,"[2] as one of the cross-pieces that hold the epistemic raft together, and that could not be replaced while the raft is afloat without causing the entire structure to sink.[3] If the network of assumptions that such statements of empirical fact and their analogues generate could never hold fast, social chaos would ensue. In short, statements of fact are the stuff of the decisions, deliberations and designs that enable modern western societies to function: they sustain the institutions that comprise these societies and that the societies legitimate.

Factuality is, however, a hotly contested issue in the present-day affluent western world both within philosophy and without it – in feminist theory and in other post-colonial critical projects. On the one hand, information networks saturate the environment with impersonal statements of fact about what "surveys show" and "experts have proved": the quotidian deliverances of an instrumental, faceless rationality mold and shape the dominant social-political-epistemic imaginary with a plethora of "facts." Yet, on the other hand, from the radical constructivism attributed to post-modernists in the second half of the

---

2 The term is R.G. Collingwood's, who writes, "*An absolute presupposition is one which stands, relatively to all questions to which it is related, as a presupposition, never as an answer.*" *An Essay on Metaphysics* (Oxford: Oxford University Press, 1939), 31 (italics in original).

3 The image of the raft comes from Otto Neurath, who represents human knowledge as a raft that floats freely. Repairs (= revisions in a system of knowledge) have to be made while the raft is afloat. No part is immune from repair, but it is vital to be able to stand on some parts in order to replace or repair others: it would be impossible to dismantle the whole structure at once.

twentieth century and articulated in the early 1980s by such feminist theorists as Liz Stanley and Sue Wise,[4] to Ruth Hubbard's now-classic declaration that "every fact has a factor,"[5] statements of fact have taken on a less matter-of-fact, neutral and innocent demeanour than they once quite naturally claimed. "Just the facts, ma'am" has, for more than one theorist, become ironically emblematic of a more naive time when it was (a-politically) reasonable to believe such a request could expect an adequate response.[6] Indeed the pull between maintaining an in-terpretation-exempt factual zone of epistemic stability and addressing the imperialistic, power-infused practices that the maintenance of such a zone has legitimated in post-Enlightenment politics of knowledge counts as one of the principal, and potentially most productive, tensions that emerged in feminist and other post-colonial epistemologies of the 1990s.

Epistemologists cognizant of the politics of knowledge need methods-methodologies that can generate and adjudicate knowledge both about the factuality of the physical-material world and about a social order whose epistemic assumptions are complicit in sustaining its own nega-tive and positive enactments. They need revisionary ways to engage knowledgeably with the real, palpable material-social interactions of "nature" and "human nature." Indeed, they seem to need an empiri-cal-realist foundation just when foundationalism counts – justifiedly – as one of the villains of the Enlightenment story. They also need ways to show how even the simplest material-observational knowledge claim is open to critical scrutiny in itself and in the circumstances of its mak-ing: none of these circumstances can be presumed innocent before the fact, and many are less innocent than they seem. This tension, I am suggesting, generates an imaginative creativity that makes it more pro-ductive than aporetic: who could presume to propose closure?

---

4 Liz Stanley and Sue Wise, *Breaking Out: Feminist Consciousness and Feminist Research* (London: Routledge & Kegan Paul, 1988).

5 Ruth Hubbard, "Science, Facts, and Feminism," *Hypatia: A Journal of Feminist Philosophy* 3, no. 1 (1988): 5-17.

6 Consider, for example, Kim Lane Scheppele, "Just the Facts Ma'am: Sexualized Violence, Evidentiary Habits, and the Revision of Truth," *New York Law School Law Review* (1992): 123-72.

The dominant epistemologies of late modernity are built around stylized examples of the very statements of fact whose status I am simultaneously affirming and interrogating: observationally-derived propositional knowledge claims whose formulation in the rubric "*S* knows that *p*" presents them for verification or falsification in controlled, universally replicable circumstances. In this exemplary mode, they function as pivotal points in the neo-empiricist theories that hold pride of place – unifying communities of practitioners around an imaginary of direct, demonstrable access to "reality" – in mainstream twentieth-century epistemologies. The apparent simplicity and separate atomicity of the facts these propositions state generates the assumptions, first, that all simple propositional knowledge claims that are amenable to observational verification are equally innocent, and the circumstances of their utterance equivalently irrelevant to their evaluation; second, that more elaborate knowledge claims are mere multiples of such simple claims, with the same apolitical status; and third that the subjectivities of knowledge-claimants are as epistemically inconsequential elsewhere as they seem to be in the stripped-down events of knowing that the cup is on the table, or the cat is on the mat.

Post-Enlightenment critics of positivistic empiricism and its offspring are at once drawn to and suspicious of these simple facts: drawn by the urgency of demonstrating the incontrovertible factuality of the material, historical, physical, social world – of its intransigence *and* its amenability to prediction and intervention; suspicious because of the injustices and harms rationalized – and naturalized – in appeals to "facts" about nature and human nature. Hence, in her now-classic paper "Situated Knowledges," Donna Haraway names *radical constructivism* and *feminist critical empiricism* as the polarities of a powerful dichotomy that both tempts and traps feminist epistemologists.[7] Haraway shows that a premature dissolution of this tension would force feminists to stop well short of the epistemological-political goal of producing "faithful accounts of a 'real' world" and critical analyses of the "radical

---

7 Donna Haraway, "Situated Knowledges: The Science Question in Feminism and the Privilege of Partial Perspective," in *Simians, Cyborgs, and Women: The Reinvention of Nature* (New York: Routledge, 1991).

historical contingency" of power-implicated knowledge and subjectivity. She thus advocates a "feminist objectivity [of] limited location and situated knowledge," in which objectivity responds to the pull of empiricism; location and situation to the pull of constructivism and diversely enacted subjectivities.[8]

My thesis in this essay is that "statements of fact" indeed acquire or fail to achieve that status *situationally* according to the patterns of authority and expertise that structure the "institution" in whose discursive spaces they circulate and in whose praxis they are embedded: institutions neither so alike as to be amenable to universal, abstract and interchangeable analyses, nor so unlike and isolated as to require separate and distinct analyses. Critical-revisionary engagement with the presuppositions that sustain their status and legitimate "normal" epistemic practice within them expose some of the complexities in the politics of knowledge that successor epistemologies have to address.

Here I take the goals Haraway articulates as my starting point for analysing two examples from specifically situated ("local" in Foucault's sense) regions of cognitive practice: law and medicine. From feminist legal inquiry, I take Regina Graycar's analysis of judicial knowledge;[9] and in medicine I concentrate on Kirsti Malterud's discussions of epistemological problems posed by women's undefined medical disorders.[10] I read these examples as salient epistemic moments within "natural" or "material" institutions of knowledge-production (to

---

8 Haraway, "Situated Knowledges," 187, 190.

9 Regina Graycar, "The Gender of Judgments: An Introduction," in *Public and Private: Feminist Legal Debates*, ed. Margaret Thornton (Melbourne: Oxford University Press, 1995). The phrase "statements of fact" that supplies the title of this essay is pivotal to Graycar's discussion.

10 Kirsti Malterud, "Women's undefined disorders – A challenge for clinical communication," *Family Practice* 9 (1992): 299-303; and "The Legitimacy of Clinical Knowledge: Towards a Medical Epistemology Embracing the Art of Medicine," *Theoretical Medicine* 16 (1995): 183-98; Kirsti Malterud and Hanne Hollnagel, "The magic influence of classification systems in clinical practice," *Scandanavian Journal of Primary Health Care* 15 (1997): 5-6.

borrow Sabina Lovibond's words).[11] My argument does not depend, however, on finding in Haraway's "situated knowledges" a ready-made solution. Insightful and compelling as her arguments are, she accords vision a more exclusive epistemic primacy than I would grant it, and she does not, at least in the 1991 essay, show how theoretical space could be made for drawing connections across diverse epistemic situations.[12]

In addressing these issues, I bring three lines of thought together. On the issue of vision – and indebted to Sonia Kruks – I look to ways of developing an epistemological position that takes praxes (hence specific practices) as primary sites of knowledge production. For connections that the escalating affirmations of difference in the 1990s have made increasingly tenuous, I examine interpretive practices that escape the subjectivist dangers of what Kruks calls "an epistemology of provenance," one of whose analogues I have called "experientialism."[13] And to show how remappings of the epistemic terrain could be achieved, taking naturalistic practices within these institutions of knowledge-making as geographical markers, I sketch the outlines of an ecological model of knowledge and subjectivity that I have begun to elaborate elsewhere.[14] Its very

---

11 In Sabina Lovibond, "Feminism and Postmodernism," *New Left Review* 178 (1989): 5-28. Lovibond sees in naturalizing epistemology an effort "to represent the activity we call 'enquiry' as part of the natural history of human beings," noting that "naturalist or materialist analyses of the institutions of knowledge-production ... have made it possible to expose the unequal part played by different social groups in determining standards of judgement" (12-3).

12 Haraway begins to engage with these questions in *Modest_Witness@Second_Millenium.FemaleMan©_Meets_Oncomouse™* (New York: Routledge, 1997).

13 See Sonia Kruks, "Identity Politics and Dialectical Reason: Beyond an Epistemology of Provenance," *Hypatia: A Journal of Feminist Philosophy* 10, no. 2 (1995): 1-22. I am indebted to Kruks's analysis in my thinking about Haraway's paper. See also my "Incredulity, Experientialism and the Politics of Knowledge," in *Rhetorical Spaces: Essays on (Gendered) Locations* (New York: Routledge, 1995).

14 See Lorraine Code, *What Can She Know? Feminist Theory and the Construction of Knowledge* (Ithaca, NY: Cornell University Press, 1991), chapter 7; "What Is Natural About Epistemology Naturalized?" *American Philosophical Quarterly* 33, no. 1 (January 1996): 1-22; and "The Perversion of Autonomy and the Subjection of Women: Discourses of Social Advocacy at Century's End," in *Relational Autonomy*, ed. Catriona Mackenzie and Natalie Stoljar (New York: Oxford University Press, 2000).

possibility is dependent upon the engaged praxis of practitioners whose commonalities and differences are always an issue in their endeavours to produce epistemic environments that are neither oppressive nor exploitative.

Crucial to this exercise in the debt that it (partially) owes to Haraway is that "situation" becomes *a place to know* in two senses: a place where epistemic activity occurs; and a place that demands to be known in its aspects that facilitate or thwart knowing. The mappings integral to this project focus attention on the structural intricacies of place, the genealogies, power relations, and commitments that shape the knowledge and subjectivities enacted there, the locational specificities that resist homogenization, the positionings available or closed to would-be knowing subjects. Situation, then, is not just a place *from which to know*, as the language of "perspectives" implies, indifferently available for occupancy by anyone who chooses to stand there.

Epistemology Naturalized?

The essay is part of a project of *negotiating empiricism* which interrogates taken-for-granted epistemological assumptions according to which empirical facts are self-announcing to the properly observant eye: that ambiguity or contestation would destabilize their factual status. Its negotiations occur not merely when scientists or secular knowers debate, at a commonsense level, about which pieces of evidence to count and which ones to leave aside. Rather, they are about how the going commitments of any inquiry generate questions about the nature of evidence and the relation of evidence to "facts"; about how or why a statement of fact (a putatively factual claim) "goes through," carries weight, or fails to establish itself, where the answer is not available in claims about replicability, or correspondence. Often the appropriate conceptual apparatus is not available for claiming acknowledgement for a set of empirical claims (at one level) or for articulating an empirically based theory (at another). So the questions this project raises are about negotiating anew what empirical knowledge claims entail.

The project enlists the resources of naturalized epistemology for feminist and other emancipatory ends, yet it locates the "natural" in places that orthodox naturalists might scorn to acknowledge, while contending that "natural," too, is a negotiable designation. It proposes that "situated knowledges" critically elaborated through analyses of institutionally located praxes, and naturalistic epistemology deflected from its scientistic course, become co-operators in charting a way forward for successor epistemologies. The project maintains an allegiance to a critical empirical-realism in its accountable (= evidence-reliant) engagement with the natural and social world, both found and made. Yet this is no spectator epistemology emanating from a value-free position; nor is it reliant either on propositional atomicity or on an abstract epistemic agency whose monologic statements of fact could count as epistemic basics. Its aim is to develop principles and guidelines for negotiating the situations in which knowledge *and* subjectivity are variously enacted on a complex, institutionally patterned and diversely populated epistemic terrain. In this essay, I am examining how certain kinds of "statement of fact" operate within this larger project.

In the late twentieth century, naturalistic epistemologists made some of the most notable moves away from a dislocated epistemology preoccupied with analysing what ideal knowers ought to do and/or with silencing the sceptic.[15] Naturalists start from an assumption that knowledge is indeed possible and work to delineate its real-world (natural) conditions. Rather than seeking *a priori*, necessary and sufficient conditions for "knowledge in general," they examine how people actually produce knowledge, variously, within the scope and limits of human cognitive powers as these powers are revealed in the same projects of inquiry. Naturalism's most successful North American version, with its originary debt to the work of W.V.O. Quine, looks to physical science as the institution of knowledge-production most worthy of epistemic analysis because of its accumulated successes in revealing "the nature of the world." It finds in scientific psychology and cognitive science sources of exemplary knowledge of human cognitive

---

15 Here I am drawing on my argument in "What Is Natural About Epistemology Naturalized?"

functioning.[16] Although Quinean naturalists draw normative conclusions from studies of knowledge production in the scientific practices they esteem, they are committed to ensuring that their project does not amount simply to turning an "is" of epistemic practice into an "ought" of epistemological normativity. Hence, although they shift from a formal epistemic mode to a descriptive method, their descriptions are no mere recordings of how people know in certain naturalized settings. Naturalism's reflexive turn commits its practitioners to a critical and self-critical stance toward the practices they examine and in which they engage: critical both of the conduct of the practices themselves and of the values and commitments that animate them.[17] In my readings of naturalistic projects, it is this reflexive stance that makes interpretive negotiation possible. Naturalists thus contend that descriptive analyses of experimental findings yield more adequate normative and evaluative principles than *a priori* epistemologies can provide; hence epistemological exhortations can become more directly pertinent to the capacities and projects of real knowers than they can in experience-remote analyses of monologic knowledge claims ("*S* knows that *p*") that are everyone's, and no one's.

These commitments notwithstanding, a tacit normative assumption that governs the work of Quinean naturalists and their associates sounds a cautionary note. It is apparent in an evaluative contrast that grants cognitive science the power to denigrate the knowledge claims

---

16   According to Hilary Kornblith, naturalism's principal questions are "What is the world that we may know it? And what are we that we may know the world?" Answers will be sought at the places where the best current theories of the nature of the world and the best current psychological theories dovetail. Hilary Kornblith, *Inductive Inference and Its Natural Ground: An Essay in Naturalistic Epistemology* (Cambridge: MIT Press, 1993).

17   Richmond Campbell argues persuasively that naturalism's reflexive turn is one of the principal sources of its value for feminist epistemology. The fact-value holism, and the meaning-value holism that Campbell elaborates from a naturalist position go a long way toward showing how a committed, value-infused political stance can promote objective knowledge of a real world. See Richmond Campbell, *Illusions of Paradox: A Feminist Epistemology Naturalized* (Lanham, MD: Rowman & Littlefield, 1998), especially chapters 7 and 8, and p. 219.

of "folk psychology"[18] in any setting other than "folksy" conversation: a move that is emblematic of the hierarchy that consistently elevates scientific knowledge above all "other" knowledge, even for naturalists. Thus the still-experience-remote laboratory retains its claim to be the natural knowledge-making setting. This move sustains the assumptions, first, that it is legitimate to represent this constructed, artificial setting as "natural"; second, that the assumptions, methods, and evaluative techniques of cognitive science are in order as they stand, translatable without negotiation across knowledge-making situations and institutions; third, that naturalism fulfills its mandate by importing into diverse locations the relative valuations of scientific versus "other" knowledge that characterize the very mainstream that naturalists contest, and in whose eyes *their* projects are transgressive;[19] and fourth that the questions I pose in my title are epistemologically *hors de question* because any adequately trained researcher would produce the same statements of fact as any other, and when human subjects are the objects of study, any "typical" member of a sample would behave like any other. Issues about epistemic negotiation thus do not and should not arise.

All of these assumptions are contestable; all come under scrutiny in feminist and other post-colonial epistemologies. Nature is neither self-announcing, nor does it "naturally" distinguish itself from culture or artefact.[20] The choice of physical science-cognitive science as natural preserves the science-dominant assumptions that govern standard

---

18 Jerome Bruner contends that the term "folk psychology" was "*coined in derision by the new cognitive scientists for its hospitality toward such intentional states as beliefs, desires, and meanings.*" Jerome Bruner, *Acts of Meaning* (Cambridge: Harvard University Press, 1990), 36 (my emphasis). Cited also in my "What Is Natural About Epistemology Naturalized?"

19 For an interesting analysis of these relative valuations, see Stephan Fuchs, "The new wars of truth: conflicts over science studies as differential modes of observation," *Social Science Information* 35, no. 2 (1996): 307-26.

20 See in this connection my "Naming, Naturalizing, Normalizing: 'The Child' as Fact and Artefact," in *Toward a Feminist Developmental Psychology*, ed. Patricia Miller and Elin Scholnik (New York: Routledge, 2000).

epistemic analyses, despite naturalism's critical stance toward more orthodox epistemological inquiry. Continuing to favour this source of "natural" knowledge, then, generates scientistic excesses that widen rather than narrow the gap between a naturalism that promises to re-locate itself "down on the ground," and the real, everyday epistemic practices that prompt many inquirers to seek revisioned justificatory strategies and methods for assessing the factuality of statements of fact.[21]

Situations

To make good my contention that scientific knowledge production is neither the only nor the most "natural" focus of naturalistic analysis, I turn to law and medicine as candidates at least as worthy: sites where empirical scientific findings are often integral to the knowledge that informs and is informed by practice and where scientific method fre-quently governs "fact-finding"; yet where science neither yields the only knowledge worthy of the label nor counts as the uncontestable epistemic master narrative. In these examples, situation is a place to know whose governing imaginary is infused with the judgement of "the reasonable man" (in law) of whom a judge is the exemplar *par excellence*; and with the remarkable successes of empirical science (in medicine) of which an objective, science-obedient diagnostician is the exemplar *par excellence*. Analyses of knowledge thus situated expose the historical-material contingency – the negotiability – of the social-political arrangements of authority and expertise enabled and enacted there.

i. Law

Having discerned markedly gendered subtexts in a range of statements of fact that inform judicial pronouncements, Regina Graycar suggests that the "doctrine of judicial notice" sanctions appeals to contestable "commonsense" knowledge that figures in their formulation:

---

21 For a useful discussion of the excesses of scientism, see Tom Sorell, *Scientism: Philosophy and the Infatuation with Science* (London: Routledge, 1991).

"knowledge," however, that requires neither corroboration nor verification.[22] Judgements, she notes, are often informed by tacit yet powerful beliefs about what "women in general" want and are like, how domestic arrangements work, what the reasonable man would think or do – or expect a woman to think or do – in allegedly typical situations. Graycar urges feminists to "confront the epistemological processes by which legal discourses construct reality and give authority to particular versions of events, while at the same time entrenching and dangerously widening ... the 'perceptual fault lines' of understanding" (281). Many of the generalizations from experience out of which a judge produces small, seemingly innocent statements of fact that generate or give rhetorical force to the content of his judgements (though not singly or without appeal to precedent and the letter of the law) are plainly just that: extrapolations from *his own* experiences, shaped by the specificities of his social-economic-gendered position. Yet they claim an authority from his elevated, power-infused status that far exceeds their empirical basis. They defy the most elementary principles of induction to yield statements of fact whose effects are to reaffirm and sustain a social order whose contribution to women's oppression – and to classism, racism, ethnocentrism, homophobia – is documented throughout feminist and post-colonial literature. Nor are these judges especially notorious persons of evil intent. Yet stereotypes and fictions circulate out of control in their utterances: of women as naturally mendacious and untrustworthy, of rape as "not a serious form of harm," and of judges themselves as so (relevantly) experienced that their common sense beliefs are reliable on matters well beyond their experience (72).

It is not surprising for a man whose endowments and credentials admit him to such a position to manifest the "prejudices," "biases"

---

22 The doctrine of judicial notice is "a construct whereby the law absolves the parties from proving by evidence everything necessary to make out a case and allows the courts to take judicial notice of certain things considered not to be contentious." Graycar notes that "Courts may use this doctrine to incorporate into their judgements common sense ideas about the world, common assumptions or, indeed, widely held misconceptions." Graycar, "Gender of Judgements," 274-5.

that these judgements bespeak.[23] Yet – and this is the crucial point – the language of biases and prejudices, which "belong" to someone, of which a judge can purge himself (or herself) with a dose of appropriate counterevidence, is inadequate here. In the dominant imaginary of objective, professional knowledge lodged in the western world's most august institutions, law shares with science that impartial seat removed from the whimsicality and vested interest that afflict more ordinary pursuits, to stand as a repository of even-handed decision-making that has thrust such idiosyncracies behind it. Graycar's reading, like other feminist and racially informed analyses, contests this imaginary absolutely,[24] exposing the secular face of law as a situated – and implicated – knowledge akin to every other. Her reading shows that it takes more than the occasional counterexample to contest its status: that only systemic, social-structural negotiations around its purportedly empirical core can destabilize the "truths" it keeps in circulation. Epistemologically, then, Graycar's argument is no mere insistence on displacing the gender-inflected statements of fact that inform judicial decision-making with statements "more factual" and less oppressive to women. The struggle here is not for simple empirical ascendency, to be won by the contestant armed with the most powerful facts, for a sexist (male) judge is not "contradicted" simply by showing him some women who do not confirm his definition, as an unnegotiated empiricism would claim. He already knows such women and they do not make enough difference: evidence and counterevidence are of little avail.

---

23 I say "man" and "he" in this part of my discussion, because female judges find it difficult not to "do it like a man." Graycar makes a similar point, although some of the judgements she cites are spoken by female judges. (In the Soon Ja Du case I discuss below, the judge is a white woman.)

24 For comparable stories, see Patricia Williams, *The Alchemy of Race and Rights: The Diary of a Law Professor* (Cambridge: Harvard University Press, 1991), and *The Rooster's Egg: On the Persistence of Prejudice* (Cambridge: Harvard University Press, 1995). See also *Race-ing Justice, En-gendering Power: Essays on Anita Hill, Clarence Thomas, and the Construction of Social Reality*, ed. Toni Morrison (New York: Pantheon, 1992); and my "Incredulity, Experientialism, and the Politics of Knowledge."

Now, although Graycar focuses her discussion on judicial statements, similar "fault lines" run throughout legal discourse,[25] prompting Nicola Lacey to argue that "differently sexed legal subjects are constituted by and inserted within legal categories via the mediation of judicial, police, or lawyers' discourse."[26] Established legal discourse, Lacey suggests, works from a set of unquestioned assumptions about "normal" human subjectivity and agency that legitimize certain ways of reading evidence and thwart others. So, for example, the conception of consent operative in sexual assault cases trades on an idea of autonomous freedom of choice, of which a rational man is by definition capable, while leaving "no space for the articulation of the affective and corporeal dimensions of *certain* violations of autonomy."[27] Thus, the restrictively dichotomous conceptual apparatus available to and perpetuated in judging such cases recirculates stereotypes of active masculinity/passive femininity in presupposing that only two forms of agency are possible in an assault case: an active freely choosing assailant and a passive, subordinate victim, who either "consents" or "submits," but will be judged either way according to patterns of "normal" rational choice. Because none of the forms of emotional-psychic damage that assault incurs, such as "violation of trust, infliction of shame and humiliation, objectification and expectation" (106) find expression in this model of the rational, autonomously choosing individual, there is no place for them among the statements of fact that allegedly generate morally and judicially adequate judgements of the harms that sexual assault inflicts. Thus, many of the "facts" that are produced by heterosexist, patriarchal distributions of power disappear behind the screen of "normal," interchangeable human sameness.

---

25 See also Carol Smart, *Feminism and the Power of Law* (London: Routledge, 1989); and Drucilla Cornell, *Beyond Accommodation: Ethical Feminism, Deconstruction and the Law* (New York: Routledge, 1991).

26 Nicola Lacey, *Unspeakable Subjects: Feminist Essays in Legal and Social Theory* (Oxford: Hart, 1998), 10.

27 Lacey, *Unspeakable Subjects*, 117 (italics in original).

Neil Gotanda tells an analogous story of racial stereotypes – Asian- and African-American – circulating out of control, in the Soon Ja Du trial of "a fifty-one-year-old Korean immigrant, mother, and store owner, [who] shot and killed ... a fifteen-year-old African-American girl in a dispute over a bottle of orange juice";[28] and in the O.J. Simpson trial. In each trial, albeit differently, the "model-minority" stereotype of the Asian-American, and the dangerous and out-of-control stereotype of the African-American are mobilized to shape "the facts" that inform judicial behaviours and decisions. Asian-Americans are represented as living just as non-white people ought to live, in order to demonstrate their awareness of the privilege of living in white society: African-Americans as trouble-makers, bound stir up trouble, and thus never truly presumed innocent. Because the stereotype of "gangness" is unquestioningly accepted as endemic in African-American youth, facts about the dead girl's family and school life that tell against the stereotype fail to cross the threshold of admissible evidence. By contrast, the "model minority" stereotype tells in favour of the shopkeeper's innocence, even as it blocks the possibility of weighing the specific facts of the case to determine whether the black girl was so dangerous that she really had no choice but to shoot her. Similarly in the O.J. Simpson case, Judge Ito's "model minority" status allowed him to appear to be "colour-blind and without 'values or history'... [as he remained] safely hidden within his judicial robes and [maintained] the invisibility of the black-white racial framework" (80). Gotanda reads these events as evidence for his claim that the law, like the media and the education, participate in racial construction: in naturalizing certain behaviours, stances, and knowings.

These stories, as I read them, tell of natural knowledge-*making*, not just of *using*, *applying* ready-made knowledge, but the point may not be obvious. A residual and tenacious *tabula rasa* rhetoric of empirical knowledge-making, both in the laboratory and in more "simple" observational moments, sustains a belief that "reality" writes itself upon a blank page when knowledge is properly *made*. Thus when a judge or

---

28 Neil Gotanda, "Tales of Two Judges," in *The House That Race Built*, ed. Wahneema Lubiano (New York: Vintage, 1997), 66.

a lawyer appeals to commonsense "facts" already in circulation, and to law established, codified, it looks as though he or she is merely applying, using knowledge, not making it. On this derivative *tabula rasa* assumption the empirical moment is indeed not negotiable: it simply records facts that command assent, verification, consolidation. These assumptions thus mask the extent to which legal deliberations and judgements participate in the continuous making of knowledge. Neither laboratory experiments nor everyday observations amount to a knowing *ex nihilo*, nor are courtroom situations unlike these more common (to epistemologists) moments of knowing, although the pieces are differently configured. Judicial robes fitting to his/her august "station and its duties" clothe not merely a judge's person but his or her practice. She or he brings perceptual-observational habit and experience to the process of fact-finding, as does everyone who observes that the cup is on the table and every participant in a controlled experiment.[29] And each act of judging confirms, alters, adds, recirculates "the facts" that give substance to his/her statements. Judging, then, is no mere repetition of the same but a subtle accumulative, altering process where "the fact" at issue is sometimes consolidated, reconfirmed – if only because now there is more; sometimes loosened from its moorings, even dislodged, should she or he contest the going wisdom. When observation and interpretation work critically together in negotiating empirical claims, no repetition is a mere re-using of the old: it is simultaneously a making of the new, reinforcing the dominant imaginary or unsettling it.

On first reading, then, judicial pronouncement may seem to have the last word: a chain of processes in and outside the courtroom coalesces in a judgement, informed by encoded law and by the common knowledge that invisibly suffuses it. But a judgement is also the first word in larger processes of critical and corroborative knowledge-making, one word

---

29 My argument here thus resists the philosophical "myth of the given," if "given" means presented to the innocent and untutored eye. For a classic discussion, see Wilfrid Sellars, "Does Empirical Knowledge Have a Foundation?" in *Empirical Knowledge,* ed. R.M. Chisholm & R.J. Schwarz (Englewood Cliffs, NJ: Prentice Hall, 1973).

among many in patterns of orthodox and less orthodox judicial knowing. It is situated within affirmations that consolidate a judge's position, and the status of "the law," within the social imaginary, and within the racial, gendered, economic structures of the social-political-moral order it sustains. But ongoing critical interrogations set in motion by the changing faces of the profession and its theorists and critics also inform the situation of judgements, as do the dissentions and debates that keep the law resistant to closure, even as its rhetorical patterns and institutional structures pull toward conservation of the same comfortable yet contestable "facts."[30]

"We" then – we "situated" epistemologists – are looking to what judges, lawyers, and their challengers and supporters bring to and take from such knowledge-making. The making that issues in statements of fact reverberates through and shapes the social order well beyond these relatively small events, subtly reinforcing, sometimes challenging the dominant social-political imaginary; sometimes entrenching it more firmly. The challenge for epistemologists, then (recalling Haraway), is to produce "faithful accounts of the real world" that work through genealogical, power-sensitive inquiry to destablize the social-political imaginaries that confer a critical immunity upon statements of fact whose historical-material contingency attests to their vulnerability to critique.

ii. Medicine

Comparable negotiations in medicine supply my second set of examples. Trained in a climate of virtually uncontested – and amply vindicated – respect for scientific medical knowledge, Kirsti Malterud learned that "the physician's task was to ask, the patient's task was to answer, and the answers were expected to fit into a universal pattern."[31]

---

30 For an important discussion of debates in legal theory over critique versus closure, see Nicola Lacey, "Closure and Critique in Feminist Jurisprudence: Transcending the Dichotomy or a Foot in Both Camps?" in *Unspeakable Subjects*.

31 Kirsti Malterud, "Strategies for Empowering Women's Voices in the Medical Culture," *Health Care for Women International* 14 (1993): 366.

What, then, to do about women's "undefined disorders," for which there are no established eliciting questions, no technologically diagnosable signs, yet the "reality" of women's physical suffering is incontestable? Two incompatible sets of "statements of fact" equally – hence impossibly – demand assent: empirical tests identify no symptoms; experiential reports attest to painful, persistent symptoms. Recurring lack of fit between "authorized" objective knowledge and patients' allegedly unstable subjective knowledge, and an ongoing realization in practice that "identical diseases might present and proceed quite differently in different patients"[32] prompt Malterud's challenge to the epistemologies that sustain *scientific* medicine as the non-negotiable locus of overriding truth. Her work contests medical science's pretensions to universal applicability and claims validity (albeit a negotiated validity) for women's subjective knowledge.

Among women's undefined disorders, Malterud counts fibromyalgic pain (chronic muscular pain) and a cardiac condition (syndrome *X*), both of whose symptoms fail to find straightforward, causal confirmation in testing by even the most sophisticated, state-of-the-art scientific-medical procedures. Fibromyalgia presents no standard symptomology; and syndrome *X* tends to slip through the net of the most refined cardiac screening procedures. Both conditions, coincidentally or otherwise, are more prevalent in women: both tend in orthodox consulting rooms to elicit dismissal as sufferings that are "all in her mind," reinforcing stereotypes of women as overreactive, irrational complainers. Their experiential reports, read through these ready-made stereotypes, meet with an incredulity that blames the patient, often for wasting the doctor's time with imaginary symptoms – that cannot be factual, because there is no corroborating evidence. As Susan Wendell comments of her experiences with Chronic Fatigue Syndrome (Myalgic Encephalomyelitis), "my subjective descriptions ... need the

---

32　Kirsti Malterud, "The Legitimacy of Clinical Knowledge: Towards a Medical Epistemology Embracing the Art of Medicine," *Theoretical Medicine* 16 (1995): 184. See also Kirsti Malterud, "Women's Undefined Disorders – A Challenge for Clinical Communication," *Family Practice* 9, no. 3 (1992): 299-303; and "The (Gendered) Construction of Diagnosis," *Theoretical Medicine*, forthcoming.

confirmation of medical descriptions to be accepted as accurate and truthful."[33] It is the kind of acknowledgement Wendell seeks that Malterud is committed to providing.

Malterud is engaged in knowledge-making practices that are respectful of her patients' testimonial evidence, and cognizant of the social-material-economic mediations that contribute to producing their symptoms. Her research-in-practice seeks to show, empirically *and* critically/self-critically, that these women's knowledge is just that: knowledge. There is no before-the-fact justification for dismissing it as folk conjecture ready to be trumped by the doctor's accredited expertise. Yet neither does it simply contradict scientific medicine, assuming that every "I feel" utterance warrants total, uncontested corroboration. A commitment to take seriously – if not always literally – what a patient knows permeates these negotiative diagnostic encounters. Doctor and patient seek meanings and treatments co-operatively, weighing the evidence, interpreting it creatively. The doctor is prepared to evaluate the patient's causal explanations as hypotheses as worthy of consideration as "the received view," even despite their incongruity with established patterns of medical etiology. She proposes solutions for deliberation: she does not impose them.

In the discourse of an observation-based epistemology that is about verifying or falsifying knowledge claims, these undefined disorders seem to represent a triumph for an old-style empiricism. By the best standard tests, they yield pretty definitive statements of (negative) fact. Yet on a different reading they expose the limits – indeed the impotence – of an unnegotiated empiricism because of the evidence it leaves unexplained; its failure to provide explanations adequate to the specificities of the complaints; the systemic-structural problems within the institution of scientific medicine that it cannot address. The causal connections these women narrate elicit no established scientific correlations, yet treatment is often successful when a doctor acknowledges that patients can "present plausible causal chains, sometimes [going]

---

33 Susan Wendell, *The Rejected Body: Feminist Philosophical Reflections on Disability* (New York: Routledge, 1996), 122.

beyond the doctor's medical imagination."[34] When physician and patient work together with such causal hypotheses, the effects often satisfy the most stringent empirical requirements.

The issue, then, is not just about saying that Malterud does not know all that she might know in the initial encounters: that she needs to include more; that soon she/we can know better. It is about the persistence and ubiquity of a social imaginary that venerates scientific knowledge to the point that it would block her methods/her knowings from extending beyond her practice. It need not prohibit them explicitly, purposefully, or even visibly in order to ensure that there is no place for them within public knowledge of the sort that could make a broader difference; that might even count as the first small steps toward a paradigm shift. What has to be factored in, then, to aspects of received medical knowledge that thwart these knowings is the force of the assumption that human beings are bodies, mechanically knowable and fixable: the mechanical model of the body that governs decisions about what counts as evidence/facts has to be dealt with on the same plane as the evidence that is accredited within it, or discredited for falling outside its purview. Thus Malterud and other like-minded doctors are caught in an imaginary in which they risk dismissal as quacks by a science-venerating public if they allow their interpretive skills to play an appropriate part in shaping their diagnostic practice.

Yet Malterud's project is no naive anti-science crusade. It neither dismisses "science" (essentialized) as the villain in the piece nor accepts the patient's every word as a source of indisputable truth: it negotiates through and away from these old tyrannies of *scientism* and *experientialism*. Nor does it seek new universals to displace the old, for it reworks claims to universality through analogy and disanalogy from locally specific mappings. Nonetheless, knowledge is made in this negotiated encounter, not just for the patient but also for the doctor, with effects that disrupt institutional patterns and taken-for-granted power structures. Nor is a simple reversal either of epistemic hierarchies the aim – a shift in the locus of knowledge from doctor to patient. The image of a twist of the kaleidoscope captures it better: knowledge made

---

34 Malterud, "Women's Undefined Disorders," 301.

in the consulting room may translate to other practices, but the *art* of medicine that is as active as the science in its making will ensure that "fit" is a matter of creative interpretation, ongoing negotiation. Analogy may only be partial, but artful practitioners will be as skilled in recognizing disanalogies as in discerning repetitions.

Standard, seemingly unnegotiated empiricist principles can be read into both of these examples. A judge structures his/her judgements around statements of fact about which others "like him/her" in relevant respects could equally appeal to observational evidence to reach the same conclusion. Years of accumulated observations (in settings arguably less "controlled" than a laboratory, but thus more "natural"), and the rhetorically sustained "wisdom" of the judicial position, confer immediate credibility on what he or she says. On a Kuhnian reading, the occasional exception to the norm that informs this thinking is merely that: an aberration. And a naturalist plucked from the laboratory would have no trouble reading the event through observational lenses ground in a laboratory setting, to corroborate both process and product. With women's "undefined disorders," empirically established diagnostic techniques used with meticulous precision, and repeated, as scientific method requires, yield no identifiable, diagnosable "facts." Since scientific diagnosis alone claims social-political-epistemic legitimacy as a producer or revealer of facts, these women's statements of fact about their symptoms – even their identical or analogous experiences – fail to achieve recognition as knowledge either singly or cumulatively, because they fail by the very state-of-the-art fact-corroborating techniques to which these women have, in good faith, appealed.

I intend these examples to support the larger claim that, although these power-infused public institutions are analogous in how knowledge functions within them, a "knowledge in general" presumption would gloss over salient *epistemological* differences. Thus, in law, I point to the circulation – the sedimentation – of "commonsense" statements of fact in legal judgements, and thence to their constitutive function in judicial decision-making, despite their empirical contestability. In medicine, subjective, experiential knowledge – which nonetheless merits the label "knowledge" (this too is integral to the argument) – slips through the grid of scientific diagnostic procedures, to remain invisible to all but the most maverick, eccentric clinician. The examples confirm that *situated knowledge* does not just announce "where it (or its articulator) is coming from," nor "situate" itself merely by select-ing examples from specific practices. Rather, it *engages critically with* situations, as natural sites of knowledge-making inhabited by par-ticular, fallible human beings. These sites may be analogically-eco-logically implicated with others; but "facts" insensitive to their local specificities cannot just be "applied" whole and uncontested, as though they counted as universal truths. Situated knowledge is ever cognizant of its own situatedness; willing to examine the specificities and implications of its positioning, to engage in self-scrutiny. Yet its negotiated dimension ensures that such scrutiny reduces neither to monologic introspection nor to an individualis-tic retreat into autobiography. These examples show that even the most venerable of facts is vulnerable to analysis that "puts it in its place," doubly, to evaluate it there, *in medias res*. Neither the judge's perceptual failures nor failures of scientific diagnosis, then, are simple empirical errors, for at issue are the imperatives and limits of an *insti-tuted* epistemic imaginary. Critique at the level of the imaginary itself, imaginatively institut*ing* critique is integral to critique of the would-be statements of fact that claim authority within it.

This inquiry, then, is about the politics of knowledge: it shows how questions about knowledge-*making*, subjectivities, and insti-tutional structures have to be integrated into epistemological in-quiry, for the minutiae of agency, structure and practice are as significant to the making of knowledge as the statements of fact that issue forth. My allusion to the impotence of simple empirical strategies to dislodge and discredit patently erroneous fact-governing assumptions shows that epistemologists need to reconfigure their regulative beliefs. Once they move from ideal-ized propositional analyses of '*S* knows that *p*' statements of fact they have to engage critically and self-critically with epistemic prac-tices located at the intersections of vested interest, background beliefs, rhetorical assumptions, and the politics of social-political hierarchy, framed within imaginaries too elastic and elusive merely to be gainsaid, yet complex enough to invite interrogative re-examination.

Haraway

Donna Haraway's "Situated Knowledges" is a pathbreaking feminist contribution in transformative science-knowledge projects. Most startling is its challenge to a dominant imaginary according to which interchangeable knowers, spectators "from nowhere," produce universally valid observational knowledge that enables them to manipulate, predict and control "the world and all that dwell therein." The pieces of her essay that bear on my inquiry are its demonstrations, first, that the universal mastery that the discourses of the mainstream assume is incongruous in its presumption that knowledge that comes from nowhere can be applicable and regulative everywhere; and second, that only self-consciously situated knowledge can break the spell of the "god-trick" that offers the pretense of dislocated transcendence. Objectivity – and objective talk about *reality* – Haraway insists, are possible only in situated knowledges, answerable for their seeings, frankly and self-critically acknowledging the mediated, embodied specificity of their knowings.

A renewed analysis of vision is central to Haraway's argument: a vision not found but made, because an untutored vision can see neither what is before nor behind its eyes. The seeing that informs an objectivity thus negotiated requires *learning* to see what is ordinarily invisible: to see from below, from the margins, and – self-reflexively – from the centre. Haraway retains no brief for the (classical empiricist) vision that sees accurately, simply by virtue of its ocular endowments. A re-educated vision cognizant of its partiality relinquishes any claim to see "everything from nowhere": it works from its "particularity and embodiment" and with the technological enhancements that modern science affords, toward a "usable, but not an innocent, doctrine of objectivity."[35] The situated epistemic subject, aware of the partiality of its location, is as fully immersed in politics and ethics as in the positionings that conspire to generate "struggles for the contests over what may count as rational knowledge" (193).

---

35 Haraway, "Situated Knowledges," 189.

The rhetorical apparatus that carries Haraway's case forward is as eccentric to sedimented epistemological assumptions as its visionary promise: its respect for ambiguity, radical interpretation, meaning-making; its recognition of the active agency of the world – the surprises and ironies it throws up to anti-reductivist knowers, its heterogeneities that disappear into the homogenizing strategies of falsely self-satisfied universalism. Yet the mobile positioning Haraway advocates is neither careless nor anti-realist: it is about the abdications of responsibility that the "god trick" allows; the urgency of preventing "gross error and false knowledge" (198) from passing as knowledgeable instruments of mastery and domination. It is about *negotiating* empiricism. It resonates with a revisioned naturalism, with a turn toward hermeneutic-interpretive analysis, and with (Foucauldian) genealogical investigations of power-infused disciplinary societies where subjugated knowledges ironically and transgressively disrupt the self-satisfaction of the epistemic order, and the panopticon is the "other self" to Haraway's mobile vision.

For Sonia Kruks, Haraway's analysis of vision is one of the most useful, yet still troubling, aspects of her argument.[36] I single Kruks's essay out for discussion because it engages subtly with Haraway's argument just where it connects with my interests here. Many of the directions Kruks proposes for epistemology after "Situated Knowledges" run parallel to mine, and where they do not, the divergences are instructive. Kruks reminds her readers of the limitations of vision as a metaphor for knowing: despite Haraway's affirmation of "the embodied and situated nature of knowledge," it is hard to grant vision epistemic centrality without "implying that knowledge is rather passively received through the senses and simply varies according to where we happen to be situated" (8). The point is well taken: by representing the senses – especially vision – as passive receptors of the world's messages, epistemologists reinforce the abstracted, "god-trick" assumptions with which Haraway and Kruks alike take issue. Haraway is careful on this

---

36 Kruks, "Identity Politics and Dialectical Reason, 7.

issue. Vision as she re-visions it, particularly in her emphasis on *learning* to see, acknowledging its partiality, being accountable for it (a meaningless requirement if the world imprints itself identically on every retina) is indeed more active than the rhetoric of epistemic passivity allows. Yet Kruks is worried by Haraway's failure to pursue the questions of how/why people are differently situated, with different "partial perspectives"; who makes the instruments of vision that are (unevenly) available to situated knowers; who has these instruments, who controls access. Haraway, as Kruks reads her, needs to engage more fully with the politics and practices where vision is physically and technologically implicated.[37] Nor are my legal and medical examples only about vision, except in an attenuated sense, but about voice and listening; about repositionings of authoritative, expert practitioners. Feminist praxis works around the judge's utterances to negotiate interpretations; in the consulting room it reconstructs the exchanges *away from* standard clinical readings of evidence to produce newly negotiated connections. Issues of seeing are involved: neither the orthodox sexist judge nor the orthodox scientistic physician has seen well enough. But the metaphor is too thin, detached where it needs to be located within the power-infused structures that enable or limit ways of seeing.

For Kruks, the issue is about connections across voices and practices; thus across *differences*. She worries that the logic of situatedness, which is indeed politically compelling, could lead feminists and other emancipatory theorists into "an epistemology of provenance" for which "knowledge arises from an experiential basis that is fundamentally group-specific and ... others ... outside the group ... who lack its immediate experiences, cannot share that knowledge" (4). Haraway does not show how "situated knowledges" avoid terminating in the logical

---

37 Haraway begins to do just this in *Modest_Witness*. Her position there is adumbrated both in "Situated Knowledges" and in "Manifesto for Cyborgs" in the bleak metaphor of an anonymous technological making and control that is everywhere and impersonally nowhere, silently making us and our vision in the most sophisticated of molds; making "identities" ever more elusive.

dead-end of a subjectivism for which experiences are so radically distinct that there can be no speaking or acting across them. In consequence, she leaves unanswered the question of how to accord privileged status to "the claims to knowledge of particular identity groups without thereby wholly evacuating claims for a more general basis for knowledge, or more general visions and projects of emancipation" (5).

In an impressive reading of the radical potential of Jean-Paul Sartre's *Critique of Dialectical Reason*, Kruks proposes a way forward. While acknowledging feminist resistance to finding a theoretical resource in Sartre, she reads past his sexism and androcentrism to extract the outlines of a position "that would privilege differences while still exploring the possibility of a project of world-wide human emancipation" (10). Sartre's beginning in situation, in the world of the embodied, "practically engaged" subject; his examination of "the purposive and transformative human activity that he calls *praxis*," mark a conviction that theory must start from what people do in the world, yet not merely as individuals. He choses an individualistic starting point heuristically "in order to be able to demonstrate that human action is in fact social through and through" (12). Sartre achieves this end well enough, Kruks believes, to establish that knowledge must be both practical and situated, and to reveal possibilities of reciprocity and mutual comprehension between subjects.

Individual praxis discovers its connections with the praxes of others not *a priori* but as it goes – and never once and for all – through the mediations of "the practical material field." It is intelligible across subjectivities because of its intentionality, its *project*, which becomes an entry point into *ontological* recognitions that other subjects are analogously, comparably engaged in projects like mine. Yet such reciprocity is no essential or enduring connectedness. It could as readily manifest itself in reciprocal antagonism as in solidarity; nor does it reductively aggregate the substance of diverse projects of transforming the "practical material field" (13).

Now Kruks is not claiming that Sartre has solved the problems Haraway and other standpoint theorists leave unaddressed. She takes from him, rather, a way of going on, showing some real-world effects of a position for which knowledge is both practical and situated, uncovering its implications for a global emancipatory politics.[38] To take her interim conclusions in a somewhat different direction, I return to Haraway's essay to draw out another of its central threads, reading it through the conceptual framework of Cornelius Castoriadis's also-Marx-indebted analysis.[39] Mixing the resources available from these three thinkers may advance the task of making theoretical space for the reciprocity, solidarity, and mutual recognition that makes negotiating differences possible.

Especially transgressive in an epistemological heritage that venerates disembodied, dispassionate reason is Haraway's claim that "The imaginary and the rational – the visionary and objective vision – hover close together" (192), to which I now turn. I have spoken of "the imaginary" in a more substantive sense, referring to an instituted social imaginary that holds in place complexes of socially informing beliefs, sustains the authority of institutions, knowledge, patterns of expertise, and perpetuates a hierarchially arranged social order. It manifests itself in a rhetoric of justifiably conferred and located power and privilege. Haraway's appeal to "the imaginary" as it contrasts with "the rational" meshes with Castoriadis's work that is germane to transformative social-political-epistemological critique, and thence also, I shall suggest, to instituting an *ecologically modelled* epistemology that could destablize the epistemology of autonomy and ubiquitous – if dislocated – individual mastery.

The complex of interlocking assumptions that enables Enlightenment reason – in Kruks's words – to "lay the world out before itself as a set of objects for [the] contemplation and dispassionate investigation" (11)

---

38 Kruks cites individual decisions of U.S. women to enter the traditionally "caring" professions as contributors to an unanticipated "consolidation of a segmented labor market"; and "third world" women's decisions to bear large numbers of children to secure support in their old age as inadvertent contributors to overextending the economic resources on which they might otherwise have been able to draw (13-4).

39 See, for example, Cornelius Castoriadis, *Philosophy, Politics, Autonomy: Essays in Political Philosophy*, ed. David Ames Curtis (New York: Oxford University Press, 1991); and *The Imaginary Institution of Society*, trans. Kathleen Blamey (Cambridge: MIT Press, 1987).

of a transcendent knowing subject is held in place by what Castoriadis calls an *instituted social imaginary*.[40] He writes:

> the socialization of individuals – itself an instituted process, and in each case a different one – opens up these individuals, giving them access to a *world* of social imaginary significations whose instauration as well as incredible *coherence* goes unimaginably beyond everything that "one or many individuals" could ever produce. These significations owe their actual (social-historical) existence to the fact that they are *instituted*.[41]

To the instituted imaginary, Castoriadis opposes the *instituting* imaginary: the critical-creative activity of a society that exhibits its autonomy in its capacity to put itself in question: in the ability of (some of) its members to act from a (collective for some collectivity) recognition that the society is incongruous with itself, with scant reason for self-satisfaction. Imaginatively initiated counter-possibilities interrogate the social structure to destabilize its pretensions to "naturalness" and "wholeness," to initiate a new making (a *poiesis* – Castoriadis claims an abiding debt to Aristotle).

Castoriadis's work carries no presumption in favour of a single, hard-edged hegemonic imaginary (no counterpart of Kuhnian paradigm-talk). His interest is in the imaginary of late capitalism that sustains social hierarchies and injustices, perpetuates a mythology of the instrumental innocence and neutral expertise of scientific knowledge, and generates illusions about benign equations between power and knowledge. It works from dubious assumptions about the relations between individual and society that legitimate the exploitation and domination known to every reader of feminist and post-colonial theory. His is in many ways a familiar Marxist critique, occupying a terrain contiguous to that of standpoint feminism. But its innovative dimension, whose effects he means to be far-reaching, is its concept of *the imaginary*, whose positive inspiration comes from Freud, Marx, and

---

40 Cornelius Castoriadis, "Radical imagination and the social instituting imaginary," in *Rethinking Imagination: Culture and Creativity*, ed. Gillian Robinson and John Rundell (London: Routledge, 1994).

41 Castoriadis, "Individual, Society, Rationality, History," in *Philosophy, Politics, Autonomy*, 62.

Kant's *Critique of Judgement*; its negative inspiration from an overblown post-Enlightenment individually "owned" reason posing as the legitimator of knowledge of physical nature and human affairs alike, which carves out its domain by relegating imagination to the merely fanciful, incapable of articulating statements of fact, thus unable to make contact with "reality."

In a provocative essay, Castoriadis argues that the ecological movement has cast in question "the whole conception, the total position and relation between humanity and the world and, finally, the central and eternal question: what is human life? What are we living for?"[42] He advances no naive claims to the effect that ecology has the solution to the problems of the modern world, but he claims that only such an imaginatively conceived and politically savvy *instituting imaginary* can effectively interrogate an already instituted imaginary. Nor is it a matter merely of opposing one imaginary, confrontationally, to another. It is about showing, variously and though diverse practices, some other possibilities, marking what is open to question, "making strange" what passes for natural. The *instituting* imaginary is a vehicle of radical social critique: it is about reconfiguring the power-infused rhetorical spaces where knowledge-making and circulating occur. The larger vision is global, but the activities will often be local – as my legal and medical examples also suggest.

The conceptual apparatus Castoriadis proposes opens a way of enlisting the insights Kruks draws from Sartre, to mobilize critical-emancipatory projects of which praxis in a somewhat different sense is a vital component. Valuable in Kruks's account is its tracing of a movement from a (heuristically conceived) individualistic starting point to an affirmation that human action is "social through and through" (12). Missing from that same part of the story is any sense of the social as both *pre-given to* and the *frame of* human practical action: the social as exceeding the sum of individual recognitions and makings, which alone could not suffice to produce the solidarity and/or antagonism that transformative, politically committed action requires. The point holds even though "the social" itself is produced out of the collective

---

42 Cornelius Castoriadis, "From Ecology to Autonomy," *Thesis Eleven* 3 (1981): 14.

efforts of social actors. Now Kruks is careful to observe that even a theory of knowledge as both practical and situated cannot supply the entire substance of a transformative politics. Thus, in my reading of Castoriadis, I am locating praxis and situation not just as originary moments that issue, cumulatively, in the social. Rather, I am positioning them – praxis and situation – within the social as "always already" given, constitutive of the world into which the knowing subject is thrown, of which he/she has to make something.

A creative addressing-interrogating stance toward what is already there is missing from Sartrean praxis in Kruks's reading (even in her references to the practical-material field) – as perhaps it must be in an ontology that retains the flavour of a commitment to radical making and self-making. Her claim that the Sartre of the *Critique* has, in consequence of the events of World War II and its aftermath, moved to acknowledge *la force des choses* is persuasive; nor is she obliged to provide a complete politics where she promises only an element. But this palpable absence of a sense of the instituted given-ness of what Castoriadis calls "the imaginary" leaves the connections she is seeking to forge across differences less manageable than they might be, even within the limits she has sketched. Sartre, as Kruks presents him, appears to remain with what "one or many" individuals could produce.

Yet the instituted imaginary is never seamless or static in a non-totalitarian society: it is always in motion, whether in maintaining itself or in critical interrogations within and around it. Its gaps, its motility leave spaces open for the instituting imaginary. Local imaginative critique, such as Castoriadis's ecology essay, prepares the way for a renewed imaginary that can shake itself free from the one that has kept standard theories of knowledge isolated from the very knowledge they have sought to explicate. I conclude with a too-brief reading of this essay to show its doubled pertinence to these issues.

The ecology movement engages with human existence at the level of its "needs," of which Castoriadis affirms, unequivocally (for the western world), "there are no natural needs" – only the needs that capitalism creates and it alone can satisfy.[43] Taking *electricity* as a

---

43 Castoriadis, "From Ecology to Autonomy," 12.

regulative, society-governing commodity, he argues that an overwhelming impulse to produce the energy to satisfy this need has generated a relationship to nature of mastery and possession that is evident well beyond attitudes to wilderness, animals, and romanticised conceptions of "our" participation in nature. This relationship underwrites patterns of domination that ultimately enslave the society: "it implies the totality of production, and at the same time, it involves the totality of social organisation" (16). Castoriadis argues that the ecological movement opens ways of transforming the technologies that an energy-addicted society has created so that they cease to enslave their creators: so that "the producers as individuals and groups are truly masters of their productive processes" (20). The movement's critical scepticism toward the pretensions of an energy-fetishized society challenges science's position as the dominant religion. The ecology movement, then, becomes a transformative praxis.

The dominant epistemologies of post-Industrial Revolution societies participate in the same rhetoric of mastery and possession: knowledge "acquired" for manipulation, prediction, and control over nature and human nature; knowledge as a prized commodity that legitimates its possessors' authoritative occupancy of positions of power and recasts "the natural world" as a human resource. The "god-trick" of the dislocated knowers Haraway takes to task is about mastery and possession, as are the self-certainties of judicial commonsense and the intransigence of scientific medicine in the face of challenges to its mastery over all the facts worthy of the name. Aggregating, amalgamating differences is also about mastery – over the wayward, the unfamiliar, the strange – in the problems about acknowledging differences while not representing them as individual possessions, discrete identities, that engage Kruks.

Here I enlist ecology metaphorically, to sketch an ecological model of knowledge and subjectivity that can yield a renewed epistemic-moral-political imaginary, where these three conjoined modes of inquiry work reciprocally, interactively together. It takes its point of departure from the – natural – dependence of knowledge claims upon one another, and upon and within sociality and location. It *situates* the negotiations that a renewing empiricism requires, contending that situation-sensitive knowledge-making practices will refuse the unimaginative, dislocated levellings-off that the epistemologies of mastery have performed. Because its effectiveness requires responsible inter-mappings (from region to region), as well as internal mappings, nego-tiating differences will be a prominent item on its agenda. Negotiating, here, includes seeking respectfully, imaginatively, and critically to know differences,[44] honouring them where practical wisdom (*phronesis*) shows them worthy of preservation; interrogating them where necessary; yet neither in stasis nor in isolation.

I conceive of this approach as a revisioned *naturalism*, because it locates epistemological inquiry within the practices and institutions where people produce knowledge and from which they enact its ef-fects. It makes no before-the-fact assumptions about "knowledge in general," yet it is committed to drawing (interim) conclusions that can map from region to region, location to location, to inform and enable global emancipatory projects, aware that the meaning of emancipa-tion varies with regional and demographic diversity.[45] It is wary of the power-infused tendencies of racial-gender-class stereotypes and of essentialized conceptions of "science" and "nature" to take on the self-fulfilling, self-perpetuating qualities that foster illusions of sameness.

An ecological epistemology counts the empirical findings of natu-ral and social science as evidence in determining how survival is best enhanced, not just quantitatively but qualitatively, while rejecting their claims to joint occupancy of the position of master meta-narrative. Thus, in its critical engagement with natural science, ecological thinking con-cerns itself (in Verena Conley's words) "with active interrelations among ... [species] and between them and their habitat in its most di-verse biochemical and geophysical properties."[46] It will, as Castoriadis

---

44 See in this connection my "Rational Imaginings, Responsible Knowings: How Far Can You See From Here?" in *EnGendering Rationalities*, ed. Nancy Tuana and Sandi Morgen (Albany: SUNY Press, forthcoming).

45 I appeal here to the idea of bioregional narratives, elaborated by Jim Cheney in his "Postmodern Environmental Ethics: Ethics as Bioregional Narrative," *Environmental Ethics* 11 (1989): 126. See also in this connection my "How to Think Globally: Stretching the Limits of Imagination," *Hypatia: A Journal of Feminist Philosophy* 13, no. 2 (1998): 73-85.

46 Verena Conley, *Ecopolitics: The Environment in Poststructuralist Thought* (London: Routledge, 1997), 42.

puts it, "have to seize part of what exists at present as technology and utilise it to create another technology";[47] and to learn, analogically and literally, from the science of ecology. It establishes its evidence in self-critical reflexivity where locally, environmentally informed studies of disciplines, their subject matters, and their interdisciplinary relations generate an ongoing sceptical suspicion of presumptions to theoretical hegemony. Ecological thinking works with a conception of embodied, materially situated subjectivity for which locatedness and inter-dependence are integral to the possibility of knowledge and action: of an ecological human subject made by and making its relations in reciprocity with other subjects and with its (multiple, diverse) environments.[48] The model is not self-evidently benign, for ecosystems are as competitive and unsentimentally destructive of their less viable members as they are co-operative and mutually sustaining. So for work within it to avoid replicating the exclusions endemic to traditional epistemologies, its adherents need moral-political guidelines for regulating and adjudicating claims to epistemic authority.

Standard theories of knowledge, with the gap they maintain between knowledge made and applied, work with residues of a unity-of-knowledge/unity-of-science assumption. In consequence, disciplines, domains of inquiry are at one and the same time kept separate by a set of border-patrolling assumptions *and* homogenized, assimilated one to another with arguments that knowledge will be methodologically-epistemologically identical from one domain to another – i.e., formally – in the conditions it observes and obeys, if it is to count, legitimately, as knowledge. Ecological thinking refuses this unity-of-knowledge assumption as a before the fact regulative (= coercive) principle. It maps locations of knowledge-production separately and comparatively; considers the specificities of the "habitat" conditions within each as a basis for deciding what analogies can reasonably be drawn, what disanalogies demand acknowledgement. Epistemological evaluation

---

47 Castoriadis, 20. Solar energy is a good example.

48 For Conley ecological subjectivity involves relating "consciousness of the self to that of being attached to and separated from the world," *Ecopolitics*, 10.

thus has to stretch to address the (empirically demonstrable) effects of knowledge, the meanings it makes and sustains, the practices it legitimates, the values it embodies and conveys. Responsibility and accountability requirements join verifiability high on the epistemic agenda as epistemic and moral-political issues coalesce, and statements of fact take on a less self-evidently-factual status.

II. Biology and Moral Discourse

CANADIAN JOURNAL OF PHILOSOPHY
Supplementary Volume 26

The Biological Basis and Ideational Superstructure of Morality

CATHERINE WILSON

If moral epistemology can be naturalized, there must be genuine moral knowledge, knowledge of what it is morally right for someone or even everyone to do in a particular situation. The naturalist hopes to explain how such knowledge can be acquired by ordinary empirical means, without appealing to a special realm of moral facts separate from the rest of nature, and a special faculty equipped to detect them. Various learning mechanisms for acquiring moral knowledge have been proposed. Most, however, have the following deficiency: What they actually explain is moral acculturation with respect to accepted or author-preferred moral norms, not the acquisition of moral knowledge. Of course, an additional premise to the effect that accepted moral norms or author-preferred norms embody moral truths would deal nicely with this problem, but at the expense of the distinction between opinion and knowledge, or true belief, in which epistemologists are necessarily interested.

A team of psychologists, anthropologists, sociologists, and students of moral discourse could, with a little effort, explain moral acculturation. We can discover what peoples' conceptions of their moral obligations are by observing them in the field, by putting them into special test situations and seeing what they do, or simply by asking them about their moral beliefs, though the last method is the least empirical and not very reliable. Approaching moral phenomena as naturally occurring phenomena, we might gradually attain an understanding of the moral novice's emotional and dispositional apparatus, and the steps by which she is brought to exercise moral judgment with respect to her own actions and the actions of others, to analyze situations using moral terms, and to denominate the virtues and vices. We might study the reinforcement and extinction of patterns of behaviour through praise and blame and show how the learner establishes a pattern in her judgments of fairness and unfairness as a result of parental attempts to adjust juvenile expectations. But just as the sociological approach to the study of scientific knowledge either flatly identifies "scientific truth" with "current accepted belief" or ignores the question of truth as a metaphysical irrelevancy, the anthropological approach to moral phenomena offers no insights into our true obligations.[1]

Reversing the common usage in the history and philosophy of science, we might term the limitation to moral belief the "weak programme" in naturalized moral epistemology. But philosophers who believe that there is genuine moral knowledge that stands to accepted belief as natural science stands to the folk knowledge of plants, animals, stars, and planets of our ancestors will demand a good deal more. The "strong programme" in naturalized moral epistemology has to provide nothing less than an account of how, given the sorts of cognitive apparatus and affective propensities humans have as a matter of their native endowment, some combination of information-gathering and analytical procedures will lead to knowledge of moral truths, or at least to the expulsion of moral falsehoods from the corpus of popular moral belief.

---

1 Sociological studies can explain why there is a given level of consensus on a given issue in the natural sciences without appealing to the truth of a doctrine. An empirical study of moral acculturation would also reveal to what extent there is moral agreement amongst humans and would explain its basis; the alleged truth of some moral judgment need play no role in explaining anyone's beliefs or behaviour. Gilbert Harman notes in this connection the absence of any genuine explanatory function for moral truth as opposed to moral belief; see *The Nature of Morality* (New York: Oxford University Press, 1977), 7.

   In natural science, it might be observed, the consensus of certified experts has normative importance. This makes the identification of truth with institutionally certified belief in social studies of science more plausible. Other things being equal, I ought to believe what credentialed persons tell me about global warming, using vitamin supplements, etc. In ethics, by contrast, the consensus of credentialed experts has little normative force for individuals. (Maybe it does for hospitals or accounting firms, who really *ought to do* what the staff ethicist tells them to.) But, like the old Protestants, the rest of us want, and mostly feel empowered, to discover "moral truth" for ourselves. This reduces the plausibility of the identification of expert-approved belief with truth, and ultimately reduces the plausibility of the claim of the moralist to be able to discover moral facts.

The purpose of this paper is to argue that the strong programme in naturalized moral epistemology is confused. We have no demonstrable obligations, and we cannot find out what our real obligations are by employing any procedure analogous to scientific method, let alone employing our intuitions. It cannot be the case that merely exposing our human cognitive-emotional apparatus to the data-stream and allowing it to experiment and play will, in time, produce good methods for acquiring moral knowledge, though, from an extremely detached perspective, this is how we have managed to discover so many scientific truths about the world. Obligations are assumed, not discovered, though our empirical discoveries about the world may influence profoundly what obligations we decide to assume. The source of the confusion behind the strong programme is the focus on moral judgments as the primary phenomenon of morality, rather than on behavioural inhibitions and prohibitory rules. If morality is a system of imperatives, its rules can be endorsed, ignored, discussed, or rejected as inappropriate, and they can be the object of other forms of approbation and criticism. It can be known that certain rules are the rules, and many other truths can be asserted about rules, but there is no truth in rules for a naturalist to discover. Moral judgments of rightness and wrongness, are, on this view, pseudo-declaratives without truth-conditions: they are orthographic variants of imperatives.[2] There

---

2 The imperative theory was defended by R. M. Hare over his fifty-year career but has fallen out of favour, though cf. Harman, *Nature of Morality*, 63-4. A clever version of moral objectivism that interprets "ought" as indicating the existence of a kind of reason was defended by the late Jean Hampton. Hampton argued that "Human beings should not be cruel to animals" "… gives us a metaphysically necessary reason not to be cruel to animals," and that by virtue of knowing about this reason, a given instance of animal torture is correctly described as morally wrong. *The Authority of Reason* (Cambridge: Cambridge University Press, 1998), 47. To say that a reason as opposed to a proposition is metaphysically necessary is I think to say that it compels universally and overridingly. But Hampton failed to show that it is metaphysically necessary reasons themselves rather than (mere) belief in (nonexistent) metaphysically necessary reasons that induces people (wrongly) to think their moral judgments are factually true. On the view defended here, "Human beings should not be cruel to animals" is a pseudo-declarative corresponding to the command to human beings not to be cruel to animals.

remains accordingly only the weak programme in naturalized moral epistemology, the explanation of how moral acculturation takes place.

Kant, who did hold an imperative-based theory of morality, concluded that we could come to know what rules it would be correct for all humans to obey through the exercise of a supersensible faculty of reason. He appreciated that that morality seems to require the suppression of much natural behaviour, for although there is plentiful evidence of native human benevolence and altruism, there is also ubiquitous selfishness, partiality, and the domination of the weak by the strong. Antinaturalists like Kant have insisted that, because morality is at war with our spontaneous tendencies, psychology and anthropology (and by implication biology) cannot explain its origins.[3] Unfortunately, they have gone on to elaborate philosophical fictions such as the noumenal self and to imagine enactments of universal legislation that cause empiricists to shake their heads. All this is unnecessary: morality is a naturally occurring phenomenon that has a foundation in native human dispositions and in the exigencies of our lives as social animals, both of which are subjects for naturalistic inquiry. All cultures have some rules that can be identified objectively as their moral rules; we can admire, endorse or deplore their rules, but nature cannot teach us that a certain rule is objectively speaking too morally lax or too morally rigorous, and a supersensible faculty cannot teach us this either.

The conviction that there is a correct answer to the question how morally rigorous we ought to be, or how morally lax we are permitted to be, explains why many contemporary normative programmes are incommensurable.[4] To defend my challenge to the strong programme, I offer in this paper a framework for understanding morality in terms of a biologically determined proto-moral core and an ideational

---

3 Immanuel Kant, *Foundations of the Metaphysics of Morals*, A 410.

4 Compare the anti-utopian programmes of Bernard Williams in *Ethics and the Limits of Philosophy* (London: Fontana, 1985), repr. 1999, and Thomas Nagel, *Equality and Partiality* (London: Oxford University Press, 1991) with the comparative rigorism of Peter Unger, *Living High and Letting Die* (Oxford: Oxford University Press, 1996) or Shelly Kagan, *The Limits of Morality* (Oxford: Oxford University Press, 1989).

214

hypermoral periphery. The key idea is that moral
gation form a set of gradients. As surprising as it
quite a simple matter to determine which formulas of obliga...
taining to behaviour amongst those entertained, believed, and enforced
in various cultures are specifically moral, and which are more or less
moral than others. So, in this sense, morality is perfectly objective; it is
a fact that compliance with Formula X is "more moral" than compliance with Formula Y. There are also facts about how the normative
self-positioning of moral agents, their adoption of some particular set
of formulas of obligation, occurs, for example, through social learning.
There are no further facts about which position or positions it is right,
permissible, or obligatory to adopt, and in this sense "nihilism" in the
sense of Harman[5] is true, though nihilism is by no means, contrary to
what is commonly believed, subversive of morality. After explaining
the details of this account, I will take up the question where it leaves
moral theory and moral argument as these are traditionally conceived.
The organization of the paper is as follows. After a few historical comments, I review the kinds of proto-moral behaviour that have been
identified in animals and humans whose use of language is still rudimentary and that are considered by some sociobiologists to be the foundation of morality. Turning to beings who formulate and entertain
propositions, I then argue that moral formulas of obligation are a sub-
class of the many and varied formulas of obligation the human mind
is naturally disposed to generate, including taboos and other social
regulations. Members of the particular sub-class are recognizable as
moral formulas because, as Nietzsche correctly perceived, they seek to
limit the personal advantage one individual or social entity possesses
over another by virtue of its superior strength. The extreme formulas
of hypermorality represent a total renunciation of natural or situational
advantage. Most people's, and most cultures', moral systems trace a
certain pattern between the core and the periphery, and metaethical
positions can also be interpreted as moral self-placements. In the last
section of the paper, I argue that the question "Where ought I to locate
myself?" or "Where ought we to locate ourselves?" is not theoretically

---

5 Harman, *Nature of Morality*, 7ff.

an ability to envision the future is mirrored in contemporary accounts that substitute the cunning of nature, or "blind" natural selection under conditions of environmental scarcity, for strategies consciously chosen in a state of anxious competition. It is evident that, under the assumption that tendencies to behave in certain ways in the presence of certain stimuli are inherited by an animal's offspring, behavioural programmes such as "Kill other members of your species wherever possible and take their food" are self-eliminating. An animal that follows this policy will reduce its stock of potential mates, impoverish its gene pool, expose itself and its descendants to predation by its own similarly programmed descendants, and fade into extinction. But programmes such as "Kill occasionally" or "Kill very troublesome individuals" may well enhance an individual's chances of survival, and may be part of a given species' genetically underpinned repertoire which expresses itself in responses to certain types of cueing. Programmes of co-operation also find a middle-ground. A programme that commands an animal to sacrifice its life in every case where another animal can be saved by this sacrifice will probably expunge itself quickly from the gene pool. A more modest programme of aid to others where it is not too costly, especially where such aid is directed at kin, or where reciprocity can be counted on, facilitates survival and reproduction.

In recent years, the sociobiological focus appears to have shifted from Hobbesian competition and reciprocal "tit-for-tat" altruism to Humean altruism. Famously, Hume is interested in the gentler systems of maternal and paternal care and in the personal qualities that make humans socially charismatic while reducing envy, and this shift of focus from aggression, territoriality and dominance-behaviour has furthered his adoption by a new generation of naturalistic moral theorists. It is not clear that Hobbes and Hume are in more than superficial disagreement over our pre-social characteristics. Hume's world of loving mothers and discreet polished charmers could be the realization of an underlying programme involving unremitting hostility and mutual interference that would erupt into a war of all against all in the absence of socially cultivated manners and morals. Nevertheless, what is now emphasized is that social primates display distinct personalities, recognize each other as individuals, and assess individuals' behaviour. They know who their children are even after they are grown, and they have fondnesses and enmities. Friendships between animals of the same sex, or between males and females, based neither on immediate sexual interest nor on close kinship may develop and last for years.[8] Animals can perceive and react to each other's needs, and they may attend to each other's health, look after one another's infants, and may make somewhat clumsy but surprisingly effective attempts at treating one another's wounds, or even the injuries of a human. Wolfgang Koehler famously described how a chimpanzee removed a splinter from his finger "by two very skillful, but somewhat painful squeezes with his fingernails; he then examined my hand again very closely, and let it fall, satisfied with his work."[9] Monkeys are however surpassed in the possession of those cognitive capacities, notably a vivid projective imagination, that facilitate the full development of empathy by human children.[10]

Observation of young children has suggested that co-operation and altruism towards familiar persons are unlearned dispositions. Very young humans are not purely selfish creatures, and boys and girls between one and three years seem to recognize the needs, feelings, and expectations of those around them. Children around one year of age begin to point out objects of interest to adults.[11] A few years later, one can observe them engaged in co-operative building tasks, taking turns,

---

8 Barbara Smuts, *Sex and Friendship in Baboons* (New York: Aldine, 1985), 61ff. Smut's research shows that these animals choose their friends much as human adolescents do. On the possible advantages of such friendships, see 251ff.

9 Wolfgang Koehler, *The Mentality of Apes* (London: Routledge and Kegan Paul, 1925), 321-2. Koehler observed that "[If] one is on friendly and familiar terms with an ape who has been injured – say by a bite – one can easily induce the creature to extend the injured limb or surface for inspection, by making the expressive sounds which indicate sorrow and regret, both among us and among the chimpanzees."

10 Dorothy Cheney and Richard Seyfarth, *How Monkeys See the World* (Chicago: University of Chicago Press, 1990), 235ff.

11 H.L. Rheingold and D.F. Hay, "Prosocial Behaviour of the Very Young," in *Morality as a Biological Phenomenon*, ed. Gunther Stent (Berkeley and Los Angeles: University of California Press, 1980), 93-108.

and trying to help their parents with household tasks like operating the vacuum cleaner. They display an ability to read the mental states of others from their behaviour and may offer toys and distractions to other children who are crying or hurt.[12] Children have a strong sense of what is "fair."

Naturalists who are impressed by such examples of innate benevolence and the inclination to reciprocity and just distribution tend to regard theoretical morality of the Kantian or utilitarian type as either redundant or excessive. If there are basic dispositions that underlie the inclination to respect life, to tell the truth, to perform one's contracts, and to give help when needed, specific duties are otiose. Correspondingly, if morality demands more of us in the way of ratiocination and exertion than what we are normally disposed, encouraged, and can be taught to do, it is excessive. Thus Bernard Williams argues that there is a central core of pre-theoretical moral beliefs that are adaptive and uncontested. Outside the core, there are only the diverse and conflicting systems of individuals and groups vying for recognition and social control.[13]

2. The Natural History of Moral Imperatives

Accounts that try to derive positive morality from universal human dispositions founder for two reasons. The first is that there is no central core of agreement that could be expressed in propositional form. The idea of a central core of universally acknowledged obligations is attractive because our moral theories seem to converge. Mosaic law, rule-utilitarianism, and Kantian ratiocination all generate the set "Don't kill," "Don't steal," etc. But what these formulas of obligation actually mean is unclear, as they invite contention and tend to be subject in practice to numerous exceptions and qualifications. As Williams concedes, regulations about killing and stealing take different forms in different societies. Propositions such as "Don't kill" do not command

---

12 Rheingold and Hay, "Prosocial Behaviour," 97-8.

13 Williams, *Ethics and the Limits of Philosophy*, 186 f.

universal acceptance and have rarely been strictly observed. There are wars, executions, and various forms of slow starving-out. "Don't steal" is ambiguous, and its applications contestable. People disagree about whether what landlords, tax-authorities and derivatives-traders do is stealing or not. Universal agreement about anything is hard to come by, despite frequent appeals to what "we" think. Michael Ruse is confident that "no one would say that it is morally acceptable for grown men to have sexual intercourse with little girls."[14] This is supposed to be an empirical statement of fact, but confidence on this score seems unjustified. Social scientists and anthropologists can surely turn up examples of human beings who believe that sexual intercourse between grown men and little girls is fully acceptable, and who can supply arguments in favour of the practice.[15] Moreover, there is a difference between what people say, and what they think and do. It is likely that some grown men do not think that sexual intercourse with little girls is morally acceptable, and would not try to defend it, but engage in it anyway. Hume is confident that no one would "tread as willingly on another's gouty toes, when he has no quarrel with him, as on the hard flint and pavement."[16] But the qualifier "given that he had no quarrel with him" is significant. Some people like to fight and will elicit a

---

14 Michael Ruse, *Taking Darwin Seriously* (Oxford: Blackwell, 1986) 212. Ruse defends his views in subsequent articles, including "Evolutionary Ethics: Healthy Prospect or Last Infirmity?" in *Philosophy and Biology*, ed. Mohan Matthen and Bernard Linsky (Calgary: University of Calgary Press, 1988), 27-74.

15 At least there are people (reputedly the Etoro of Papua-New Guinea) who consider sexual intercourse with boys as young as ten to be a good thing and so presumably morally acceptable, since it is considered to preserve male powers by restricting the circulation of valuable and nutritious semen to men. (Thanks to my colleague John Russell for bringing this to my attention.) The practice may have some hidden fitness-increasing population-control rationale, but it is not dignified by the beliefs concerning human excellence surrounding it. It involves the use of underage subjects who have little choice in the matter, and probably helps to consolidate the men's power over the women of the tribe too.

16 Hume, *An Inquiry Concerning the Principles of Morals*, 2d ed., ed. L.A. Selby-Bigge (Oxford: Clarendon, 1902), V. II, 226.

provocation and manufacture a quarrel in order to provide a reason and stimulate their desire to hurt someone. The psychological motivations to what "we" think of as gratuitous cruelty are poorly understood. The perception of vulnerability in another sometimes triggers pity in humans but functions at other times as an incitement to aggression. Weakness in another can be an encouraging sign to proceed.[17]

Biology, then, radically underdetermines the specific formulas of obligation an individual or group subscribes to and by which it regulates its behaviour; any positive morality can only represent a selection and cultivation of some spontaneous tendencies and a selection and suppression of others. Game-theory tells us that we cannot be a population of hawks, or, in Nietzsche's terms, "eagles," and ethology tells us that we are, on occasion, empathetic and helpful to kin and even to non-kin. But biology hardly licenses Ruse's inference that morality essentially involves happiness-conferring care for those in our neighbourhood, or Robert Richards's conclusion that "community welfare is the highest moral good."[18] This makes it difficult to understand the propositional morality embodied in formulas of obligation otherwise than as a derivation *a priori* with the accompanying difficulties.

A second problem with the presentation of morality as an game-theoretic equilibrium is that the Hobbesian *a priori* approach and sociobiology both assume a certain level of homogeneity or uniformity in their populations. An evolutionarily stable strategy I is defined by John Maynard Smith as a strategy such that "if almost all members of a population adopt I, then the fitness of these typical members is

---

17 Richard Wrangham and Dale Petersen describe high levels of interspecies injury and killing amongst some populations of chimpanzees, a species to which we are closely related. *Demonic Males: Apes and the Origins of Human Violence* (London: Bloomsbury, 1996). Infanticide, Sarah Blaffer Hrdy, concludes is a widespread and well-established reproductive strategy of primate males. *The Woman That Never Evolved* (Cambridge: Harvard University Press, 1981), 76ff.

18 Robert Richards, "A Defence of Evolutionary Ethics," *Biology and Philosophy* 1 (1986): 286.

greater than that of a possible mutant."[19] The assumption on which Hobbes's notion that a mutual non-aggression pact will be rational for all his contractors to agree to is that they are all fairly equal in the degree of force they can individually exercise and desire to exercise. Hobbes does not begin with the assumption that some are born weaker, less aggressive, or less competent than others, and the same assumption is present for obvious reasons in game-theoretic sociobiological framework: a measurably less "fit" organism will not be in the game to start with, its genes having been expunged long ago. Maynard Smith has, to be sure, pointed out that evolutionarily stable strategies do not require homogeneity down to the level of individuals; they may be instantiated in distributions of traits in polymorphous populations, and Robert Trivers takes stable strategies to correspond to the frequency with which individual members display certain forms of behaviour. In either case, "hawkish" and "dovish" tendencies and responses as well as "faithful" and "promiscuous" conduct can be modelled in terms of patterns that are resistant to self-extermination and invasion alike. But neither approach to the emergence of ethics starts from the premise that individual creatures in the state of nature at the relevant scale level are very differently endowed and behave differently in various contexts. In any real-world population of social animals, some are cleverer, or stronger, or more ruthless, or more attractive than others, and can exercise social dominance; others are correspondingly dimmer, weaker, gentler, and less charismatic. (The latter are not "less fit." Their own hidden-from-view mosaics of physical and psychological traits serve them just as well in the struggle for existence.)[20] And if we narrow our focus not just to differences between animals, but to the dif-

---

19 John Maynard Smith, *Evolution and the Theory of Games* (Cambridge: Cambridge University Press, 1982), 14.

20 Extreme shyness in a male, for example, might be thought *a priori* to reduce his breeding capacity. Let's pretend for the sake of the argument that there are "shy genes." These have nevertheless remained in the human population for perhaps one hundred thousand years, so either the assumption that shyness interferes with breeding is wrong, or shyness confers compensating benefits, or it is inexorably linked with some trait that does.

ferent roles they assume in particular interactions, it is evident that many such interactions place one animal in an advantaged position. By contrast with Hobbes and Hume, Rousseau and Nietzsche, despite their obvious differences from one another, take morality to pertain to relations between unequals. In doing so, they capture a powerful intuition about morality – that it involves a transfer of benefits from stronger to weaker – while leaving it mysterious how such a peculiar institution could arise in nature.

It is not surprising that biologists are divided on the question whether natural selection alone, without social learning, can explain the persistence of traits such as reciprocal altruism.[21] If we look at populations from a great distance, as effectively homogeneous (Hobbes), it is easy to do so. But if we look at them up close, as composed of dominant and subordinate individuals (Rousseau), the contractualist approach is no longer effective. To put the point simply, powerful individuals, unlike weak individuals, cannot expect to receive a benefit from any contract they could arrange; a powerful individual does better without any constraints.

One way around these two problems is to consider humans from the anthropological point of view as rule-making and rule-using animals.[22] Considered in this way, formulas of obligation may turn out to have an ideational reality as imperatives and optatives that have little or no significance in terms of natural selection. We are aware and semi-aware, on many levels, that our actions are constrained by internalized canons of appropriateness, decency, taste, and civility that forbid us certain things and that we wish others to respect to some degree as well. Such rules govern what we eat, how we dress, what we

---

21 Maynard Smith, *Evolution and the Theory of Games*, 171.

22 The classic work of this genre is Wilhelm Wundt, *Ethics*, 3 vols., tr. Margaret Floy Washburn, Julia Gulliver and Edward Titchener (London: Swan and Sonnenschein, 1897-1908). Alan Gibbard, however, notes our "broad [natural] propensity to accept norms, engage in normative discussion, and to act, believe, and feel in ways that are somewhat guided by the norms one has accepted." *Wise Choices, Apt Feelings: A Theory of Normative Judgement* (Cambridge: Harvard University Press, 1990), 27.

talk about and what words we use, how we greet people, and how we move through the world. The study of rules has both an empirical and a logical dimension. Rules are plausibly seen, as David Braybrooke suggests, as "in origin physical blocking operations that prevent people from acting in ways prohibited, or, better, systems of blocking operations."[23] Verbal rules are substitutes for physical movements that prevent others from performing certain sorts of action. Cultures all have rules, practices governing their rules, and theories about their rules – for example, theories explaining their supernatural origin. Some rules are strictly enforced while others are not; some rules are believed to apply universally while others are believed to apply only to members of one community or class, and some rules are believed to be categorical and to admit of no exceptions, whereas others are regarded as defeasible.[24] The logic of rules in general appears to be non-monotonic.[25] Nevertheless, almost all cultures believe that there are some rules that admit of no exceptions and bind categorically.[26]

Restrictive and prohibiting rules have always been subjects of special interest to anthropologists and psychologists. Freud, who noted the depth, universality, and supra-rationality of anti-pleasure mechanisms, suggested that they might "throw light on the dark origin of our own

---

23 David Braybrooke, "The Representation of Rules in Logic and Their Definition," in *Social Rules*, ed. D. Braybrooke (Boulder, CO: Westview, 1996), 3-20.

24 Robert B. Edgerton, *Rules, Exceptions and Social Order* (Berkeley and Los Angeles: University of California Press, 1985), 221ff.

25 This is one way of reading Williams's discussion of "Gauguin" in "Moral Luck," reprinted in *Moral Luck and Other Essays* (Cambridge: Cambridge University Press, 1983). Gauguin has in his possession a powerful excusing condition from a *prima facie* matrimonial obligation; he is a talented, destined-to-be-great-in-the-future artist! (Or he has correctly guessed that he will acquire this excusing condition.) The critical discussion surrounding this famous essay indicates that altering the contextual information about a given "case" alters our assessment of whether something wrong was done or not.

26 Edgerton, *Rules, Exceptions, and Social Order*, 254.

'categorical imperative'."[27] Asceticism is associated by humans with sanctity, power and control, and prohibitions are accordingly encoded in all major religious and medical texts. Their variability from epoch to epoch and place to place contrasts markedly with the beliefs of participants that absolute right and wrong are at issue, absolute moral peril and perfect safety. As "self-enforcing" norms that do not require the application of external sanctions, taboos seem to be naturally occurring precursors of morality and have been theorized as such.[28] Both taboos and moral prescriptions are culturally transmitted codes of behaviour; they prescribe what must not be done and what ought to be done. Both are cultural creations that are referred to sources outside of culture, to higher reasons, and higher authorities. Both identify prohibited actions that correspond to temptations – to curiosities, wishes, opportunities, that are aroused in individuals and quelled by them. In moral systems, as well as in taboo systems, transgression of the code is regarded as defilement, and as injurious to a person's ritual status. The stain or impurity of moral transgression is wiped away by confession, apology, atonement, regret, exclusion, and perhaps punishment. Restoration of the offender's pure status in the case of taboo violation requires more than acknowledgment; it is effected by ceremonial performances such as washing or transference of the uncleanness to an animal or inanimate object, or the making of sacrifices. In taboo, there is an implicit realism about the dangerous powers of certain objects, while in moral prescriptions there is an implicit realism about the intrinsic goodness or badness of certain actions. It is widely believed

---

27 Sigmund Freud, "Taboo and the Ambivalence of Emotion," in *Basic Writings*, trans. and ed. A.A. Brill (New York: Modern Library, 1931), 824. Samuel Scheffler recapitulates Freud's theory of the development of the superego in *Human Morality* (New York: Oxford University Press, 1992), 80ff, noting that "psychoanalytic theory has the resources to offer serious explanations of the way in which moral concerns resonate through human personality," and that it is in a better position than standard accounts to respond to Kant's challenge to naturalism" (83). Freud's may, however, be an unnecessarily specialized theory that overexplains the tendency to ritualism and ascetic motives in the human personality.

28 Hutton Webster, *Taboo* (Stanford: Stanford University Press, 1942), 370.

that amoral behaviour is in some way harmful to the soul of the agent, not just to his victim. Moral prescriptions then might be seen as corresponding to rationalized taboos, in which expiation is accomplished by performances indicating an inner change in the subject, rather than external ceremonies of purification.

The existence of harsh and complex taboos contradicts Ruse's assumption that "natural selection has made us in such a way that we enjoy things which are biologically good for us and dislike things which are biologically bad."[29] It suggests that natural selection has made us so that we do not always know where to stop when it comes to inventing rules and restrictions, and that our intuitions about appropriate conduct are powerful but unreliable when dangerous actions and experiences – those pertaining to liminal states such as adolescence, marriage, childbirth or the end of life – are concerned.

Some taboos do not seem to resemble moral rules at all, but rather rules of etiquette. It is hard for us to see how they could be associated with powerful aversive or attracted feelings. For example, the high priest of Jupiter in Rome, according to Frazer,

> was not allowed to ride, or even to touch a horse, nor to look at an army with arms, nor to wear a ring which was not broken, nor to have a knot on any part of his garments; he might not touch or even mention by name a goat, a dog, raw meat, beans, and ivy; his hair could only be cut by a freeman and with a bronze knife; ... and his hair and nails when cut had to be buried under a lucky tree.[30]

The existence of such seemingly arbitrary rules is significant. It raises the question whether the rules invented and enforced by humans, including moral rules, always subserve definite social ends or whether they are, in some cases, principally expressive gestures. Functionalists insist that the former alternative is correct. The purpose of taboo rules may be transparent – keeping the King safely isolated; limiting the population by selective infanticide. Or it may be veiled. It has been suggested that arbitrary-seeming taboo regulations aim at the

---

29 Ruse, *Taking Darwin Seriously*, 236.

30 J.G. Frazer, article "Taboo," *Encyclopedia Britannica*, 9th ed. (New York: H.G. Allen, 1888), Vol. T- , 13.

mnemonic marking of privileged states for the maintenance of social hierarchies; the isolation of rulers who might be too powerful if their lives were not hampered by numerous restrictions; or the focussing of communal attention on persons in a vulnerable position. But, as Radcliffe-Brown argued, any system of codes that produces anxiety and relief and requires to be mastered by members of the society enhances group understanding and solidarity.[31] Where morality is concerned, it is clear that modern cultures as well as old ones strive to maintain a certain level of anxiety about the rules, and that, in doing so, they weave ever more elaborately the fabric of social meanings. At the same time, the requirements of morality seem to surpass what can be directly accounted for in functionalist terms.

3. Morality as Compensation

We have so far considered morality in three ways: as a biologically programmed strategy for sustainability; as founded in sympathetic and benevolent impulses; and as belonging to the sector of the inhibitory formulas of obligation that humans seem disposed to generate and respect, and with which they enforce conformity. But the problem of how a naturalist should account for the existence of rules that are accepted throughout an entire population but that are in the interest of the weak rather than the strong is still unsolved. Moral rules do appear to represent this special class of prohibitions and restrictions. Consider the following set of rules from a school handbook:

1) Girls are allowed to wear plain studs or sleeper earrings…. The wearing of rings is prohibited.

2) You are required to sign out whenever you leave the school premises.

3) To sell an item above the value of £5, you need permission.

---

31 A. R. Radcliffe-Brown, *Taboo* (Cambridge: Cambridge University Press, 1939), 39.

prohibitions (No. 2 prohibits students from leaving ̣ without signing out.), and all can be given explan-ble or not, referring to the welfare of the pupils and ̣ the institution, but only No. 3 is clearly a moral rule. Its evidei̥ ̣urpose is to prevent substantial financial transactions taking place amongst students. Experience has shown that when there are relatively large sums of money about, clever and cunning students may find ways of getting it away from more foolish or impulsive ones. Moral rules are different from other restrictive rules in that their purpose is solely to counteract the natural or situational advantage possessed by the better-endowed or currently dominant members of a social group – the strong, the beautiful, and, above all, the clever and versatile. As noted, Nietzsche perceived this clearly; his dislike of morality was based on his view that the strong, beautiful, and clever should be able to press their advantages.[32]

But how could such compensatory mechanisms have evolved through natural selection? As Hans Kummer, the student of baboon-societies, notes:

> Many moral rules appear as a cultural attempt to revert to nonopportunism.... To a biologist, this seems at first rather striking. Why should biological evolution produce a species endowed with superb behavioural flexibility and then "allow" a superimposed cultural development to undo just that achievement and, as it were, regress to rigid behavioural rules?

Kummer's answer is that "Behavioral versatility is an advantage only in certain contexts." Flexibility and unpredictability make animals dangerous to each other. They bring about a situation in which, as Hobbes suspected, too many resources are "wasted" monitoring the behaviour of others, detecting their stratagems, and defending oneself. "If we assume," Kummer argues, "that man's preadaptations offered no way to evolve a brain that was shrewd with tools, predators, and prey, but simple and predictable in dealing with his companions, the

---

32 Friedrich Nietzsche, *The Genealogy of Morals*, trans. Walter Kaufmann and R.J. Hollingdale (New York: Random House, 1969), 34.

228

evolution of moral capacities might have been the adaptive answer: a selective suppression of shrewd flexibility in the social context."[33]

Compensatory mechanisms are a common feature of biological systems; nature likes to build layers of controllers and releasers that regulate the behaviour of a system at a lower level. But Kummer does not explain how natural selection could favour a self-suppressing strategy. Group-selection is a possibility.[34] But the classical evolutionary theorist may prefer to regard behavioural rigidity as a defensive strategy evolved in response to "punishment" by other animals for being too clever. Robert Trivers notes that punishment of "cheaters" sometimes appears to be all out of proportion to their offences. But "since even small inequities repeated many times over a lifetime may exact a heavy toll in inclusive fitness, selection may favour a strong show of aggression when the cheating tendency is discovered."[35] Correspondingly, natural selection may favour a strong show of morality for self-protection. Once established, a reduced level of shrewd flexibility remains resistant to invasion by a clever, unpredictable animal.

The general characteristics of morality as a system of compensatory control of the clever and powerful will be that it is simple, inflexible, and counteracts opportunistic advantage-taking facilitated by superior skill, knowledge, beauty, influence, or strength. Morality in any culture will consist of a set of policies and practices designed to subvert natural relations of dominance and subordination and to moderate appropriation by those who simply find it easy to take. If intelligence consists in part in the development of a "Machiavellian" ability to divine the real internal psychological states of others, to predict their true intentions accurately, while hiding one's own state of mind and intentions, this divinatory and self-concealing intelligence can also be put to use in limiting advantage-taking. The possibility of deceiving others requires cognitive empathy;

---

33 Hans Kummer, "Analogs of Morality Among Nonhuman Primates," in *Morality as a Biological Phenomenon*, ed. Gunther Stent, 43-4.

34 Scorned by biologists since the Williams vs. Wynne-Edwards event, group-selection has risen from the ashes and is forcefully defended by Elliot Sober and David Sloan Wilson throughout the first half of *Unto Others: The Evolution and Psychology of Unselfish Behavior* (Cambridge: Harvard University Press, 1998).

35 Robert Trivers, *Social Evolution* (Menlo Park: Benjamin Cummings, 1985), 388.

we must put ourselves in the position of the rival to guess what he is likely to believe about us. But once we have empathy, it can be used for morality, as the feathers of ancient birds formerly served for warmth, but, once evolved, came to be used for flight. The ability to hide one's real actions and intentions facilitates the development of politeness and self-control. It is inconceivable however that natural selection alone is responsible for the moral phenomena we now take for granted, and this follows from what was said earlier about the difference between large-scale (homogeneity-assuming) and small-scale (heterogeneity-assuming) levels of analysis.

History shows us vividly what happens with individual differences in desire for power and self-advancement and ability to exercise it come into full play in the absence of countervailing moral ideation. It shows us that the contract pretended by Hobbes simply did not take place, and that tit-for-tat is not a sufficiently powerful evolutionary strategy to prevent the slaughter of enormous numbers of human beings. What strikes the reader of chronicles of ancient history in this connection is the high degree of emotional unpredictability of powerful rulers and the wide scope afforded to their agency. The "cult of frightfulness" prescribing wartime rape, execution, and the torching of villages and cities, that re-emerges under certain historical conditions from the Assyrians onwards is a latent potential of humans in groups. And it is not only the excitement of the moment that is to blame; it is remarkable how much tolerance the spouses, clients, and royal counsellors of bloodthirsty monarchs who readily killed their close kin and the children of their rivals to maintain power displayed in former times. Such actions are no longer accepted as an inevitable aspect of political demeanour. Modern leaders still commit atrocities, passively approved by their henchmen, but they no longer commit them as openly, and if the claim that there has been moral progress since ancient times tends to draw skeptical frowns, we should nevertheless acknowledge that the world of Hume's Stuart rulers was already a different world from that of Cambyses.[36] Modern people seem to have

---

36 As Arnold Gehlen argues, morality leads to a "stabilisation of the inner life" so that it is not ruled by affective impulses or subject to psychologically costly and inefficient reflection. *Moral und Hypermoral*, 2d ed. (Frankfurt and Bonn: Athenaeum, 1970), 97.

fewer personal "enemies" than ancient people did, as Kenneth Dover pointed out in his study of Greek popular morality.[37]

The behaviour, not just of our hominid ancestors, but of our historical ancestors was highly responsive to context, clever and inventive. When the Egyptian king Sesostris and his sons were invited to a banquet by his brother, according to Herodotus, his brother set fire to their path:

> As soon as Sesostris realized what was going on, he turned to his wife because he had brought her along with him too, and asked her advice. She suggested that he have two of his six sons lie down over the flames and act as a bridge across the fire, so that the rest of them could walk on them and escape. Sesostris did this, and although it resulted in two of his sons being burnt to death, this made it possible for their father and the others to escape.[38]

It is very difficult to imagine a modern royal or, for that matter, presidential couple finding themselves in such a situation, in which modern intuitions about our natural partiality to our kinfolk do not fit. The story does not present a tragic dilemma faced with great anguish; the "agent-regret" of Bernard Williams does not enter into it. Rather, a problem is solved in a most intelligent manner. And politics and human relations in general were characterized in former times by a flexible, situation-responsive opportunism that has become unusual if not unthinkable. Mary Douglas describes the Hundred Years War in Bordeaux in the thirteenth century as follows:

> Each leader scanned his host, calculated who among his vassals was weakening in loyalty so as to renew attempts to hold them, and would equally scan the followers on the other side whom he might hope to win over. With veiled threats and blandishments he would warn his own men against the evil machinations of the enemy. Between the main ranks of adversaries stood a confused crisscross of lords who sniffed the wind, weighed the risks of a change of allegiance,

---

37   Kenneth Dover, *Greek Popular Morality in the Time of Plato and Aristotle* (Oxford: Blackwell, 1974), 181.

38   Herodotus, *The Histories*, trans. Robin Waterfield (Oxford and New York: Oxford University Press, 1998), 135. I am trying to allow for Herodotus's famously dim view of foreigners.

and passed from one camp into another, trafficking in loyalty. Raymond IV, Vicomte de Fronsac, owner of a river fortress, changed sides five times from 1336-1349.[39]

In private as well as in public life, resoluteness, moral vigilance, and the enforcement of regularity of conduct have tended to increase. Modern people place a great value on protracted intermental deliberation; they appear to think that one should deliberate a lot and not change one's mind too much after it is made up.[40] While too extreme a reduction in versatility and intelligent concern for one's own advantage has been criticized as morally perverse,[41] it is well to keep in mind the distinction between highly moral behaviour and all-things-considered reasonable behaviour.

4. Formulas of Obligation

Unlike both our natural behavioural dispositions and taboo-prohibitions, moral formulas of obligation are not dyadic; they do not relate persons as members of certain categories to persons and things as members of other categories. This feature of moral rules has been widely noted. Hume suggested that the possibility of expressing formulas in general language conferred a kind of impartiality upon our

---

39 Mary Douglas and Baron Isherwood, *The World of Goods* (London: Allen Lane, 1979), 34.

40 Dover reports various ancient sayings to the effect that the wise man readily changes his mind in *Greek Popular Morality*, 122. The context makes it clear that these references are to the effect of rational deliberation, not endorsements of erratic behaviour. Williams is a typical antimodernist on this point.

41 Martha Nussbaum, for example, praises Henry James's Maggie Verver's use of her social intelligence and talent at prevarication as exemplifying a better morality than adherence to rigid rules and formulas in "Flawed Crystals: James's *The Golden Bowl as Moral Philosophy*," in *Love's Knowledge* (London: Oxford University Press, 1990), 125-47. Human needs can overrule morality, and perhaps Maggie Verver's predicament is an example of where they might be thought unproblematically to do so, but Maggie need not be considered an example of a higher morality.

judgments.[42] Moral formulas are characterized, as Kummer observes, by their wide scope. "As regards killing, respect of possession, or false information, they tend to prescribe the same course of conduct in (nearly) all situations and toward (almost) all conspecifics. Advanced codes include nongroup members, alien races, and even all animate beings among the favoured."[43] As Jack Goody remarks, the "over-generalized" moral formula is a distinctive characteristic of literate societies. "Enshrined in the written word, passed down from century to century, the generalized, decontextualized statement becomes the touchstone of moral rationality. It implies that all men should be treated in the same way, that status, relationship, age, and sex are irrelevant in making judgments about the conduct of mankind."[44]

These observations suggest a model of morality different from the model of a central, non-theoretical core of moral propositions subscribed to by all humans and a contested periphery. The biological centre of morality contains no verbal formulas at all. It is a set of species-specific inhibitions and dispositions, somewhat variable from individual to individual and population to population, evolved in the early adaptive environment of the species and dependent for performance on immediate contextual cues and on the animal's mood. Food-sharing and grooming, for example, are elements of the biological core and will be performed when animals give each other the right signals and feel like doing so. Incest with conspecifics recognizable by their shape, smell, or voice as close kin will be avoided when alternatives are available, insofar as it leads to a concentration of deleterious genes and reduces diversity and flexibility in the population, and murderous aggression expressing itself against close companions has presumably been selected against. But morality cannot be identified with this central core, but with a set of centrifugal extensions and generalizations. Mothers for the most part care naturally and intensively for their

---

42 Hume, *Inquiry*,V, II, 228ff.

43 Kummer, "Analogs of Morality," 43.

44 Goody, "Literacy and Moral Rationality," in *Morality as a Biological Phenomenon*, ed. Gunther Stent, 161.

children, and adult males seem to be at least somewhat disposed to care for infants.[45] Siblings and cousins who grow up together are often though not always loyal to one another. But the notion that one has a *duty* to care for one's offspring and relatives, whether parentally inclined or not, whether one likes them as individuals or not, is a moral extension. There are people who, in the absence of social and legal pressures, would leave their relatives in the lurch. Some succeed in doing so despite those pressures. The further notion that one has a duty to behave in a comradely fashion towards strangers or provide personal care to nonrelatives is a further extension, and the physicians and Mother Teresas who provide personal care of great intimacy to total strangers are engaging in high-level moral behaviour.

Like taboos, moral formulas of obligation may have little to offer the selfish gene, and their observance may even militate against the practitioner's chances to survive and reproduce. "Kill no one," "Do not eat animals," and "Never lie" may represent fatal strategies for individuals. By eating nothing that had ever been alive except fruit fallen from the tree, one might compromise one's reproductive health. By refusing to practise infanticide and continuing to feed infants during a short period of extraordinarily harsh conditions, one might exterminate one's whole tribe. However, even profoundly inhibited behaviour need not be deleterious, and even extreme "hypermoral"[46] systems need not be self-annihilating, as long as they remain restricted to a subculture, or as long new recruits can be attracted to them. In the meantime, certain behaviour from the biological centre that formerly increased fitness – murderous retaliation, infanticide – may no longer

---

45 Smuts observed in the case of baboons that 'paternal" behaviour is not necessarily directed at a male animal's own offspring. Its function may be to gain favour with a mother and increase the likelihood of future mating opportunities. *Sex and Friendship in Baboons*, 181ff.; 250ff.

46 I use the term "hypermoral" with approximately the same meaning as Arnold Gehlen, *Moral und Hypermoral*, passim. Gehlen's useful analysis of hypermorality's evolution is however directed towards a questionable attack on the feminization of culture, decadent art, and other supposed ills of modernity. See 146 ff.

the belief that it does so is superstition. But it is not the epistemic qualifications of the background beliefs that make this practice antimoral.
Rather, what is wrong with sacrificing virgins for the good of the community is that it instantiates a common pattern of social inequality and
advantage-taking. Virgins are less able and less likely to put up resistance to priestcraft than young men or adult women with children and
therefore attract more persecution. Remarkably, Richards is led by his
theory to maintain that members of the Ku Klux Klan are "probably
quite moral people" who happen to have empirically false beliefs about
the differences between races and international conspiracies.[50] On my
account, the Ku Klux Klan are clearly not moral, and we do not have to
investigate the truth-status of their biological and political beliefs to
know this. The xenophobic behaviour of the Klan is ungeneralized and
thoroughly non-compensatory, in that it is directed at further dimin-
ishing the happiness, security, and lifespans of a group with a long
history as an object of social aggression.

We might represent moral phenomena as a sphere pierced by numerous axes, marked by positions located at points some distance out
from the biological centre. Warlike communities who fight their close
neighbours remain close to the centre on that axis; just war theorists
are positioned somewhat father away, pacifists a good deal farther
away, at what we might call the "hypermoral edge." Practitioners of
infanticide under conditions of social stress or upheaval are near the
centre, opponents of late-stage abortion are farther away, and opponents of contraception are on the hypermoral edge. Omnivorous
humans are close to the centre, tribes that avoid eating their totem animal are some distance out, and those sects whose veneration for life
extends so far that they eat only fallen fruits are on the periphery. Sects
that regard marriage as lifelong, whether or not children issue from it,
and as exacting the strictest fidelity from both partners, are located at
the hypermoral edge, while systems of periodic reshuffling of mates
guided solely by attraction belong near the centre. In between are mar-
riage-systems that moderate the importance of attraction by adding a
long-term economic or responsibility component to pairings. Political

---

50   Richards, "A Defence of Evolutionary Ethics," 285.

solvable. There is a powerful human centrifugal tendency towards hypermorality that is countered by a powerful centripetal tendency towards the core. Acknowledging that this is the case may give an individual a reason to edge away from the periphery – or towards it.

1. Altruism as a Context-Specific Behaviour

Beginning with Hobbes, philosophers have imagined and portrayed in their works a historical or conceptual process that takes humans from a premoral state to a moral state. The motor of the moralization process – what gets a creature across the nonmoral-moral divide – has been identified variously as reason, emotion, and experience. Hobbes, for instance thinks that a blend of fear and reason induces men to re-nounce hostilities and submit to a central commander and legislator, permitting them to live "securely, happily, and elegantly." Though Hume's account of the origins of government is not very different,[6] he implicitly distinguishes between the formation of the civil state and the formation of civil society. Experience and sympathy, not fear and reason, create the moral world. Hume argues that people are naturally somewhat disposed to perform just and benevolent actions. Moreover, he thinks, people are naturally disposed to approve just and benevolent actions on account of their individual and social utility and to attribute merit to those who perform them.[7] Regard for and approval of their merit increases people's propensity to perform just and benevolent actions and decreases their propensity to perform mean actions. Bene-volence, merit, and approval thus form a positive feedback loop, and neither arduous deductive systems nor ascetic exercises of self-denial pertain at all to the establishment or maintenance of morals.

Hobbes and Hume have been taken as forerunners of Darwinian evolutionary ethics. Hobbes's notion that co-operation and submis-sion to a central authority are rationally motivated decisions based on

---

6 David Hume, *A Treatise of Human Nature*, ed. L.A. Selby-Bigge, 2d ed. (Oxford: Clarendon, 1978), II:III:VII, 535 ff.

7 Hume, *Treatise*, II:III:II, 500.

groups that deny the appropriateness of any distribution from families to strangers belong near the centre; communists are at the edge.

Some moral phenomena might appear difficult to bring under the rubric of advantage-reducing imperatives. The requirements to tell the truth and to perform one's contracts appear to be all-or-nothing moral rules that lack the compensatory aspect – for telling the truth or performing a contract may put me in a horrific state of disadvantage with respect to my accuser or the opposite signatory. But the appearance of conflict is superficial. A situation in which promises are not regarded as irrevocable simply in virtue of the words that have been spoken, and in which contracts are not regarded as inexorable simply in virtue of the words that have been written down, favours the sophisticated over the naïve. For the sophisticated can induce the naïve to believe that they will act in such-and-such a way in the future by deploying their persuasivness, charm, and intelligence. Generally, then, such rules benefit the weak, since the strong do not normally require fiduciary undertakings from the weak. (Reciprocal marriage vows of mutual everlastingness are interesting to analyze in these terms, since both parties are conceived as "weak" for different reasons. The promise or contract offers protection for the wife, who is disadvantaged by her presumptive economic incompetence, and for the husband, who is disadvantaged by his practical inability to exercise total vigilance over the paternity of his offspring. The fact that the promise or contract offers a mutual benefit is explicable only in terms of these presumptive weaknesses and the situation of "exploitation" that would occur in its absence.) In individual instances, the enforcement of such reciprocity rules, especially when a contract or promise between equals becomes a contract or promise between parties whose situation is now strongly unequal, becomes itself a violation of morality. The forgiveness of debts and the suspension of contracts are perceived as morally required in certain situations.

Some social rules that are regarded as basic moral rules, such as the rule that merit should be rewarded and that private property should be respected, seem to refute our proposal that moral rules are essentially advantage-reducing, since they appear to give to him who hath already. Three responses are possible depending on how the rule is understood and applied: First, the rules may not be moral rules. Certain of their applications may actually be contrary to morality (overcompensation, certain landlord-tenant arrangements). Second, the rules may be morally neutral but serve some nonmoral social purposes such as stimulating development and favouring the balance of trade that is considered important and that borrows the dignity of morality. Third, the rules may be applied as genuine moral rules, i.e., when some meritorious action would go unremarked and unrewarded, injuring the agent, were it not for the application of the rule, or when it is seen that harm would be done to a subject by dispossessing her of her holdings. Whether a given formula of obligation really is compensatory in intention or realization is often debatable. For instance, the notion that persons who are behaving destructively ought to be immobilized and that it is right to apprehend, imprison, and punish them is obviously based on the perception that the criminal is gaining an advantage from his or her strength and willfulness. We seize a child who is misbehaving, or band together to control an angry person, pinioning him on the ground or tying his hands behind his back. Much of our imaginative literature, especially mystery stories and novels, deals with the attempt to find and immobilize a dangerous something that is "loose." This disposition is generalized in our behaviour towards criminals, who are detained and locked up, whether it actually does them or anyone else any good or not. It is also extended and elaborated into such measures as torturing people for holding abstract beliefs (to immobilize their thinking), or throwing criminals into dungeons or cutting off their hands (to render them incapacitated). Such extensions, though they show an imaginative capacity for elaboration and generalization, do not seem to be hypermoral in the sense of vegetarianism, pacifism, etc. This intuition can be explained by pointing to the way in which the accentuation of divisions between good and evil stands in contrast to generalizing thoughts such as "There but for the grace of God go I" or "Even the mass murderer is a human being."[51] The immobilizing

---

51 From one perspective, the mass murderer is not a full human being, insofar as he or she lacks the normal complement of empathy, inhibition, and sound judgment about consequences. The notion that this empirically "monstrous" creature is nevertheless a human being in an honorific sense is "metaphysical." Moral thoughts often do seem to require metaphysical language for their expression (e.g., "spiritual brotherhood.") Is this a vindication of Kantianism in

238

impulse, when exaggerated, reverses the presumed advantage when it results in sadism by guards and officials. Similarly, chivalry may begin as the moral extension of protective impulses towards women, but become the wily exercise of power for the purpose of suppression and exclusion.

An individual's moral system can be represented as a set of points corresponding to formulas of obligation located along the various behavioural axes. Modern post-industrial societies are composed of subcultures with various local moralities, and individuals in them have more latitude in their moral self-positioning than members of smaller tribal societies. But even in the smallest society, there will be more or less pious individuals, harder workers and lazy slackers, more and less conscientious parents. Some persons will be more interested in morality, sterner with themselves and others, and others less so. Note that a given group or a given person may orient itself close to the centre in some dimensions, far in others. A religious sect requiring lifelong monogamy may be opposed to all manifestations of central government including redistributive taxation. Some vegetarians are not pacifists, as surprising as this might seem, and many defenders of abortion-rights are vegetarians. Such composite positions have their inner rationales, in that adherents may strive to and may actually manage to produce an account of why their views are coherent.

Some individuals recognize and feel compelled not just by first-order formulas of obligation, but by second-order moral formulas, such as the obligation to bring one's primary formulas of obligation into what John Rawls famously termed reflective equilibrium. They may even feel compelled by third-order formulas, such as the obligation to be a moral universalist about formulas of obligation that have been brought into reflective equilibrium. Moral theories, such as Kantianism and utilitarianism, represent philosophical attempts to systemize adherence to a particular set of formulas of obligation, to decide in advance future adherence, and to give a reason to others to conform to the

---

ethics? Not quite: Kant never thinks of metaphysics as a belief-system that can be described by the anthropologist. It is in some objective way "higher" than all the descriptive sciences, and noumenal causality is even thought to have real workings in the empirical world.

systematizer's own pattern of adherences. Individuals with a second-order belief that they ought to seek reflective equilibrium will adjust their theories to conform to their intuitions about their behaviour, or they will strive to alter their intuitions so that their theories will predict or confirm them. But all such formulas are purely ideational, and, prior to the voluntary adoption of a normative stance, they have no more actual power to "bind" rational agents than the most trivial dictates of fashion, which some people nevertheless experience as overwhelmingly motivating. Moreover, people's actual behaviour, as well as their self-acknowledged behaviour, may trace a different shape inside or outside the polygon marked out by the formulas of obligation to which they give weak or strong allegiance.

It should be understood that in describing certain positions as more or less moral than others, the present author is not advocating any of, let alone all of, vegetarianism, pacifism, monogamy, non-contraception, or, as a meta-theory, moral universalism. Like other people, the present author is "for" some of these things, "against" others, but this is irrelevant to the argument thus far. It is a genuine question for each of us how moral we think we would like to be, and on what basis we propose to make this decision. The view that it is obligatory to be as moral as possible, or that moral considerations override all others – nutritional, hedonistic, etc. is another metaethical position. Universalism is, by definition, a more moral meta-theory than relativism, insofar as it is more general, but it does not follow that a uniform system of moral principles is something to strive for. In exchange for an intellectually clear definition of what morality is and how it is related to biological dispositions on one hand and generalization and abstraction on the other, we need to relinquish the notion that it is inexorable and binds absolutely. But in doing so we also need to jettison the idea that relativism, as another meta-theory, could possibly be true, as opposed to representing another decision how to think about morality. Relativists are correct in observing that, from a descriptive point of view, moral systems are very different, and there is no criterion that we are all compelled to use in deciding which is to be preferred. But they are mistaken if they infer that these facts about moral phenomena could license any particular system of conduct on their part.

5. Moral Epistemology

Defenders of the strong programme hope to show how a human data-collecting machine that accumulates enough experiences will be able to refine its own information-gathering and analytical procedures in order to weed potentially all moral falsehoods from the corpus of popular moral belief.[52] The moral truths that remain will be overriding. It will always be wrong to perform an action that has the property of moral wrongness, and always good to perform an action that has the property of moral rightness. The strong programme implies the possibility of writing this ideal moral system down in precise detail, the way we write down physics and chemistry. But it strains the imagination to believe that a machine, left to run long enough and, through the feedback it acquires, allowed to devise corrective strategies for data sampling and interpretation will eventually give us the correct and non-overridable verdict on all issues on which people profoundly disagree and on which a multiplicity of minutely differentiated positions can be taken. No one is going to discover the precise criteria for just wars, find out what morally acceptable forms of surrogate motherhood are, or figure out the exact formula for morally permissible redistributive taxation. Natural science results in increasingly precise knowledge, and moral inquiry cannot emulate it in this respect.

What then should I do? Where should I position myself is not a theoretically solvable problem in moral philosophy. But it is constantly solved in practice. Insofar as we have made some headway with the weak programme, we know that the formulas of obligation that are articulated and respected by a particular community that has a long history behind it are often the ones that members believe ought to be

---

52 Peter Railton in "Moral Realism," *Philosophical Review* 95 (1986): 163-207, argues that the sheer pressure of reality over the long term has to mould institutions into forms better suited for human beings, thanks to the negative feedback people exert against forms of life unsuitable for them. This is an impressive idea, but it faces several unaddressed problems: 1) the operation of opposing and perhaps equal antimoral forces in the social world; 2) adaptive preferences; 3) trade-offs.

respected.[53] In some subcultures (in which the sum total of experience has not been markedly different), it is believed that formulas that have some prized logical characteristic, for example, the property of having a negation that is not universalizable, are those that ought to be respected. In still other subcultures, it is believed that all permissible fall under a general formula such as "Maximize happiness and minimize suffering." In asserting that a given norm's plausibility or a given particularization's representing a legitimate inference is a reason for conforming to it, the theorist tries to provide a non-historical reason for doing so. None of these methods bears any relationship to the method by which our experiences in nature lead to the development of instruments and experimental and analytical techniques that enable us to separate scientific knowledge from folk belief. The "track-record" of a moral theory in retrodicting successfully a number of judgments by informants does not force them to accept the theory's next prediction about what it is right to do.

Deciding to regulate one's future behaviour according to a theory whose internal consistency one admires and whose particular formulas command actions that seem appropriate is something anyone can in principle do, but it is unclear why decisions of this type have more moral merit than others. That reflective equilibrium is an intellectually satisfying state for creatures with our cognitive apparatus to find ourselves in carries no implication for the correctness of the moral views of the subject who finds himself in it. Why should I, as an opponent, concede anything to the proponent of capital punishment whose fundamental moral principles are nicely symmetrical ("A life for a life") and whose present deduction is in accord with them and meshes tidily with his other beliefs?

Although moral epistemology cannot be naturalized in terms of the strong programme, inquiry into the empirical dimensions of morality contributes to reflective self-positioning. An understanding of the actual variety of moral systems, the ways in which social learning of moral

---

53 A sophisticated version of this position that allows for moral evolution is defended by Alasdair MacIntyre, *After Virtue*, 2d ed. (Notre Dame: University of Notre Dame Press, 1984).

rules occurs, and the rationalizations given of moral practice influences our acceptance of norms. Understanding morality as an ideational superstructure built upon a biological basis can move us in either of two directions. It can push us away from hypermoral systems, which we can recognize as products of the same imaginative and elaborative tendencies that lead to baroque excess in other departments of life, at costs that are not always apparent in the moment of construction. We may no longer wish to be weighed down, like our ancestors, in yards of brocaded fabric, constricting corsets, and masses of jewels, or their analogs in morality. We can concede that Mother Teresa is objectively far more moral than the rest of us in the personal-care-of-strangers dimension, but recognize that, although not emulating Mother Teresa may be a very bad failing from an individual's point of view, it cannot be a failing from an objective point of view, as there is no objective mandate to be as moral as possible. Empirical inquiry can help us to discriminate between social rules that owe more to archaic concepts of purity and hierarchy than they do to morality proper.[54]

At the same time, however, understanding morality as an ideational superstructure can help us to perceive the depth and ubiquity of the moral motive in the species, even where the reasons for the existence of a particular practice or institution involve the overlay of a moral reason with nonmoral reasons. The existence of doctors, nurses, and public transport workers has moral significance, even if the persons occupying these social roles are not conscious of the moral dimension of their work and think of it wholly in terms of professional status,

---

54 For example, unwed motherhood and drug addiction are considered major social problems. Many people appear to think that both are paradigms of immoral behaviour. Clearly, both unwed motherhood and drug addiction are deeply impractical in the modern world and incompatible with economic success. They also symbolize personal defilement and represent and may really entail a loss of personal control and autonomy. But they are only immoral, as opposed to undesirable for other reasons, if they involve advantage-taking of the weaker by the stronger. When it is felt that some social phenomenon is very bad, and that extreme measures are needed to change it or make it go away, it is important to sort out the respects in which it is impractical or violates a taboo from the respects in which it is morally objectionable.

personal satisfaction, or pecuniary rewards.[55] It is salutary to realize that even if the existence of many of our social institutions appears to be sustained exclusively by opportunism, and that even if self-interest is frequently theorized as a magic power source for achieving everything desirable, morality in the sense of advantage-reduction is nevertheless ubiquitous. Such institutions exist for the sake of those who are temporarily or for the longer-term, less capable or less fit in a non-evolutionary sense than others. There is no necessary incompatibility between the existence of institutions whose *raison d'être* is the compensation of inequalities and power-imbalances and the provision of opportunities for individual ambition. Thus, one currently very popular objection towards social levelling – that it is necessarily destructive of autonomy and hostile to talent – is removed. We can be moved further towards the hypermoral periphery, as we come to perceive the residuals of our proto-moral history, and appreciate how much remains of advantage-taking by the strong and gifted in our behavioural repertoires and our social institutions. One way to make principled decisions might be to take formulas of obligation at the hypermoral edge as representing the default position, ethically and metaethically. The subject could simply decide to be as moral as possible in all possible dimensions, and to be a moral universalist to boot, unless there was some very good reason to adopt a weaker formula, whether the reason was aesthetic, emotional, nutritional, or practical. This would be a no less rational procedure than acting according to a theory, and no less rooted in actuality than acting according to tradition. After casting away the idea that there is a correct morality that is *per se* overriding, everyone would be free to live as closely as they wished to the hypermoral edge.

---

55 It might be objected that the physician may have only these motives. Nevertheless, unbeknownst to her, her actions belong to the realm of social phenomena that are recognizably moral. The same is true of ambulance drivers, even if they regard their jobs much as bus drivers do. Driving a bus is, in my view, a somewhat moral activity (since it helps to compensate for the limited mobility of persons without cars or chauffeurs.) Bus transportation is part of the public sector, which has important advantage-reducing concerns, and this would be obvious to, say, a visitor from Mars, though it is less evident, for various reasons, to people inside the system. I ignore complications deriving from the objection that health-care and public transportation serve to maintain an enslaved class of low-paid workers at subsistence level, etc.

CANADIAN JOURNAL OF PHILOSOPHY
Supplementary Volume 26

All the Monkeys Aren't in the Zoo: Evolutionary Ethics and the Possibility of Moral Knowledge

MICHAEL STINGL

The error theory of moral judgment says that moral judgments, though often believed to be objectively true, never are. The tendency to believe in the objectivity of our moral beliefs, like the beliefs themselves, is rooted in objective features of human psychology, and not in objective features of the natural world that might exist apart from human psychology. In naturalized epistemology, it is tempting to take this view as the default hypothesis. It appears to make the fewest assumptions in accounting for the fact that humans not only make moral judgments, but believe them to be, at least some of the time, objectively true.[1] In this paper I argue that from an evolutionary perspective, the error theory is not the most parsimonious alternative. It is simpler to suppose that mental representations with moral content arose as direct cognitive and motivational responses to independent moral facts.

The argument will not address several large and important questions. First, it will not address the question of whether primates other than humans can really possess mental states that might reliably represent the world around them; nor will it address the questions of whether these representational states, should they exist, must be

---

1 J.L. Mackie, *Ethics: Inventing Right and Wrong* (Harmondsworth: Penguin, 1977), 30-46, and Michael Ruse, *Taking Darwin Seriously: A Naturalistic Approach to Philosophy* (Oxford: Basil Blackwell, 1986), 252-6. Mackie traces this view back to Hume in *Hume's Moral Theory* (London: Routledge and Kegan Paul, 1980), 71-3, 121-3, and 147-50. Gilbert Harman's version of the error theory is discussed below; see note 13.

propositional in content, or whether such states, should they exist, should count as knowledge. I will thus ignore the deep philosophical questions of whether naturalized epistemology is really epistemology, or whether all knowledge of the world must involve a relationship between a knower, something known, and a proposition.

Although these are all contestable questions, plausible lines of argument exist for supposing that the minds of other primates do contain representational states that reliably correspond to the world around them, and further, that states such as these need not be propositional to count as knowledge.[2] My purpose here is to ask what follows from these claims, if they are correct, regarding the possibility of moral knowledge.

Let us start simply. A chimpanzee, moving through a grassy area, surprises a lioness and her cubs; the lioness roars. Suppose that the sight of the lioness and the cubs, along with the ensuing roar, puts the chimp into a particular representational state, a state that represents the lion as dangerous. I have put the contents of this state into a propositional form, but that is because you and I, as speakers of a language, naturally represent things in terms of propositions, or at least we appear to. This fact about us may or may not be relevant to how representations work in the heads of chimps.

Let us further suppose that such representations in the heads of chimps are reliable, and that indeed, when reliable, they count as knowledge about the world inhabited by chimps. What is it that a chimp knows, when he or she knows that a lion is dangerous? What, that is, counts as a dangerous thing for a chimp? One plausible suggestion is that dangerous things, for chimps, are things that may physically and immediately harm them. Chimps have evolved a capacity that enables them to be wary of such harmful things and to steer clear of them when they can. This capacity, and the mental states it generates, is at once both cognitive and motivational.

------

2 For the first argument, see Frans de Waal, *Good Natured: The Origins of Right and Wrong in Humans and Other Animals* (Cambridge: Harvard University Press, 1996); for the second, see Richmond Campbell, *Illusions of Paradox: A Feminist Epistemology Naturalized* (Lanham: Rowman & Littlefield, 1998), 47-9, 70-9, and 169-75.

Morality is tied up with harms, but not directly with harms. The sorts of harms that morality concerns itself with are unjustified harms. So this is what moral knowledge regarding harms must represent: the unjustifiable nature of a harm, and not just the harmfulness of a thing or situation. So let us return to our chimp, and grant that he or she may know that certain things are harmful. Can the chimp reliably recognize when certain harms are unjustified?

There is evidence to suggest that the answer to this question is yes. Consider a kind of case reported by Frans de Waal: a group of chimps is presented with a bundle of branches and leaves from one of their favourite trees. In this sort of situation, the foliage must be shared. If a chimp grabs too many branches, he or she faces punishment from the most dominant male, and thus, encouragement to return some of the branches to others in the group. If the dominant male goes too far in meting out the punishment, however, the older females in the group may attack the dominant male, thus encouraging him to desist in his own attack.

Not getting your foliage when others in your group are getting theirs probably counts as a harm for chimps, a harm they may be reliably aware of when it occurs. However, sharing only occurs under certain conditions: scarcity and abundance, for example, both lead to an absence of sharing behaviour. In scarce conditions, one chimp may beg another for food, but will not reliably get any. Again, we might suppose that this is recognized as harmful, not getting food when there is some food to be had. But in these instances, unsharing behaviour goes unpunished. Assuming as we are that chimps can detect situations in which they are harmed, it seems reasonable to suppose, on the basis of examples like these, that they can also recognize when such harms are justified or unjustified, or, at least, when such harms call for punishment and when they do not. Moreover, given their consistent ability to tell the two kinds of cases apart, we might suppose that their recognitional capacity in this regard is extremely reliable.

A similar point might be made about punishments – group members can tell when a certain level of harm is justifiably imposed on another chimp and when it is not. Some acts require more punishment, some less, and the dominant male had better be able to tell which situations are which or receive punishment of his own. The upshot of these examples is that it appears that chimps can tell when the imposition of harm by one chimp on another is justified and when it is not. Thus, in a simple sense, it seems that chimps can tell right from wrong.

With this claim we might have two worries that it is interesting to juxtapose. On the one hand, we might worry that at this particular point in chimp psychology, action based on representational knowledge gives way to a simpler story about stimuli and responses. Although the chimps can certainly *detect* the difference between the two different kinds of situations, they cannot really *tell the difference* between harms that are justified and harms that are unjustified. Their representational capacities are limited, and knowledge of right and wrong surpasses those limits. Seeing that the alpha male's attacks are disproportionate to a particular grabbing of too many branches is not what motivates the older females to attack the alpha male; instead, given a certain environmental stimulus that they don't like, the females respond by attacking the alpha male.

Whether or not this is so is an empirical question. But before we consider it, let us first consider a diametrically opposed worry: do chimps directly see that certain harms are unjustified, or do they only *think* that they see that certain harms are unjustified? This is the error theory of moral judgments. The central claim of the error theory, as it has been applied to human moral judgment, is that it is simpler to suppose that when we judge something to be right or wrong, it only appears to us that the thing is right or wrong, and that we are geared, by evolution, to mistake such appearances for reality. There is no fact of the matter about what is right or wrong; there is just human agreement about right and wrong, which agreement we naturally mistake for objective knowledge about the world.

So how would the error theory work when applied to chimps? That harms are harms is an objective fact about the world that chimps inhabit. But that some harms are unjustified and others justified only appears to be objectively true, to the deluded chimps, insofar as they are psychologically programmed to mistake appearances for reality in precisely this sort of way.

This seems a strangely complicated story to tell about chimpanzee psychology. One reason for its strangeness is the fact that the chimp mental states with supposed moral content seem to be firmly anchored in the chimps' social world in ways that similar mental states in humans are not. Our moral representations seem to be much more freely floating above and beyond the social worlds we actually inhabit: over the course of time, we are readily able to change our moral beliefs, in an apparently endless variety of directions. So part of what makes the error theory plausible for humans but not for chimps is that we are able to change our moral codes in ways that chimps are not. On our best moral behaviour, we debate our moral beliefs with one another, and over the course of history these beliefs change, sometimes, we think, for the better, but sometimes for the worse. The chimps' moral world, on the other hand, is much more static: if the rules chimps follow change, it is not because they have made a conscious decision at either the individual or group level to change them, at least not as the result of rational reflection or discussion. The rules that guide their behaviour are part of the real world of chimp interaction that evolution has created for them. That they can recognize this aspect of their world to whatever degree that they can is no doubt an important part of its having evolved into its current state, but that it evolved is a real fact about their evolutionary history. The bare fact that chimps have evolved to the point that they can begin to recognize certain actions as being right or wrong is hardly reason to suppose that they must be mistaken about this important aspect of their social environment, and that what they recognize to be so only appears, to them, to be so. That such things are so may, on the other hand, help to explain why chimps recognize them to be so.

Had he been thinking about chimpanzees and other less psychologically sophisticated primates, such as capuchin monkeys, perhaps Alan Ryan would not have been so quick to dismiss the importance of precisely this point in his otherwise elegant and insightful account of John Dewey's ethical and political thought.[3] In response to the social Darwinists at the turn of the last century, T.H. Huxley had argued that moral values are not to be found in human evolution.[4] Happily for us, humans have evolved to a point of view from which we can rise above

---

3 *John Dewey and the High Tide of American Liberalism* (New York: Norton, 1995), 132.

4 "Evolution and Ethics," 1893 Romanes Lecture, published in T.H. Huxley, *Evolution and Ethics* (London: Macmillan, 1894), 46-86, and reprinted in *Issues in Evolutionary Ethics*, ed. Paul Thompson (Albany: SUNY Press, 1995), 111-50.

the blind, evolutionary process that has produced us, to a superior point of view from which we can decide how to change our social relationships for the better, despite what evolution may itself have planned for us. Like Dewey, I want to argue that this idea is in part true, but only in part; in another part, we have the morally significant point of view that we do because of the way in which we evolved as a particular kind of social creature.

Dewey's point against Huxley, who believed, as Richard Dawkins and other sociobiologists seemingly continue to believe, that evolution can only produce creatures that are fundamentally selfish at the level of unreflective but nonetheless conscious motivation, was that in social environments such fundamentally selfish motivations would not be likely to be fitness enhancing.[5] Ryan's objection to this point is that by talking about social environments, Dewey is cheating.[6] In accounting for the evolution of moral sentiments, Dewey cannot build into the environment that produced them those very sentiments, under the guise of what others are motivated to accept as socially appropriate responses on the part of any given individual. But what examples of capuchin and chimpanzee behaviour suggest is that this explanatory move is not viciously circular: while capuchins behave in apparently unintentional ways to punish unsocial behaviour, chimps behave in very similar sorts of ways, except for the fact that they seem to be

---

5 Dewey, "Evolution and Ethics," *Early Works, 1882-1898*, vol. 5 (Carbondale: Southern Illinois University Press, 1972), 34-53, reprinted in *Evolutionary Ethics*, ed. M.H. Nitecki and D.V. Nitecki (Albany: SUNY Press, 1993), 95-110. (First appeared as an article in *The Monist* in April of 1898, 321-41.) Dawkins' official view, of course, is that it is our genes that are selfish, not us. But he is not always so careful, nor are other sociobiologists. See the quote on p. 6 of *Good Natured* and the discussion on pp. 13-20.

6 Ironically, in an article eleven years earlier to the one that is the focus of Ryan's discussion, Dewey himself makes a similar claim against those who, before him, were arguing for the possibility of an evolutionary ethics, namely, that they illicitly took the existence of moral order in human social relations as both explanans and explanandum. See his "Ethics and Physical Science," *The Early Works, 1882-1898*, vol. 1 (Carbondale: Southern Illinois University Press, 1969), 216-7. (This article originally appeared in 1887.)

conscious, at least to some degree, of what they are doing. What this suggests is that social behaviours first evolved as such, and that secondly, the reliability and efficiency of these behaviours was greatly enhanced by mechanisms of conscious recognition and motivation. That such mental states, as they were evolving, would themselves have become part of the environment affecting their further evolution is an interesting hypothesis worthy of more exploration, not an illicit assumption about the way in which the evolution of moral sentiments might have occurred.

Let us return, then, to the empirical question of what chimpanzees might be said to know about morality, and to recent empirical evidence regarding the social behaviour of chimpanzees. At the centre of de Waal's work on chimpanzees and their moral tendencies are two mental states, empathy and sympathy, for which de Waal thinks there is ample evidence in his subjects. According to de Waal, empathy is a cognitive mental state which involves the capacity to feel, and thus to understand, the distressed mental state of another. Sympathy, on de Waal's usage, is caring enough about this unhappy state of another to want to do something to ameliorate it. Just as one feels one ought to do something to ameliorate such states when they are directly one's own, one feels that one ought to ameliorate such states in others, at least for some others some of the time. According to the error theory, of course, it is a mistake to think that the strength or significance of this second sort of "ought" inheres in the objective facts of situations in which individuals feel sympathy for one another; instead, the true motivational strength of moral oughts comes from an illusory belief that moral values are objective facts pertaining to *some other* aspect of the world. This is true at least for a more cognitively sophisticated species like our own, where social groups are able to develop religious beliefs, for example, to underwrite the apparent fact that we really ought to do what we apparently ought to do.

In addition to the motivational oughts that might arise from empathy and sympathy, chimpanzees may also experience motivational oughts that arise from prescriptive rules aimed at some degree of social equality. To return to our earlier example, a chimp may grab too many branches and a fight may ensue between the chimp and his or her neighbours. If so, the alpha male is likely to break the fight up, and, in so doing, favour not his friends or allies, but the situation's underdog individual or group. Again, if the alpha male shows favouritism in his mediation of fights or excess in his punishments, he is likely to fall from the hierarchical grace accorded him by the other members of the group, including, importantly, the older females in the group, who may switch their allegiance to a rival for the top spot in the male hierarchy. De Waal himself is uncertain whether such rules are genuinely prescriptive, because he is not sure that they are prescribed as such from above; i.e., no one is actively teaching anyone socially beneath them the rules they have to follow. The rules are enforced, but they are apparently not taught. Thus it may be, for example, that alpha males simply don't like certain things, like fights, and so they disrupt them. The rest of the group doesn't like it if these fights are ended in certain ways – e.g., in a way that favours the alliances of the alpha male – and so they respond in a negative manner when the alpha male ends fights in these sorts of ways.[7]

There is, on the other hand, a way of understanding prescriptive rules that makes it possible to suppose that chimps do know what they are doing when they act in accord with rules such as those described above. In *Logic on the Track of Social Change*, Braybrooke, Brown, and Schotch develop a definition of prescriptive rules as intentional blocking operations.[8] According to this definition, blocking operations need not be linguistic – they may be purely physical or vocal – although they must be intentional. Putting an arm out every time your toddler moves from the sidewalk toward the street is a blocking operation of the right sort, which the toddler might come to understand as such, whereas as parking your car in such a way that the toddler's access to the street is impeded is not. Despite this intentional element in Braybrooke, Brown, and Schotch's definition of rules, it is possible, and indeed probable, that blocking operations got their evolutionary start in unintentional blocking behaviours. From the receiving end of

---

7 De Waal, conversation. The worry here is that while the behaviour of chimps may be rule governed, they themselves might not be consciously following any rules.

8 David Braybrooke, Bryson Brown, and Peter K. Schotch, with Laura Byrne, *Logic on the Track of Social Change* (Oxford: Clarendon Press, 1995), chap. 2.

such blocks, it would be advantageous to be able to understand their extent and limits, and so we might suppose that blocks first entered consciousness as blocking operations from the bottom up, rather than from the top down. Since all tops except the very first would have begun their lives as curious bottoms, once rules became prescriptively understood, they would have been prescriptive from both perspectives, bottom and top alike. Additionally, there would be no need to teach the rules explicitly to bottoms if they already had a reliable means of learning them. That such a means exists in the case of chimpanzees is suggested by the systematic teasing younger chimps address to those older than themselves. In persistently testing the limits of how much they can get away with before they experience a threatening response, young chimps may be building increasingly accurate representations of how far one chimp can go with regard to his or her impositions on another.

So it may be that chimps not only have mental representations tied up with sympathy, but as well, they have mental representations of rules with moral content, for example, that when mediating disputes, the interests of the powerful ought not trump the interests of the less powerful. If these mental representations have sufficient cognitive salience and motivational force to override selfish motivations in chimps often enough to preserve group cohesiveness, then for chimps at least it seems like this is the end of the story: chimps are not given a further motivational push in the direction of morality by a chimpanzee version of the error theory. But maybe the general psychological tendency postulated by the error theory is necessary for an extra push in humans, precisely because we can reflect about our mental states in ways that chimpanzees cannot. Thus, paradoxically, moral knowledge might be possible for chimps, but not for us.

To see why this is unlikely, consider a general argument about sympathy and selfishness recently presented by Sober and Wilson in their book *Unto Others*.[9] Sober and Wilson offer three conditions that, absent well-developed empirical tests, might be used to differentiate between the plausibility of various evolutionary hypotheses. The two

---

9 *Unto Others: The Evolution and Psychology of Unselfish Behavior* (Cambridge: Harvard University Press, 1998), 304-24.

hypotheses they consider are a form of psychological egoism, according to which all actions are ultimately selfish, and a form of evolutionary altruism, according to which some actions are at least in part ultimately caused by sympathy. This second hypothesis leaves open the possibility that many altruistic actions might be motivated by both self-interest and sympathy.

The three conditions against which Sober and Wilson measure these hypotheses are *availability*, *reliability*, and *energetic efficiency*. To explain these conditions let me apply them, as Sober and Wilson do, to the two hypotheses described above. The first hypothesis tells us that whenever parents, for example, appear to be motivated by sympathy to help their children, lurking beneath this sympathy is self-interest, for example, the good feeling a parent normally gets when he or she helps a child. The second hypothesis tells us that at least some of the time, or at least in part much of the time, parents act directly out of sympathy for their children. Sober and Wilson point out that, for sympathy to be ultimately motivated (and hence explained) by self-interest, sympathy must already be assumed to be available as a separate psychological trait, one that might be capable motivating action all by itself depending on the pressures of natural selection.

One of these pressures is surely reliability – how often action motivated by sympathy alone or sympathy grounded in self-interest actually helps to maximize the reproductive fitness of the actor through promoting the fitness of his or her child. Sober and Wilson argue that sympathy alone, or sympathy working at times in concert with self-interest, is likely to be more reliable that sympathy based ultimately in self-interest. What's directly good for a parent, as an individual organism, is only tenuously linked to what is good for a child, and thus to the parent's own reproductive fitness. To take the hedonistic form of the psychological egoism hypothesis, perhaps the most likely form for most non-human altruists, doing what's good for one's child may in many instances not feel very good for the parent. Or, to twist a well-known phrase of Bernard Williams', to think that in benefitting my child I benefit myself is to think exactly one thought too many.

This last point leads us to the idea of energetic efficiency. If sympathy and self-interest are both equally "ultimate" motivations, sometimes they will clash, and adjudicating between the two in these clashes will take psychological energy. But so too if sympathy is motivated by self-interest: self-interest favouring one action can clash with self-interest favouring an alternative, requiring psychological energy to resolve the clash. Conflicts of interest take energy to resolve, and it is not clear that conflicts between sympathetic interests and self-interests would take any more energy to resolve than conflicts between self-interest with sympathy and self-interest absent sympathy.

As Sober and Wilson point out, these conditions hardly settle the empirical question of the ultimate motivation of altruistic actions, or perhaps we should say, the empirical questions, since species may well differ in this regard. But what these considerations do show is that psychological egoism is certainly not the default hypothesis with regard to the possible sources of moral motivation. A similar point pertains with even more force to the error theory.[10]

As a first hypothesis, let us suppose that sympathy sometimes wins out over self-interest, or even that self-interested reasons somehow in support of sympathy sometimes win out over self-interested reasons not in support of sympathy. On a second hypothesis, that of the error theory, this would not happen, or would not happen often enough, unless the psychological forces of sympathy were further bolstered by a false belief, namely, that the "oughts" of sympathy somehow track an objective world of moral values. Now, although chimps seem capable of both false beliefs and astonishing acts of deception, that they are capable of false ideologies about moral value is wildly implausible on current evidence. So quite apart from the general reliability of ideologies about moral value, and the amount of energy it takes to create and maintain reliable ideologies, it seems that for chimps the requisite false beliefs are simply unavailable as a psychological trait that might be open to selective pressures.

This is of course not true for humans. Our attraction to ideologies of all sorts is well attested by an abundance of evidence. Even so, while such ideologies might be enlisted in support of "oughts" that originally arise out of a psychological trait like sympathy, it is hard to see

---

10 This argument was first suggested, as far as I am aware, in John Collier and Michael Stingl, "Evolutionary Naturalism and the Objectivity of Morality," *Biology and Philosophy* 8 (1993): 47-60, reprinted in Thompson, *Issues in Evolutionary Ethics*, 409-29.

how they might entirely underwrite these oughts, or how they might be motivationally necessary to get sympathy off the ground. It takes a while to get an ideology itself off the ground, and apart from that, ideologies can be extremely unreliable at least over parts of their histories, particularly as one ideology supplants another. If the foundational connection between sympathy and self-interest might be considered to be a Rube Goldberg arrangement, then the error theory postulates a Rube Goldberg device *par excellence*. Ideologies are easily detached from sympathy, as in the story of Abraham and Isaac, and such detachments can be extremely energy inefficient, as again both Abraham and Isaac might tell us.

The argument is that, from an evolutionary perspective, ideological support for moral beliefs is too little and too late. Early humans, we might plausibly suppose, would have been closer to chimps than to us in terms of the direct connections between sympathy and prescriptive rules with moral content, on the one hand, and moral behaviour on the other. Ideologies and the capacity to take them seriously might thus have come to reinforce the cognitive and motivational force of the moral knowledge these early humans would have already had, but the fact remains that they would have already had the knowledge in question. Beliefs in objectivity postulated by the error theory might have helped them to act on this knowledge when they otherwise might have hesitated, but these beliefs could not have created the appearance of such knowledge in the first place. On the other hand, ideologies can lead humans astray, to avenues of social interaction where both chimps and angels might fear to tread. I will briefly return to this problem at the end of the paper.

Interpreting the error theory as I have, exclusively in terms of ideology and belief, might seem to miss its most important aspect. Perhaps what is at the core of the error theory is simply the mind's propensity, in Hume's phrase, to spread itself on external objects.[11] So the idea would be that this general propensity is the direct result of the evolutionary development of the human mind, and that what ideological beliefs about morality reinforce are certain of its rudimentary illusions

---

11 Mackie, *Ethics*, 42.

rather than the rudimentary forms of moral knowledge that might otherwise be supposed to arise from psychological traits like sympathy. On Hume's side, there is certainly ample evidence of this propensity with regard to a great many supervenient qualities, for example, the current fashionableness of different styles of car or of clothing. What looks unmistakably chic one seasons looks miserably drab or simply absurd the next. But consider the dangerous things that chimpanzees might come into contact with, and the dangerous things that our common ancestors would have come into contact with. These things really were dangerous, and we developed a capacity to recognize this and to avoid them. Similarly important to our survival as the social species that we are would have been our ability to recognize and to act on the morally good and bad things disclosed to us by sympathy and by the internalization of rules regarding justified and unjustified harms.

The earliest forms of moral knowledge would thus have been found in certain representational states with moral content. Sympathy allows one individual to recognize that the suffering of another is bad: not necessarily bad for survival, but bad as such. Similarly, attention to prescriptive rules of the kind discussed above enables individuals to recognize that not getting one's fair share of something – such as food or punishment – is a bad thing. Again, not bad for survival, but bad as such. A sufficiently intelligent species might later make the not unimportant connections to survival and to reproductive success, but these connections seem unlikely to be part of the content of the original cognitive and motivational mental states. If such states can be supposed to reliably represent the world inhabited by their possessors, then they would count as moral knowledge on the assumption of a naturalized epistemology.

What does it mean to say that something is good or bad *as such*? Consider a somewhat more straightforward example. Through evolutionary processes, roughage arises as good for the health of certain kinds of organisms. Roughage is tied to health, which is tied to survival and reproductive success. But not directly: reproduction is not always good for an organism's health, and making an otherwise healthy choice may lead to an organism's early demise. Health, in and of itself, is a generally good kind of thing that arises as a result of evolutionary processes. As such, its goodness is not the same thing as the goodness of survival or reproductive success, whatever it might mean to say of these other two things that they are good. How does this point pertain to morality? For co-operative species with a certain level of intelligence, responding to the needs of others seems to be a generally good kind of thing. What kind of good thing? Given what we have come to refer to by the word "health," health itself turns out to pertain to well-functioning bodies; given the general sort of thing we refer to by "morality," and given the foregoing argument, morality itself seems to pertain to well-functioning social groups, the members of which have reached a certain level of cognitive development. Responding to the needs of others might thus be an empirically discoverable moral good, a generally good kind of thing that arises as part of the evolution of social co-operation. Just as lions really are dangerous, responding to the needs of others really is good, and indeed, morally good. Although such goods are ultimately tied to reproductive fitness, this is not what makes them good in the sense in which they are good, good just as the kinds of things that they are. Conscious awareness of these goods has additional reproductive value, but the goods arise first, the consciousness of them second.

Here it is important to resist the common view that when natural selection explains the function of something, then the function of that something is to pass genes to the next generation, that is, to increase fitness.[12] To take another example: the main function of an eye is to process information about important aspects of the natural world, aspects of the world that are visible to organisms with the kind of eye in question. Eyes are of course the result of natural selection, but their most direct function is to enable organisms to see. Moreover, some kinds of organisms may be able to see better than others. Some kinds of eyes, that is, may be better than others at disclosing what there is to be seen.

---

12 For discussion on this point see Larry Wright, "Functions," *Philosophical Review* 82 (1973): 139-68, reprinted in *Conceptual Issues in Evolutionary Biology: An Anthology*, ed. Elliott Sober (Cambridge: MIT Press, 1984), 347-68; Philip Kitcher, "Function and Design," in *Midwest Studies in Philosophy* 18, ed. Peter A. French, Theodore E. Uehling, Jr., and Howard K. Wettstein (Notre Dame: University of Notre Dame Press, 1993), 379-97, reprinted in *The Philosophy of Biology*, ed. David L. Hull and Michael Ruse (New York: Oxford University Press, 1998), 258-79; and Peter Godfrey-Smith, "Functions: Consensus Without Unity," *Pacific Philosophical Quarterly* 74 (1993): 196-208, also reprinted in *The Philosophy of Biology*, 280-92.

Let us call an organism's psychological mechanism for processing information about the morally important aspects of its natural environment its moral capacity. Different kinds of organisms may have better or worse moral capacities, and so for example humans may have a better moral capacity than chimps. We may, that is, have a much better idea than the chimps of what counts as good and bad, right or wrong. But what, on this view, might we suppose the human moral capacity to look like? What might moral facts look like? If we are not simply always making a mistake when we make moral judgments, we, like the chimps, must have a moral capacity that enables us to become cognitively aware of morally important aspects of the world. On the view being developed here, such a capacity would give us our initial and most immediate access to such moral facts; so to know anything about the nature of moral facts, we first need to know something about the nature of our moral capacity.

It may be that we need blaze no new trails here. Our moral capacity, and moral facts along with it, may turn out to look pretty much like we might expect them to look. To see how this might be so, let us briefly consider a well-known, general argument for moral scepticism, one which includes a rudimentary version of the error theory.

According to Gilbert Harman, the most parsimonious explanation we can give for the fact that humans seem to make moral observations involves no reference to "moral facts" apart from the social and psychological facts that we adopt conventions to regulate our social lives and that these conventions are then internalized into the developing human mind through the mechanism of something like a Freudian superego.[13] The dictates of the superego, however, are really nothing more than socially useful fictions; luckily for social stability, they are fictions that humans cannot easily rid themselves of.[14] Things are different with

---

13 *The Nature of Morality: An Introduction to Ethics* (New York: Oxford University Press, 1997), see esp. chaps. 1, 2 and 5.

14 Harman, 62. I have changed Harman's own misleading wording of this point, according to which the superego itself is a fiction; what he surely means is that the belief that the dictates of the superego ought to be obeyed is fictitious, rather than the superego itself.

regard to empirical observations, like the trail we observe in a cloud chamber. In this sort of case, the most parsimonious explanation of our making such an observation involves the physical fact of something's having left the trail, a proton or something like an proton, as it passed through the cloud chamber. Yet when we (apparently) observe the wrongfulness of some hooligans setting a cat on fire, we need suppose nothing about the world other than that as humans we are apt to choose conventions that make this sort of thing wrong, and that we have a matching psychological capacity that directly enables us to see, or feel, that such things are wrong. That it is wrong to set cats on fire is not true independently of our thinking it to be so, at least according to this particular appeal to an inference to the best explanation.

Harman does not have much to say about the details of the superego, probably because he supposes that something like this sort of psychological mechanism must simply be part of the explanation of human moral beliefs and hence morality itself. But what the earlier argument of this paper establishes is that this sort of sceptical hypothesis is not the default hypothesis when it comes to explaining human beliefs about morality. If chimpanzees are cognitively responding to natural facts of their moral environment, it is not unreasonable to suppose that humans are as well. To be sure, our moral knowledge grows, or at least changes, in ways that chimpanzee moral knowledge does not; and Harman is probably right in suggesting that what marks such change is the adoption of new social conventions. But before there were conventions to be subsequently internalized by something like the superego, there may well have been a human moral capacity with both cognitive and motivational dimensions. Why not suppose that this capacity would have been, and might still continue to be, an important part of the development and adoption of social conventions regarding morality?

In attempting to explain moral change empirically, we might regard Harman's scepticism as a sort of null hypothesis: as we survey the history of changes in moral convention, all we need suppose to account for any of these changes is groups of individuals, each of whom knows his or her position in the group, agreeing to conventions that will hold them together in a more or less stable social union. Some of these individuals may have other-related preferences, some not. According to Harman, people can generally be supposed to be self-interested. But many other factors may also be presumed to affect choices of conventions: the will to power, personal and systemic hatreds, nepotism, greed, and many other more or less pleasant aspects of human nature. All these factors will be relevant for any hypothesis involving the human capacity for adopting conventions with moral content. The question is, if we are to move beyond Harman's hypothesis, what empirically testable constraints might a specifically moral capacity put on the sorts of conventions that may or may not be adopted, as we examine the actual history of moral change.[15]

To know what to make of this question, we need some idea of what a specifically moral capacity might look like. Let me briefly consider several alternative hypotheses, ignoring questions of whether their proponents would like them to be regarded fully as empirically testable claims about the form of a human moral capacity that is the result of evolution. My point here is that an evolutionary moral capacity, and moral facts along with it, need not be supposed to be deeply mysterious, or to be divorced completely from mainstream moral theory. Secondarily, I want to emphasize the apparent fact that human moral belief seems, at least at a very general level, to be twigging to the same sorts of things as chimpanzee moral belief.

According to David Gauthier in *Morals by Agreement*, evolution might be supposed to have made humans constrained maximizers.[16] The Hobbesian moral contract is unavailable to purely rational agents, says Gauthier, because they cannot always be expected to keep their agreements. Luckily for humans, we have evolved a capacity for morality that enables us to genuinely care about others, and hence, to keep our agreements with them even when rationality would tell us not to. Gauthier talks about a "capacity for morality" rather than a "moral capacity" because he thinks that the capacity in question will take as its input whatever is output as "morality" by our rational capacity. So according to the theory of morals by rational agreement, our capacity

---

15 For the sort of thing I have in mind here, see Thomas Haskell, "Capitalism and the Origins of the Humanitarian Sensibility, Parts I and II," *American Historical Review* 90 (1985): 339-61 and 547-66.

16 David Gauthier, *Morals by Agreement* (Oxford: Clarendon Press, 1986), 187-9, 326-9, and 337-9.

for morality adds no real moral content of its own to our agreements regarding moral conventions. Such a "capacity for morality" would nevertheless seem to be less plastic than Harman's "superego," insofar as it is already geared to make us care about others, and insofar as it is fully geared to limit this care in precisely the ways that rationality requires. For the evolutionary aspect of Gauthier's argument to work, the fit between rationality and the capacity for morality has to be pretty good, if humans are not to suffer the fate of the purely rational agent. To do the job required of it by the theory of morals by rational agreement, our capacity for morality would seem to require more internal structure than Harman's superego.

Eschewing Hobbesian versions of a rational contract basis for morality, Richmond Campbell argues on the basis of evolutionary considerations for a Kantian model of human contractors.[17] According to Campbell's argument, Gauthier is probably right about more primitive stages of human morality: our earliest dispositions may have been dispositions of pure reciprocity. But, says Campbell, as these dispositions increasingly came into conflict with one another, there would have been selective pressure for some sort of psychological mechanism for resolving such conflicts in ways acceptable to all parties involved, if not to the group as a whole. The willingness to recognize and treat others as ends in themselves, not just as means to reciprocal benefits, would be the right sort of psychological mechanism, according to Campbell.

Empirically, this understanding of our moral capacity may be related to the sorts of concerns that chimpanzees have for social rules of sharing and punishment. Mediation that favours the underdog rather than the mediator's ally seems, that is, to suggest some sort of rudimentary concern for all members of the group, even the weakest, as ends in themselves. The weaker are not to be interfered with by the stronger in unjustified ways, and everybody knows this. But we might also look to sympathy as a source of our capacity for morality. When I respond sympathetically to the plight of another, I see that individual's interests as being as important as my own. This suggests an impartial point of view which is agent neutral in form: interests matter as interests, not because

---

17 Campbell, *Illusions of Paradox*, 98.

they are the interests of this or that particular individual or agent. Put more bluntly: I recognize suffering as bad wherever I spot it, in myself or in another, it doesn't matter. I defend this sort of non-Kantian, agent-neutral model of our moral capacity in an earlier paper.[18]

Biologically, both Kantian and agent-neutral models of our moral capacity are suspect. Both require us to be impartial between our ends or interests and those of all others, regardless of the degree of closeness of their relationships to us. More biologically sensible, according to de Waal and others, is a graduated sense of sympathy or impartiality: the closer my relationship to another, the more sympathetic or more concerned about the other's ends I am likely to be.[19] This hypothesis builds a set of internal constraints into the structure of our moral capacity, constraints that arise from the biological importance of selfishness, kinship, and reciprocity. But these factors might also serve to limit our moral capacity externally, through a set of separate psychological traits. A sense of familiarity with or dependence on another individual may help to engage my sympathy more readily than it otherwise might without these traits being a part of that capacity. Absent empirical tests of more well-developed hypotheses, there is not much to choose between internally and externally constrained versions of otherwise similar hypotheses about the general form of our capacity for morality. At this point, internally limited sympathy or impartiality is not the default hypothesis.

---

18 "Evolutionary Ethics and Moral Theory," *Journal of Value Inquiry* 30 (1996): 531-45. In addition to distinguishing between Kantian and agent-neutral hypotheses about a human moral capacity grounded in evolution, this paper also develops a rudimentary typology of possible systemic errors in human systems of moral belief.

19 De Waal, *Good Natured*, 212-4; Ruse, *Taking Darwin Seriously*, 234 and 239-42. Interestingly enough one gets the same graduated view of sympathy in Nell Noddings' attempt to work out the sort of contextual ethics suggested in the work of Carol Gilligan; see Noddings, *Caring: A Feminine Approach to Ethics and Moral Education* (Berkeley: University of California Press, 1984) and Gilligan, *In A Different Voice: Psychological Theory and Women's Development* (Cambridge: Harvard University Press, 1982). That this is not the best way to work feminist concerns into an empirical theory of the human capacity for morality is argued by Campbell, *Illusions*, chap. 9.

So what, then, might moral facts look like? Pretty much like what we might expect them to. As a matter of moral fact, the hooligans' setting the cat on fire is wrong. Wherein does its wrongness lie? In the unjustified harm suffered by the cat, and in the hooligans' inflicting this harm on someone smaller and weaker than they are. Among social creatures that have evolved to a certain level of intelligence, such things are in fact morally bad; we ourselves have evolved the capacity not only to recognize such facts, but to feel it imperative to do something about them.

I have listed off the preceding set of hypotheses about the human moral capacity to emphasize the fact that we do not get to assume the sceptical hypothesis for free. It is one of several alternatives, none of which is the default hypothesis. At least some of the time when we make changes to our social conventions regarding morality, we may be acting on the basis of an evolutionary moral capacity linked, in some way, to sympathy or impartiality. What may really be at issue in many of the choices we face is just how sympathetic or impartial we can or need to be. According to the view suggested here, the "need" part of this question can only be answered through the actual workings of our moral capacity, along with the other factors that affect our social decision-making. Knowing more about the capacity may, of course, affect how well we are able to make it work. The "can" part of the question, on the other hand, is more purely empirical in nature, and it looks toward the future as well as back to the past. On the one hand, the historical record of moral changes provides a testing ground for hypotheses about our moral capacity. On the other hand, we may not know the true limits of our moral capacity until those limits are severely tried.

As we humans observe the moral behaviour of other primates, it is fairly easy to see the limits of their capacities. With close observation, we can see fairly readily how far chimpanzee sympathy and the readiness to follow rules aimed at the common good will take them before self-interest becomes too big a force to resist. We might even speculate, with some claim to accuracy, about what sorts of changes to their environment might drive them to extinction. Given the limits on their more rudimentary moral capacity, certain changes might well be expected to lead their social groups to collapse. Of such a social collapse, we might say that the chimps just didn't know any better.

It is of course harder to observe whether there are similar limits on our own moral capacity. It may be that, under certain conditions, say those of advanced capitalism, our moral capacity is up against its outer limits and unable to save us from the destruction of our environment or the networks of trust that our societies have up until now depended upon to prevent internal collapse. Knowing how best to respond to the needs of others may simply elude us in such circumstances, and second best may not be good enough. From the outside, of course, all this might be fairly obvious. We might thus imagine a species as intellectually superior to us as we are to capuchin monkeys doing a post mortem on the demise of human society and life on the planet earth: the human social and material environment changed in ways that their moral capacity was unable to cope with. The possibility of moral knowledge does not necessarily bring along with it, alas, the certainty of moral wisdom.[20]

---

20 My apologies to that repository of American moral wisdom, Der Bingle, and to all those apes who find some amount of comfort in the knowledge that they are not really monkeys. My thanks to Richmond Campbell for pushing me to be clearer where my argument was murkiest. The argument of this paper is directly related to the argument of an earlier paper (note 10) written by John Collier and myself.

CANADIAN JOURNAL OF PHILOSOPHY
Supplementary Volume 26

*Word and Action: Reconciling Rules and Know-How in Moral Cognition**

ANDY CLARK

Abstract

Recent work in cognitive science highlights the importance of exemplar-based know-how in supporting human expertise. Influenced by this model, certain accounts of moral knowledge now stress exemplar-based, non-sentential know-how at the expense of rule-and-principle based accounts. I shall argue, however, that moral thought and reason cannot be understood by reference to either of these roles alone. Moral cognition – like other forms of 'advanced' cognition – depends crucially on the subtle interplay and interaction of multiple factors and forces and *especially* (or so I argue) between the use of linguistic tools and formulations and more biologically basic forms of thought and reason.

1.   Introduction: A Balance Lost?

Aristotle and Kant, occasional publicity notwithstanding, held some quite delicately nuanced views regarding the balanced roles of rules and know-how in moral thought and reason. Each author depicted moral cognition as involving an interplay between the appreciation of rules governing correct action and some kind of know-how, or practical wisdom; wisdom instilled by exposure to exemplars and honed by

---

*   Thanks to Bruce Hunter for some very helpful comments on an earlier draft.

the needs of daily personal interaction and moral decision-making. Kant, it is true, emphasizes the role of universal laws and demands that morally correct action be rooted in the endorsement of such laws, and the conformity of one's actions to them. But (as Sterba 1996, 249-50, nicely points out) Kant also, and simultaneously, held that the application of such rules to specific situations is not *itself* rule-governed, and that exposure to exemplars (in which rules are deployed in concrete cases) can be indispensable in promoting the capacity to properly apply the rules (see, e.g., Kant 1781, 134; 1787, 174). In a related vein, Onora O'Neill (1989, chap. 2) reminds us of Kant's clear insistence, in the *Critique of Practical Reason*, on the importance of practical reason (see Kant 1977, 120-2; for some discussion, see Khin Zaw 1996, 264). It is Aristotle, of course, who is (quite properly) depicted as the true champion of practical wisdom. But even Aristotle[1] allowed that the kind of systematic understanding gained by explicitly formulating policies of action could play an important role in both legislation and in the promotion of individual moral virtue. Aristotle's *Nicomachean Ethics* is, moreover, replete with unqualified universal principles (such as "bravery is a virtue"), although these do not, for Aristotle, play the same kind of role that universal moral laws play for Kant. For Aristotle, they are not rules to be consciously endorsed and followed, so much as principles *others* may use for judging and evaluating actions. (They are thus instances of what Goldman 1986, 25-6, called "non-regulative" rather than "regulative" normative schemes.)

Nonetheless, both Kant and Aristotle were concerned, in part, with the delicate and important *interplay* between explicitly formulated rules and practical wisdom or know-how in the moral domain. Recent cognitive scientifically inspired work[2] in moral philosophy has tended to ignore or downplay this interplay and has promoted instead a vision of moral reason that is based almost entirely on practical wisdom and

---

1 Thanks to Bruce Hunter for pointing this out, and for some related comments concerning Kant.

2 I have in mind the powerful and exciting (but, I'll argue, somewhat distortive) treatments of Churchland (1996) and Johnson (1993). An unusually balanced treatment is Sterba (1996).

skilled know-how. This new development is closely associated with work on Artificial Neural Networks, in which something like skilled, supra-sentential know-how is depicted as the basis of all forms of knowledge and reason.

A prime exponent of such a view is P.M. Churchland, who links the neural-network-based vision to Aristotle's emphasis on practical wisdom and suggests that:

> This portrait of the moral person as one who has acquired a certain family of perceptual and behavioral *skills* contrasts sharply with the more traditional accounts that pictured a moral person as one who has agreed to follow a certain set of rules.
> P.M. Churchland (1996, 106)

I shall argue that such bald opposition is a mistake: a distortion of the complex nature of moral reason and one that obscures the real source of much human moral expertise. For human moral expertise is made possible only by the potent complementarity between two distinct types of cognitive resource (or "mind-tool" – Dennett 1996, chap. 5). One is, indeed, the broadly pattern-based, skill-learning capacity that we share with other animals and artificial neural networks. But the other is, precisely, the very special modes of learning, collaboration and reason made available by the tools, of words, rules, and linguistic exchange. A mature science of the embodied mind will, I suspect, have at its very center a sensitive account of how advanced thought and reason emerges only from the complex and iterated interactions of these two kinds of resource.

2. Moral Expertise

One driving force behind the cognitive scientific endorsement of the "practical wisdom" model of moral knowledge is an influential model of expertise. It is a model grounded in both cognitive psychological studies and in attempts to replicate expert skill using artificial neural networks. With this model of basic biological cognition, I have no quarrel – indeed, it is one that I positively endorse (see Clark 1989; 1993). What I shall be questioning, however, is the concomitant down-playing of the role of actual human talk and discourse in exposing and navigating the moral realm: a down-playing evident in comments such as:

> Stateable rules are not the basis of one's moral character. They are merely its pale and partial reflection at the comparatively impotent level of language.
>
> P. M. Churchland (1996a, 107)

> The skill development model we are proposing ... demotes rational, post-conventional moral activity to the status of a regression to a pre-expert stage of moral development.
>
> Dreyfus and Dreyfus (1990, 252, 256)

What, then, *is* the cognitive scientific vision that is meant to lead us to such dramatically "anti-sentential" conclusions? It is, in large part, the demonstration that certain kinds of neural network device (of which biological brains are plausibly an example) are capable of extracting and encoding information (knowledge) in forms whose richness, fluidity and context sensitivity far outstrips anything that could be supported by a set of linguistically couched action selection rules, principles or maxims. At the heart of the alternative conception is a daunting story about vectors, prototypes, high-dimensional state spaces and non-propositional, distributed encodings: a story nicely laid out in, for example, McClelland et al. (1986), P.S. Churchland and T.J. Sejnowski (1992) and elsewhere. This computational story dovetails well with cognitive psychological work suggesting that much human knowledge is organized around encodings of prototypical cases rather than via the use and storage of rules and definitions (see Rosch 1973; Smith and Medin 1981). For one way to think of the way knowledge is encoded in a neural network is to think of the experienced network (the network after extended training on example cases of input and desired output) as commanding a rich and context-sensitive battery of prototypes ready to be deployed in response to incoming stimuli.

A prototype, as it emerges in this kind of model, is just the statistical central tendency of a set of exemplars each of which displays a range of features. Typical neural network learning algorithms take as input a set of exemplars (or "training instances") and yield a knowledge-base in which the most typical features and the most typically co-associated feature groups become highlighted and play an especially potent role in driving future recall, generalization and problem-solving. One way to think of the extracted prototype is as a point or region in a space which has one dimension for each possible feature.

The learnt prototype of a dog may thus subsist in a feature space whose dimensions include height, weight, aggressiveness, color and so on. Exposed to a variety of dog exemplars, the connectionist system learns the most common features and combinations and hallucinates a "typical dog" – one whose precise feature combinations need not correspond to that found in any actually encountered exemplar, but which reflects the overall statistics of the training set. Churchland (1995) notes that a mature human brain may command a variety of such prototypes: not just ones for concrete objects, but ones for (e.g.) economic, social, moral, political and scientific concepts and ideas. In fact, all human knowledge, according to Churchland, is encoded in this same general way. (For further discussion, see Churchland 1989; 1995, Clark 1989; 1993, Fodor and Lepore 1993).

The potential importance of all this for our conceptions of moral knowledge and moral reason rests on two specific consequences. The first concerns the grain and nature of the knowledge itself. The second concerns the acquisition of such knowledge and the development of moral expertise. Concerning grain and nature, the now-familiar (see, for example, Churchland 1996a; Goldman 1993; Flanagan 1996; Johnson 1993; Clark 1996) point is that our moral knowledge may quite spectacularly outrun anything that could be expressed by simple maxims or moral rules. For the mode of storage and organization, combined with the sheer capacity of biological neural networks, reveals simple sentential formulations as, in Churchland's words, nothing but "a one-dimensional projection of a [high] dimensional solid" (1989, 18). The project of reducing the knowledge (know-how) encoded in a biological neural network to a set of summary moral rules is every bit as intractable as that of capturing the knowledge of an expert bridge or chess player in a set of such maxims. Such maxims, as Dreyfus and Dreyfus (1990) suggest, are of great value to the novice. But they cannot replace the finely tuned pattern recognition skills of the expert who (we now assume) deploys a highly trained neural network of great dimensionality, tuned by exposure to countless instances and minor variations, and organized around a multiplicity of stored prototypes representing the fruits of long, hard hours of play and practice. The second important consequence is now also apparent. The development of moral knowledge and expertise is thus crucially dependent on rich and varied moral experience. It cannot be successfully instilled by exposure to simple sets of moral maxims, any more than great (or even good) chess play can be achieved without dense and repeated practice. Seen in this light, the provision of 'moral tales' and (even better) our occasional immersion in rich, often morally complex or ambiguous, novels takes on a new importance. Such "virtual moral experience" affords just the type of training that begins to approximate the kinds of rich, real-world experience needed to instill genuine moral expertise.

Churchland (1995; 1996a) also offers a vision of moral debate and moral progress firmly grounded in this story concerning supra-sentential individual moral know-how. The account has three important features. First, it depicts moral knowledge as fundamentally similar to non-moral (e.g., scientific) knowledge. Second, it depicts moral debate as a clash between the different prototypes to which a real-world scenario might be assimilated. And third, it depicts moral progress as real (genuinely occurring), but as consisting in something like increasing knowledge of how to match ones behavior to the social framework in which one finds oneself.

The picture, with a little more flesh, is this. The child finds itself in a complex physical and social setting and must acquire a set of perceptual and behavioral skills to flourish. This is not, or not primarily, a matter of learning a set of rules, so much as learning how to act and respond in fluent, highly context-sensitive ways. And it is accomplished by the slow, experience-basic training of complex on-board neural networks. The successful learner develops both "skills of recognition" and "skills of matching ... behavior and the moral circumstances at hand" (Churchland 1996a, 105). The processes by which we acquire such skills are not, however, specifically moral. They are the very same processes involved in all kinds of skill acquisition, and the knowledge obtained is in no way special. Scientific knowledge, according to Churchland, is ultimately practical knowledge: knowledge of "how to navigate the natural world." Moral knowledge, likewise, is just knowledge of "how to navigate the social world" (Churchland 1996a, 106). Moral and scientific knowledge thus emerge as equally 'objective' – answering to a set of constraints imposed by a reality not itself constructed by the individual brain that seeks to comprehend it. And each domain allows for genuine – though pragmatic – kinds of progress in thought and understanding, as we (both as individuals and as a species) learn better and better ways to navigate both physical and social space. Moral disagreement, to complete the picture, arises when different agents or groups use different prototypes to characterize a situation. Moral 'debate' then consists, largely, in the attempt to assert one prototypical understanding (e.g., the fetus as person) over another (e.g., the fetus as internal growth). Churchland says little about how such debates are resolved, but presumably any good resolution must ultimately turn on the relative usefulness of the prototypes as aids for navigating complex social space.

This concludes my thumbnail sketch of Churchland's connectionist-inspired story about moral thought, argument and progress. It is a story wonderfully grounded in some of the most powerful developments in recent cognitive scientific thought. But it is a story marred, I believe, by a failure to engage with a crucial dimension of human thought and reason in general: a dimension, moreover, whose role in enabling moral thought is especially critical. The missing element, to repeat, is a better appreciation of the complementary role of moral language and practices of moral debate in both the construction and the communal navigation of 'moral space.'

3.   Talk and Thought

The connectionist image of moral thought and reason (in particular) and of advanced thought and reason (in general) is incomplete. It fails to do justice to the profound effects of various species of "external scaffolding"[3] on human cognition. One striking effect of this failure is an impoverished view of the role of public language and public discourse in moral reason.

It is all too easy, I have claimed (Clark 1996) to allow the stress on supra-sentential moral know-how to blind us to the profound

---

3 This broad notion of external scaffolding is based on Vygotsky's (1962/1986) observations about the role of linguistic rehearsal in learning, but extends the image to include all the kinds of social, linguistic and technological support that transform the problem spaces confronting the naked biological brain. See Clark (1997b) for the full story.

importance of linguistic exchange and moral maxims. Even if is true that individual moral understanding typically far surpasses anything that a few words can capture, it is *also* true that moral reasoning and decision-making is quintessentially a communal and collaborative affair. It involves the attempt, in a large class of morally crucial cases, to communally negotiate a course of action that meets the differing constraints of multiple individuals and interest groups: identifying these constraints and displaying a course of action as fair and reasonable is at the heart and soul of much contemporary moral thought and reason (think, for example, of the debates concerning the social acceptability of euthanasia, or the delicate balancing acts involved in setting legal constraints on internet activity). Yet this process – of negotiating a practical course of action that meets the needs of multiple different groups and individuals – is linguistically mediated through and through. It begins with the attempt to articulate, often in quite summary ways, the leading ideas, needs and desires of various parties, and proceeds via the repeated exchange of linguaform formulations until some vaguely acceptable compromise is reached. Such a process, as long as it is guided not simply by local expediency, but also with an eye to more global moral issues, underpins all our attempts to discover fair, communally acceptable, co-operatively developed solutions to moral, social and political problems.

In Clark (1996), I argue, in much more detail, that the marginalization of summary linguistic formulations and sentential reason found in Churchland (1989; 1995; 1996a) and in Dreyfus and Dreyfus (1990) is a mistake. Summary linguistic formulations are not (as, for example, Dreyfus and Dreyfus claim) mere tools for the novice. Rather, they are essential parts of the socially extended cognitive mechanisms which support communal reasoning and collaborative problem solving, and are thus crucial and (as far as we know) irreplaceable elements of genuinely moral reason. They are the tools that enable the co-operative explorations of moral space: a space which is intrinsically multi-personal and whose topology is defined largely by the different – but interacting – needs and desires of multiple agents and groups.

But language, I now want to suggest, may play an even more fundamental role in the development of moral knowledge and the exercise of moral reason: a role associated not simply with the communal search for better moral understanding, but with the very process by which the moral realm "comes into view" as an object of human cognitive endeavor.

There is a substantial case to be made that abstract, 'higher-level' thought of all stripes is possible – for biological brains whose basic computational profile is much as Churchland suggests – only in virtue of a kind of cognitive augmentation rooted in the use of signs, labels and words. In much this vein, Dennett (1996) speaks of the role of multiple *mind-tools* in enabling human cognitive success, while Clark (1997a,b) stresses the complementary cognitive benefits of stable, linguistic tokens and fluid pattern-associating styles of individual processing. There are two distinct (but deeply related) dimensions to such benefits, and it is worth treating each in turn.

The first dimension concerns learning and the initial "bringing into focus" of the moral domain. Concerning learning in general, it can be shown (Clark and Thorton 1997) that all known learning algorithms – both connectionist and classicist – flounder in the face of a certain kind of complexity in the training data. Very roughly (see the previously reference for a lot more detail) such algorithms (assuming they are essentially unbiased, i.e., not provided with antecedent domain-specific knowledge) are likely to uncover only relatively superficial statistical regularities in the input data. To help uncover deeper ("hidden," relational, and higher-order) regularities, a powerful strategy is to re-code the input data so that complex, "hidden" regularities show up as simple surface regularities. For example, if you re-code two poker hands (9, 10, J, Q, K and 10, J, Q, K, A) as "straight" and "straight" the deeper relational commonality between the two sequences of cards emerges as a simple surface commonality in the labels. The bulk of the work, in such cases, is done not by the basic learning device but by the re-coding, however that is achieved.

Now suppose we view public language, with its convenient stock of moral terms and labels as – from the point of view of individual reason – a kind of "found" reservoir of potentially useful re-codings: reifications of complex patterns and tendencies in the underlying web of events. Such items, societally accrued by the painful, slow processes of extended search, trial and error over cultural time, will serve to reduce complex, otherwise "cognitively invisible" patterns to tractable, learnable regularities and will enable individual brains to pursue a deeper and more penetrating exploration of moral space. Such exploration is *possible*, for basic biological intelligences like ours, only in virtue of the repeated transformations of understanding achieved by the use of the linguistic signs and labels. When we learn about promises, duties, rights, obligations and so on, we are not just learning labels for morally relevant states of affairs. We are learning to see the world through a new lens –one in which ever deeper patterns (of interactions and conflicts among entities such as rights and duties, etc.) are revealed as potential objects of thought and reason. Language, on this account, is the special tool that brings the moral realm into focus for biological, pattern-based engines of reason, by displaying a "virtual reality" in which morally salient patterns and descriptions are the concrete objects of subsequent thought and reason.

Lest this all seem too speculative, abstract and unanchored in concrete cognitive scientific research, it is worth pausing to consider a simple – but I think striking-demonstration. In recent work with chimps (*Pan troglodytes*), Thompson et al. (in press) show that the provision of simple arbitrary tokens as "names" for relationships allows the chimps to discern complex higher-order relationships which are otherwise invisible to the basic (non-token-augmented) chimp brain. Chimps trained to associate the relation of sameness (two shoes, two cups, etc.) with one arbitrary tag (a plastic token), and the relation of difference (e.g., a shoe and a cup) with a different arbitrary tag, prove capable of learning to spot the presence of higher-order relations. Of a display containing two cups and two shoes, they can then judge that the *same* relation is displayed (sameness in each case). Ditto for a display containing two pairs of unmatched items (cup/shoe, ball/banana) – here the same relation is again displayed, although it is the relation of difference. Given one pair of matched and one of unmatched items, the higher-order relation is correctly judged to be difference: one pair displays sameness, the other difference, hence the higher-order relation is difference. Chimps lacking the history of token training cannot learn to solve these higher-order problems. A compelling conjecture is that the higher-order task becomes tractable because each visually presented pair recalls an image or representation of the appropriate plastic token, thus reducing the higher-order task to a lower-order one (are the two mentally recalled tokens the same or different?). The image is thus of a potent cascade in which culturally acquired tags and labels make available a new quasi-perceptual space in which biologically basic capacities of pattern-recognition can be used to negotiate new and otherwise cognitively invisible realms.

Notice, then, that even the process of moral development (learning to see the moral domain itself) involves a complex interaction between linguistic tokens and signposts and our fine-grained (perhaps ultimately prototype based) appreciation of the situations in which they apply, and of the kinds of actions that may or may not be appropriate. For it is our exposure to moral labels (labeling acts as kind, greedy, selfless, misguided and so on) that enables our pattern-sensitive brains to isolate morally salient patterns that might otherwise remain buried beneath the noise of more superficial similarities and dissimilarities. When Dreyfus and Dreyfus (1990) depict linguaform slogans ("don't tell lies," etc.) as mere tools for the novice, they have in mind a less potent role: the role of enabling a *roughly* acceptable response while we are busy developing (via repeated experience) more precisely honed skills. The developmental image presented above accords moral talk and maxims a more fundamental role: they actually *make possible* the kinds of pattern-and-experience-based learning that Dreyfus and Dreyfus celebrate, at least in those cases in which the target patterns are abstruse and easily swamped by other surface regularities.

There is, of course, a second dimension to this kind of (broadly) language-based cognition enhancement. For the line between learning and mature reason is not hard and fast, and the cognitive benefits of linguistic encoding are by no means restricted to the processes by which we come to learn about complex moral reality. Indeed, the picture of linguistic tokens as the stable anchor points around which to organize ever-more-abstract forms of (in this case) moral perception and reason applies equally well to the case of mature thought. A version of this claim is ably defended by Jackendoff (1996), who suggests a number of (what he terms) "indirect" effects of language on thought. The idea is that language makes thoughts and complex trains of thought and argument into objects available for attention and inspection in their own right. The linguistic formulations help stabilize complex ideas in working memory and help keep separate the various elements of complex thought and arguments, allowing further scrutiny and repeated re-visiting from different argumentative perspectives. In this vein,

Jackendoff (1996) asserts that "language is the only modality that can present to consciousness abstract parts of thought like kinship relations, reasons, hypothetical situations and the notion of inference."

Moral maxims and recipes are thus the anchor points for moral thought and reason. They are the re-visitable islands of order that allow us to engage in exploratory moral discourse, approaching practical moral problems from a variety of angles while striving, nonetheless, to maintain a sense of our targets, priorities and agreed-upon intermediate positions. While Churchland and others are surely correct to insist that the maxims *themselves* cannot do justice to the depth and sensitivity of our moral understanding, they are wrong to depict them as shallow reflections of our real understanding. Instead, they are tools for focusing, holding steady, and refining moral understanding. And without them, our explorations of moral space, if possible at all, would be shallow indeed.

But why should public language be so well fitted to play the role Jackendoff describes? The answer, I think, turns directly on the two roles for linguistic tokens scouted earlier. The first role was as a medium of collaborative effort, and to that end public language is already well-shaped as a tool for interrogation, criticism and the pursuit of reasons. The second role was as a source of new stable entities standing-in for complex patterns and relations. The potency of linguistic formulations as anchor points for mature thought and reason flows directly from these more basic attributes. Public language is the favored means by which pattern-completing biological brains bootstrap their way into the realm of cascading abstraction, detailed self-criticism, and the reflective pursuit of arguments and reasons: clear pre-requisites, surely for any advanced form of moral sensibility.

A partial parallel may exist in the human capacity for mathematical thought. One suggestion recently supported by an impressive array of cognitive psychological and neuroscientific evidence (see Dehaene 1997; Dehaene et al. 1999) is that the distinctive human ability to do arithmetic depends on the coordinated interaction of two quite distinct kinds of "mind-tools." The first is an innate biological competence at low-grade approximate arithmetic: a simple number sense shared with prelinguistic infants and other animals, to detect a few absolute quantities (one, two, three) and to appreciate changes in quantity and relative quantities (more, less). The second is a culturally acquired and

278

numerical-symbol mediated capacity to pick out other exact quantities (22, 103, etc.) despite the lack of any biologically basic capacity to distinguish, e.g., thoughts about "53-ness" from thoughts about "52-ness," etc. Genuine arithmetical understanding, Dehaene argues, is possible (for brains like ours) only courtesy of the complex interplay between culturally constructed (and initially external) symbolic systems and the rougher innate sense of simple numerosity.

It is not my purpose to critically discuss this suggestion here (but see Clark in press), but merely to display the form of the conjecture. For it once again suggests ways in which basic biological brains may rely on the complementary resources of public symbols and codes to successfully penetrate and navigate otherwise intractable regions of intellectual space.

The larger picture that is emerging is thus one in which neither of the two extreme poles (the emphasis on explicitly endorsed moral principles or the stress on practical wisdom) captures the subtlety, power and complexity of human moral intelligence. Instead it is the cognitive *symbiosis* between basic, prototype-style, pattern-based understanding and the stable surgical instruments (for learning, criticism and evaluation) of moral talk and discourse that conjures real moral understanding. A mistake to be avoided in displaying this complex interplay is that of depicting linguistic formulations as merely low-grade approximations to the finer-grained moral sensibilities realized in on-board neural networks: the mistake of seeing the linguistic ideas as pale, partial and somewhat impotent reflections (recall Churchland 1996a, 107) of real moral understanding. To do so is like suggesting that the rake and the plough are merely pale, partial and somewhat impotent reflections of our real ability to farm. Better by far to see the rake and plough as special tools that effectively transform the space in which the farmer's native skills of physical action are deployed and which allow her to tame and exploit terrain that would rapidly repel any unaugmented advances. The image to abandon is the image of simple translation: linguistic items do not benefit us solely in virtue of their problematic translation into some finer-grained inner code. Instead, they act by complementing, and being brought into co-ordination with, the kinds of prototype-based knowledge celebrated by Churchland, Dreyfus, and others.

It may be objected that this account, even if correct, does not yet establish a *crucial* role for *regulative* rules of conduct in either the development or the mature pursuit of moral reason. A regulative rule (see Goldman 1986) is one which is to be consciously adopted and followed, while non-regulative rules are simply tools for the evaluation of *other's* actions and choices. The worry (which was brought to my attention by Bruce Hunter) is thus that even if the use of linguistic labels aids moral learning and enables substantive moral discourse, it does not follow that any moral *rules* come to play regulative roles in the generation of individual action.

My response to this is two-fold. First, I claim that even if this were correct, it would still be important to appreciate the deep role of moral talk and discourse in constructing our understanding of moral space – a role which cannot be fully appreciated as long as the implicit model of language – to – inner code relations is one of translation rather than co-ordination and complementarity. But second, I would take issue with the notion of a firm regulative/non-regulative divide. Thus consider the morally crucial notion of self-evaluation. Having acted, or settled on a course of action, we must often step back and evaluate our own choices. In so doing, we bring to bear a wealth of tricks and tools, including knowledge of a variety of explicit evaluative criteria. Is this a decision that is consistent with my larger plans, goals and beliefs? How would I feel if someone else did as I am proposing to do? Does my choice display bravery, cowardice, greed? And so on. In engaging in such modes of reflection, we draw heavily on our experiences of public normative discussions and critiques: we engage, in essence, in a kind of evaluative exercise involving a variety of inner critics – a process sometimes called "dialogic reasoning."[4] Dialogic reasoning, I suggest, is crucial to the whole complex of second-order thought by which we judge and criticize our own reasoning and actions. And it is both developmentally[5] and conceptually linked to the notion of multiple

---

4 See Bakhtin (1981), Todorov (1984).

5 See, e.g., Berk's (1994) review of results concerning children's self-developed speech and problem-solving.

inner "voices" speaking for, and from, different perspectives. Such inner dialogues are part of the mental machinery that enables us to be sensitive and self-critical moral agents, as well as effective partners in collaborative endeavors.

In sum, I doubt that the distinction between regulative rules and criteria used to evaluate the actions of others is as firm as it may initially appear. For the element of self-evaluation, which is arguably especially pertinent to moral reason, blurs the divide between evaluation and the rational control of present and future action.

4. Situated Moral Epistemology

A situated moral epistemology, as I am using the term, will offer an account of moral knowledge and moral reason which is sensitive to the critical roles of a variety of non-individualistic elements. Such elements include the social role of language in collaborative problem-solving (Clark 1996), the scaffolding effects of larger-scale institutional and organizational contexts (for an 'economic reason' based foray, see Clark 1997a), and (see above) the cognitive and developmental benefits conferred by the framework of moral discourse and moral labels through which our neural engines of reason confront the world.

Among the consequences of any shift towards a more situated moral epistemology are, first, a somewhat different perspective on the issues concerning moral progress and the possibility of genuine moral knowledge, and second, a concomitant shift in our ideas about the natural systems in which moral thought and reason inhere.

Concerning moral progress and the possibility of genuine moral knowledge, it is again useful to compare the situated approach with Churchland's more ruggedly individualistic stance. For where Churchland stresses the potential for steady moral progress and convergence, a more situated story suggests historical path-dependence and multiple divergent explorations of an exponentially large space of moral possibilities. Churchland's position, recall, is that moral knowledge is fundamentally like scientific knowledge. Both are best seen as bodies of know-how, represented (connectionist-fashion) in the head, and subject to the same kinds of selective pressure: pressure to successfully engage the natural world, on the one hand, and the social world, on the other. Churchland thus emphasizes:

> The practical and pragmatic nature of both scientific and broadly normative knowledge [and] the fact that both embody different forms of know-how: how to navigate the natural world in the former case, and how to navigate the social world, in the latter.
> P. M. Churchland (1995, 292)

Flanagan (1996) is critical of this parallel, detecting in Churchland a kind of "naïve enlightenment optimism about moral progress and convergence" (35). Where Churchland draws a parallel between moral and basic scientific understanding, Flanagan suggests instead that the moral realm is less constrained and less likely to support strong notions of objectivity, convergence and progress. Moral knowledge, Flanagan plausibly asserts, is intrinsically more local and is better compared to the multiplicity of successful strategies characteristic of a complex ecology. Critique and debate is thus always "perspectival," rooted in the local moral ecology. And there are enough different, but equally successful, ways of living (niches) to undermine any simple appeal to a "best way" to negotiate social space.

Something like Flanagan's picture can be illuminated, I suggest, by further reflection on the role of linguistic labels and other forms of external scaffolding in influencing the shape and course of moral thought and reason. For the ultimate source of Churchland's "blindspot" is his implicit commitment to an essentially individualistic and non-constructivist naturalization program: one in which moral thought and reason is depicted as a property of individual biological brains, each seeking only the safe navigation of an essentially independent social space.

By contrast, our explorations of moral space are – on my account – highly constrained by the specific linguistic frameworks that both enable and restrict human thought and reason. The provision of labels and tags aids us, as we saw, by creating new "virtual worlds" in which to bring to bear basic biological capacities of pattern-based reasoning. But every choice of moral vocabulary is likewise restrictive, rendering *other* patterns invisible to all but the most breathtaking ("revolutionary") exercises of individual thought. This would not matter if the shape of the social world really did enforce certain practices of labeling and talking, as Churchland seems to suggest. But such a view looks to get the descriptive cart well before the constructive horse. For surely, in *at least* equal measure, it is our communal practices of talking, labeling and categorizing that create the special kinds of social space whose successful navigation becomes the 'goal' of the child's brain. And these communal practices, as Flanagan again points out, are dictated by multiple practical forces and local and historical contingencies. As a result, there simply is (in one sense) no such thing as "the social world," existing independently of our moral frameworks and capable of forcing those frameworks into shape. There is, I will allow, a useful (though famously elusive) notion of human flourishing which affords some partial anchor for our moral sensibilities. But here too, there are simply untold numbers of ways to flourish, and (as Flanagan stresses) social niches in which and do so. The overall result is indeed a kind of naturalized, pragmatic pluralism, in which moral knowledge is relative to a niche which is partially, as least, constructed by the very apparatus (of moral talk, labels and categories) with which we confront it.

This idea may be better appreciated by way of an analogy. Consider for a moment the case of "financial knowledge and reason." Financial reason, as Arthur (1994) nicely points out, involves dealing with an evolved financial ecology that is, in a very concrete sense, partially created by our own activities of labeling and exchanging. You begin with something relatively basic – the trading of valuable items ('underlyings,' currencies, debts, soybeans, etc.). But with this structure in place, increasingly complex swaps and trades become possible. We can buy and sell futures, which are contracts to deliver an underlying at a fixed later date, or options to buy. These options and futures then *themselves* constitute new kinds of underlying, that can be traded as valuable items in their own right. Which in turn opens up the space of options on futures and so on. (For the full story, see Arthur 1996.)

What I hope to draw from this example is a sense of the power of tags and labels to at once *create and explore* complex spaces. The creation is not unconstrained, nor *ex nihilo*. But the spaces themselves become available for exploration only courtesy of the linguistic practices themselves.

Moral thought and reason seems to share at least something of this nature. A recent example is the emergence of whole new domains of moral and legal complexity surrounding the use of the internet and cross-boundary trading (see, e.g., Johnson 1999). Another case, suggested to me by Carl Wellman, concerns the right to refuse medical treatments even when necessary to prolong life. This right has recently been labeled (the label being recognized, though not yet approved, in *Cruzan* vs. *Director*, Missouri Health Department (1990) 4 97 U.S. 261 and 277) as the "right to die." Should such a label become approved, it is easy to see, as Wellman suggests, how it may help reconfigure the space of local moral, ethical and legal argument. For it then invites a rights-based argument in favor of physician-assisted suicide.[6] In a similar vein, Nancy Fraser (1989) traces the way changes in the way we talk about spousal abuse have gone hand-in-hand, historically, with changes in the way we evaluate such behavior.[7] No doubt examples could be multiplied. The point, however, is just to suggest – once again – that the forces that shape our communal explorations of social and moral space are highly diverse, and that social practices of talking and labeling are potent tools that simultaneously shape moral space and make it accessible to pattern-based biological reason. Doing justice to this complex dance must be a primary goal of any situated moral epistemology.

All this has clear implications, it seems to me, for the broader business of "naturalizing moral thought and reason." For such a project cannot hope to succeed – if I am right – without recognizing that moral reason is a function not simply of our individual psychological profiles, but of the larger social, cultural, and linguistic systems in which they participate: larger systems that display a marked historicity and path-dependence, and in which change, progress and evolution are determined as much by their own intrinsic dynamics as by the actions or choices of the individuals "within" them. In studying and attempting to understand these systems, we should not be tempted to reduce their dynamics to the dynamics of individual biological brains, but *neither* should we assume all the interesting work is done by the larger social and organizational structures alone. For the moral machine is genuinely a complex ecology in which there has evolved a fit (for better or worse) between individual agents' practices and expectations, and the social, legal and political institutions and structures in which

---

6　For a useful discussion of the emergence of new legal rights, see Wellman (1999).

7　Thanks to Joel Anderson for drawing this example to my attention.

they are embedded. There has been co-evolution between all the elements of this matrix. Moral debate influences the development of moral (social, political, legal and educational) infrastructure. But moral thought and reason *is itself* constantly and profoundly affected and transformed by this infrastructure (think of the role played by the U.S. Constitution in sculpting contemporary American debates over pornography, gun control and so on). Our pattern-completing brains are thus directed not at some bare, noumenal version of "moral space," nor even at the more mundane space of practical social living. They are directed, so I claim, at the (communally constructed) space of local moral infrastructure: a space populated by laws, constitutions, formal and informal norms and a persistent host of summary moral maxims, as well as by the less visible, but equally constraining, structures of commerce, industry and educational practice.

5. Conclusions: The Cognitive Complementarity of Rules and Know-How

Moral knowledge, even Churchland admits, must involve a mix between praxis and theoria (see Churchland 1996b). But having conceded this much, he goes on to claim that "the brain draws no distinction between them: both kinds of knowledge are embodied in vast configurations of synaptic weights" (305). I have tried to argue for an alternative view: that moral knowledge is made possible by, and consists in, a carefully orchestrated interplay between the kinds of rich, nuanced, know-how directly embodied in neural states, and the genuinely different cognitive tools provided by moral talk and language. Such tools function not by simple translation into 'neuralese,' but by providing a new and importantly different class of objects on which to target our individual modes of understanding. Moral talk and labels, on this account, transform the space of moral reason as thoroughly as the invention of money transformed the space of trade and bargaining.

Sensitivity to this transformative role reveals a narrow but navigable pathway between two superficially competing visions of moral knowledge: the rule-based and the know-how/exemplar-based approaches to moral cognition. Between these poles, we should again perceive, however dimly, a middle territory. A territory in which genuine moral knowledge is *essentially* a function of the complementarity between two sets of mind-tools: the tools of rich, context-sensitive practical wisdom celebrated by Churchland, and the linguaform tools that allow us to deploy those basic biological resources in increasingly abstract, complex, collaborative and self-evaluative domains. Human moral reason, thus construed, is structurally akin to human mathematical reason, each depending crucially upon the coordination of our basic biological sensitivities with the new tools of linguistic labels and public exchange and debate.

There are other conflicts, too, that may be at least partially reconciled by this kind of treatment. These include the debate over the role of large-scale embedding structures in explaining human action (Marxist ideas about structural determination vs. Mill's ideas about individual free action, for example)[8] and the debate between moral realists and relativists. But such topics I leave for another day. In closing, I would stress only the highly preliminary nature of these remarks and speculations. Moral thoughts and moral talk do, I believe, form a deeply interanimated whole. But the specific shape and nature of the crucial interactions is not yet clear, nor the ultimate implications of such interactivity for our conceptions of moral knowledge and reason. Getting this picture right is surely essential if cognitive science is to make a sensitive contribution to moral epistemology.

---

8 For an excellent treatment, see Andrew Sneddon, "Agents and Actions," Unpublished doctoral thesis, Queen's University, Canada.

References

Aristotle. 1972. *The Nicomachean Ethics*. London: Oxford University Press.

Arthur, W. B. 1994. "On the Evolution of Complexity." In *Complexity: Metaphors, Models, and Reality*. Ed. G.A. Cowan, D. Pines and D. Meltzer. Reading, Mass.: Addison-Wesley.

Bakhtin, M. 1981. *The Dialogic Imagination*. Ed. M. Holquist. Austin: University of Texas Press.

Berk, L. 1994. "Why Children Talk to Themselves." *Scientific American*, November: 78-83.

Churchland, P.S., and T.J. Sejnowski. 1992. *The Computational Brain*. Cambridge: MIT Press.

Churchland, P.M. 1989. *A Neurocomputational Perspective*. Cambridge: MIT/ Bradford Books.

Churchland, P.M. 1995. *The Engine of Reason, the Seat of the Soul*. Cambridge: MIT Press.

Churchland, P.M. 1996a. "The Neural Representation of the Social World." In *Mind and Morals*. Ed. L. May, M. Friedman and A. Clark. Cambridge: MIT Press.

Churchland, P.M. 1996b. "Flanagan on Moral Knowledge." In *The Churchlands and Their Critics*. Ed. R. McCauley. Oxford: Blackwell.

Clark, A. 1989. *Microcognition: Philosophy, Cognitive Science and Parallel Distributed Processing*. Cambridge: MIT Press.

Clark, A. 1993. *Associative Engines: Connectionism, Concepts and Representational Change*. Cambridge: MIT Press.

Clark, A. 1996. "Connectionism, Moral Cognition and Collaborative Problem Solving." In *Minds and Morals*. Ed. L. May, M. Friedman and A. Clark. Cambridge: MIT Press.

Clark, A. 1997a. "Economic Reason: The Interplay of Individual Learning and External Structure." In *The Frontiers of the New Institutional Economics*. Ed. J. Drobak and J. Nye. London: Academic Press.

Clark, A. 1997b. *Being There: Putting Brain, Body and World Together Again*. Cambridge: MIT Press.

Clark, A. in press. "Minds, Brains and Tools: Comments on Dennett." In *Philosophers of Mental Representation*. Ed. H. Clapin. Cambridge: MIT Press.

Clark, A., and C. Thornton. 1997. "Trading Spaces: Connectionism and the Limits of Uninformed Learning." *Behavioral and Brain Sciences* 20: 57-67.

Dehaene, S. 1997. *The Number Sense*. Oxford: Oxford University Press.

Dehaene, S., E. Spelke, et al. 1999. "Sources of Mathematical Thinking: Behavioral and Brain Imaging Evidence." *Science* 284: 970-4.

Dennett, D. 1996. *Kinds of Minds*. New York: Basic Books.

Donagan, A. 1977. *The Theory of Morality*. Chicago: University of Chicago Press.

Dreyfus, H., and S. Dreyfus 1990. "What is Morality? A Phenomenological Account of the Development of Ethical Expertise." In *Universalism vs. Communitarianism: Contemporary Debates in Ethics*. Ed. D. Rasmussen. Cambridge: MIT Press.

Flanagan, O. 1996. "Ethics Naturalized: Ethics as Human Ecology." In *Mind and Morals*. Ed. L. May, M. Friedman and A. Clark. Cambridge: MIT Press.

Fodor, J., and E. Lepore. 1993. "Reply to Churchland." *Philosophy and Phenomenological Research* 53: 679-82.

Fraser, N. 1989. *Unruly Practices: Power, Discourse and Gender in Contemporary Social Theory*. Minneapolis: University of Minnesota Press.

Goldman, A. 1986. *Epistemology and Cognition*. Cambridge: Harvard University Press.

Goldman, A. 1993. "Ethics and Cognitive Science." *Ethics* 103: 337-60.

Jackendoff, R. 1996. "How Language Helps Us Think." *Pragmatics and Cognition* 4: 1-34.

Johnson, D. 1999. "Emergent Law and Order." In *The Biology of Business: Decoding the Natural Laws of Enterprise*. Ed. J. Clippinger. San Francisco: Jossey-Bass.

Johnson, M. 1993. *Moral Imagination: Implications of Cognitive Science for Ethics*. Chicago: University of Chicago Press.

Kant, E. 1781 (=A). *A Critique of Pure Reason*. London: Macmillan.

Kant, E. 1787 (=B). *Critique of Pure Reason*. London: Macmillan.

Kant, E. 1977. *Critique of Practical Reason*. Indianapolis: Bobbs-Merrill.

Khin Zaw, S. 1996. "Moral Rationality." In *Minds and Morals*. Ed. C. May, M. Friedman, and A. Clark. Cambridge: MIT Press.

McClelland, J. L. 1989. "Parallel Distributed Processing – Implications for Cognition and Development." In *Parallel Distributed Processing: Implications for Psychology and Neurobiology*. Ed. R.G.M. Morris. Oxford: Clarendon Press.

McClelland, J. L., D. Rumelhart, and G. Hinton. 1986. "The Appeal of Parallel Distributed Processing." In D. E. Rumelhart, J. L. McClelland and the PDP Research Group, *Parallel Distributed Processing: Explorations in the Microstructure of Cogntion*. Vol. 1. Cambridge: MIT Press.

Mill, J. S. 1884. *A System of Logic*. London: Longmans, Green & Co.

O'Neill, O. 1989. *Constructions of Reason*. Cambridge: Cambridge University Press.

Rosch, E. 1973. "Natural Categories." *Cognitive Psychology* 4: 324-50.

Smith, E., and D. Medin 1981. *Categories and Concepts*. Cambridge: Harvard University Press.

Sterba, J. 1996. "Justifying Morality and the Challenge of Cognitive Science." In *Mind and Morals*. Ed. L. May, M. Friedman and A. Clark. Cambridge: MIT Press.

Thompson, R., D. Oden, and S. Boyson. In press. "Language-naive Chimpanzees judge relations between relations in an abstract mapping task." *Journal of Experimental Psychology: Animal Behavior Processes*.

Todorov, T. 1984. *Mikhail Bakhtin: The Dialogical Principle*. Minneapolis: University of Minnesota Press.

Vygotsky, L. 1986. *Thought and Language*. Cambridge: MIT Press.

Wellman, C. 1999. *The Proliferation of Rights*. Boulder, Co.: Westview.

CANADIAN JOURNAL OF PHILOSOPHY
Supplementary Volume 26

Rules, Know-How, and the Future of Moral Cognition

PAUL M. CHURCHLAND

Professor Clark's splendid essay[1] represents a step forward from which there should be no retreat. Our *de facto* moral cognition involves a complex and evolving interplay between, on the one hand, the *non*discursive cognitive mechanisms of the biological brain, and, on the other, the often highly discursive extra-personal "scaffolding" that structures the social world in which our brains are normally situated, a world that has been, to a large extent, created by our own moral and political activity. That interplay extends the reach and elevates the quality of the original nondiscursive cognition, and thus any adequate account of moral cognition must address both of these contributing dimensions. An account that focuses only on brain mechanisms will be missing something vital.

I endorse these claims, so compellingly argued by Clark, for much the same reasons that I also endorse the following claims. Our de facto *scientific* cognition involves a complex and evolving interplay between, on the one hand, the *non*discursive cognitive mechanisms of the biological brain, and, on the other, the often highly discursive extra-personal "scaffolding" that structures the social-scientific world in which the brains of scientists are normally situated, a technologically and institutionally intricate world that has been, to a large extent, created by our own scientific activities. That interplay extends the reach and elevates the quality of the original nondiscursive cognition, and

---

1 Clark, A., "Word and Action: Reconciling Rules and Know-How in Moral Cognition," this volume.

thus any adequate account of scientific cognition must address both of these contributing dimensions. An account that focuses only on brain mechanisms will be missing something vital.

I draw this parallel for many reasons, as will emerge, but a salient reason is that, whatever theoretical story we decide to tell about "situated" cognition, it must meet the experimental test of, not one, but at least *two* important domains of human cognitive activity. A second reason is to emphasize that Clark's (entirely genuine) insights about the "situated" character of our moral cognition do nothing to distinguish it, in any fundamental way, from human cognition in general, including our scientific cognition. And a third reason is that each of these two cognitive domains – the broadly scientific, and the broadly moral – may have a good deal to teach us about the other, once we appreciate that, and how, they are brothers under the skin.

1. The Role of Discursive Rules

While Clark finds an important role for discursive moral rules, within the context of the nondiscursive, connectionist, prototype-centered account of moral knowledge, we must be mindful that the role he finds is profoundly different from the role that tradition has always assumed moral rules to play. I do not mean to suggest that Clark is under any illusions on this score, but many of his readers will be, and so it is appropriate to begin by emphasizing the novelties that we here confront. Clark's story on moral cognition is in no way a critique or a rejection of the recent nondiscursive neural-network models of human and animal cognition.[2] Rather, it is an important and appropriate

---

2 For a quick and accessible introduction, see P.M. Churchland, *The Engine of Reason, The Seat of the Soul: A Philosophical Journey into the Brain* (Cambridge: MIT Press, 1995). For a sketch of its applications to moral theory in particular, see P.M. Churchland, "Toward a Cognitive Neurobiology of the Moral Virtues," *Topoi* 17 (1998): 83-96. For a more thorough and more neurophysiologically focussed introduction, see P.S. Churchland and T. Sejnowski, *The Computational Brain* (Cambridge: MIT Press, 1992). For a more philosophically oriented introduction, see P.M. Churchland, *A Neurocomputational Perspective: The Nature*

augmentation of that approach. It is a local reflection of his views on situated cognition in general, as outlined in his 1997 book.[3] That more general view is interesting because it finds a significant portion of the machinery available to cognition, and a significant portion of the activity of cognition, to lie *outside* the brain. It lies in the extra-personal public space of drawn diagrams, written arithmetic calculations, spoken and printed arguments, tools of measurement and manipulation, and extranumery "cognitive prosthetics" of many other kinds as well. The idea is that the brain learns to "off-load" certain aspects of some needed computational activity into some appropriate external medium of representation and manipulation, because the job can there be done more easily, quickly, or reliably than inside the brain. Deploying the familiar grade-school recursive procedures ("write down the 6, carry the 1") with pencil on paper, to compute large arithmetical sums, would be a prototypical instance of the "off-loading" phenomenon he has in mind, and you can easily begin to generalize from this mundane example. In particular, you can begin to see a cognate role for the linguistic machinery of moral conversation, moral argument, and moral directives.

Now this externalist vision, I believe, is the *right* way to see the role of discursive representations. But it is vital to appreciate that it involves a major shift away from the avowedly *internalist* perspective that dominates traditional moral theory of almost every stripe. According to that tradition, to be moral is to have embraced, accepted, or otherwise internalized a specific set of behavior-guiding rules, which stored rules are then deployed in appropriate circumstances as a salient part of the internal cognitive mechanisms that actually produce intentional behavior. (Once these assumptions are in place, the principal philosophical questions are then pretty much fixed: which of the many pos-

---

of Mind and the Structure of Science (Cambridge: MIT Press, 1989). For a rigorous mathematical introduction, see R. Rojas, *Neural Networks: A Systematic Introduction* (New York: Springer-Verlag, 1996). The bibliography of any of these will lead you stepwise into the larger literature.

3 Andy Clark, *Being There: Putting Brain, Body, and World Together Again* (Cambridge: MIT Press, 1997).

sible rules are the truly correct or morally binding rules? And what metaphysical, apodeictic, or empirical circumstance – e.g., God's command, a social contract, pure reason, utility maximization, maxi-min choice from behind a veil, etc. – bestows that vaulted status upon them?) What goes unnoticed in this highly general perspective on moral philosophy, at least until recently, is that it surreptitiously presupposes a background theory about the nature of cognition, a theory that we now have overwhelming reason to believe is empirically false, a theory for which we already possess the outlines of a neuronally based and mathematically embodied alternative, specifically, the vector-coding, matrix-processing, prototype-activating, synapse-adjusting account held out by cognitive neurobiology and connectionist AI.

What changes does this new cognitive perspective require? Several. First and foremost, it requires us to give up the idea that our internal representations and cognitive activities are essentially just hidden, silent versions of the external statements, arguments, dialogues, and chains of reasoning that appear in our overt speech and print. That conception is an old and venerable one, to be sure, for it is the constituting assumption of our dear beloved "Folk Psychology." And it is also a *natural* one, for, how *else* should we conceive of our inner activities, save on the model of outer speech, our original and (until recently) our only empirical example of a representational/computational system?[4] How else indeed?

But in fact there are other ways, and ignorance of them has been our excuse for far too long. Nonlinguistic creatures (that is, most of the

---

4 The reader will here recognize Wilfrid Sellars' well-known account of the origins and nature of our Folk Psychology, as outlined in the closing sections of his classic paper, "Empiricism and the Philosophy of Mind," chap. 3 of *Science, Perception, and Reality* (London: Routledge, 1963). Ironically (from our present perspective), Sellars was blissfully convinced that Folk Psychology was an *accurate* portrayal of our inner cognitive activities. (I recall finding it advisable to down-play my own nascent eliminativism during my dissertation defense, a meeting chaired by that worthy philosopher.) But Sellars' conviction on this point notwithstanding, Folk Psychology had invited systematic scepticism long before the present, and for reasons above and beyond the recent flourishing of cognitive neurobiology. See, for example, my "Eliminative Materialism and the Propositional Attitudes," *Journal of Philosophy* 78, no. 2 (1981), now twenty years old.

creatures on the planet) provide the initial motivating cognitive examples. For it is not plausible to portray them as using the same discursive, linguaformal thought processes that we so routinely ascribe to ourselves. After all, why conceive of all animal cognition on the model of an isolated discursive skill that is utterly unique to a single species? But neither is it plausible to dismiss all nonhuman animals as thoughtless, stimulus-response driven brutes. They are far too clever for that. Plainly, we need a third approach, free from a procrustean anthropocentric romanticism, on the one hand, and from the dismissive deflation of animal cognitive powers, on the other.

2.   A Nondiscursive Conception of Cognition

When, in a comparative spirit, we examine the *brains* of terrestrial creatures – their large-scale anatomies, their filamentary microstructures, and their physiological and electrochemical activities – we find a striking *conservation* of form, structure, and function across all vertebrate animals, and especially across the higher mammals, and most especially across the primates, humans included. The basic machinery of cognition is the same in all of us, and it has nothing to do with the structure of declarative sentences, with the rule-governed drawing of inferences from one sentence to another, or with the storage and deployment of rules of any kind. Instead, that machinery is wonderfully designed by evolution to subserve the acquisition and deployment of a panoply of *skills* and *abilities*.

Those skills include, most obviously, a broad range of *perceptual* skills, for a creature must learn to discriminate not only colors and shapes, but to recognize such things as the peculiar locomotor gaits of its typical predators and typical prey; the entreaty or hostility in the facial expression of a conspecific; the gathering weariness of an infant, or an adversary; the existence and profile of kin relations and social alliances within one's group; the opportunities to forge and share in such alliances; and the appropriate occasions to express the commitments – such as defense, comfort, and sharing – that go with those alliances. Perception, plainly, can involve considerable conceptual sophistication.

No less important are the *motor* skills that must be acquired. A creature must learn to walk, to run, to climb, or to fly, and so forth. But it must also learn to chase its prey, to groom its conspecifics, to fend off an attack, to make a nest or burrow, to assemble an electric motor, or, if one is an administrator, to do such things as take a company public, or launch the Allied invasion of Normandy. Motor skills, like perceptual skills, can also involve a high degree of conceptual sophistication.

Finally, and not to be sharply separated from the skills already discussed, are the various skills of sensorimotor *coordination*, the skills of matching one's behavior to one's current perceptions, or of using one's ongoing perceptions to steer and modulate one's ongoing behavior. Importantly, much of one's perception involves the recognition of proto-typical *processes* that unfold in time, such as falling bodies, flying insects, swimming fish, and fleeing mice. Moreover, the perceptual recognition of such processes consists in the activation of a previously learned proto-typical *sequence* of activation-patterns in the relevant neuron population. Accordingly, a creature with sensorimotor coordination can *anticipate* the unfolding of its perceptual environment, for at least a few fractions of a second into the future, and then steer its motor behavior to suit that anticipated environment. It can dodge the falling body, swat the flying insect, and catch the moving fish or mouse. In this basic capacity for sensorimotor coordination lies the origins of all intelligence, and one obvious measure of the degree of intelligence that any creature has achieved is *how far* into the future and across *what range* of phenomena it is capable of projecting the behavior of its environment, and thus how far in advance of that future it can begin to execute appropriately exploi-tative and manipulative motor behavior. What distinguishes the intelligence of humans from that of all other creatures is not some cogni-tive discontinuity such as the possession of language. More likely, it is our pre-eminent talent in something we share with all cognitive creatures: we can see farther into the future, and execute motor behavior to exploit that future, than any other creature on the planet.

To complete this thumbnail sketch of the basic and nondiscursive cognitive activities common to all terrestrial creatures, suppose now that many species of animal acquire the ability to play and replay, "off-line" (that is, in some fashion that disconnects them from their normal motor sequelae) the various prototypical sequences of activation patterns – both perceptual and motor – that prior experience of the world has taught them. The reader will recognize these activational excursions as instances of day-dreaming or projective imagination. As launched in specific perceptual circumstances, they will constitute episodes of "vicarious exploration" of the environment. That is, they will constitute episodes of subjunctive and practical *reasoning*. We are here contemplating a conception of high-level cognitive activity that is recognizably true of ourselves, but which contains no hint of discursive representations and rule-governed activity. That basic conception is all the more interesting because an explanatorily fertile theory of its general nature (i.e., the vector-processing story of connectionism) is already in place, and because that abstract functional theory coheres very nicely with the implementation-level story of neurons and synapses provided by the empirical neurosciences. Indeed, it was our study of the latter that originally inspired our development of the former.

3. Moral Cognition and the Novelty of Rules

"Oh, very well," one might reply, a tad impatiently, "so a nondiscursive form of cognition underlies all of the more advanced forms; but don't we leave that original and primitive form behind when we enter the domain of morality and complex social cognition?"

Not at all. We can see this vital fact immediately by looking at all of the other social mammals on the planet – baboon troops, wolf packs, dolphin schools, chimpanzee groups, lion prides, and so on – and by observing in them the same complex ebb and flow of thoughtful sharing, mutual defense, fair competition, familial sacrifice, staunch alliance, minor deception, major treachery, and the occasional outright ostracism that we see displayed in human societies.[5] Most importantly, for the present issue, none of these other instances of complex social order possesses a language, or any other form of external "cognitive scaffolding," on which to "off-load" some of their social/moral cognition.

---

5 Appeals to ethology are not always welcome in moral philosophy, but we had better get used to them. The traditionally unquestioned gap between "Rational Man" and "the unreasoning brutes" is no more substantial than is the division, so long revered in ancient Cosmology, between the "sublunary realm" and the "superlunary realm." For a recent and exemplary exploration of what the animal kingdom may have to teach us about the nature of morality, see A. MacIntyre, *Dependent Rational Animals: Why Human Beings Need the Virtues* (Chicago: Open Court, 1999).

Their social cognition is conducted *entirely* within the more primitive and nondiscursive form of cognition we have here been discussing. And so, quite evidently, is the greater part of social cognition in human society as well. Typically, it is only when something goes *wrong* with our well-oiled social interactions that the discursive scaffolding of rules and moral argument and laws and court procedures is brought into play.

Even when that external machinery does get deployed, it is the original and more basic form of cognition that does the deploying. Rules are useless unless the capacity for reliable *perception* of their categories is already in place, and such perception depends utterly on the inarticulable processes of vector coding and prototype activation. Moreover, as neural network models have taught us, a perceptually competent network embodies a great deal of *knowledge* about the general structure of its perceptual environment, knowledge that is embodied in the configuration of its myriad (in humans, 10^{14}) synaptic connections, knowledge that is largely or entirely *inarticulable* by its possessor. There is no hope, to repeat the point, that we can capture the true substance of any human's moral knowledge by citing some family of "rules" that he or she is supposed to "follow," nor any hope of evaluating that person's character by evaluating the specific rules within any such internalized family. At the level of individual human cognition, it simply doesn't work that way.

I have pressed this point, perhaps over-pressed it, partly because I wished to uproot an almost universal misconception about the nature of human moral cognition, but also, and correlatively, because I wish to emphasize the genuine *novelty* represented by the evolutionary emergence of language and the cultural emergence of discursive rules. Their emergence makes an enormous difference to the character and quality of our collective moral life. They constitute, as Hooker and Christensen would put it,[6] and Clark would surely agree, a *new level of regulative machinery* to help shape the conduct of our collective affairs, a kind of

---

6 C.A. Hooker, *Reason, Regulation, and Realism: Toward a Regulatory Systems Theory of Reason and Evolutionary Epistemology* (Albany: SUNY Press, 1995). This provocative book presents a general theory of the nested hierarchy of regulatory mechanisms that biological, social, and intellectual evolution have progressively assembled on this planet.

machinery that had never existed before. They provide us with something the other social animals still do not have. First, they provide a medium for the accumulation of useful social doctrine over periods far in excess of an individual human's lifetime. Second, they provide a system for the collective discussion and local application of that (presumptive) practical wisdom. And third, they enable procedures, consistent across time and circumstance, for identifying and penalizing violations of the discursive rules that (partly) embody that wisdom. They do *not* bring moral reasoning into existence for the first time, and they do *not* provide a conceptual model remotely adequate to the phenomenon of moral cognition in single individuals and nonhuman animals, but they *do* change our lives profoundly.

In fact, as I shall now turn to argue, they change our lives even more profoundly than Clark has urged, and they hold the potential to *further* transform human life, to a degree and in dimensions that his own discussion does not begin to suggest. Specifically, I believe his own position concerning the importance of extra-cortical cognitive scaffolding holds the key to understanding how human moral *progress* is not only possible and actual, but still lies mostly ahead of us.

Let me approach these claims by looking at the sorts of rule-based regulative machinery displayed in ancient but post-cursive societies. The Judeo-Christian Old Testament provides a roughly typical example: a handful or two of rules, plus a tradition of rabbis, priests, or village elders to officiate their application and enforcement.

In this case, the rules are the now-curious Ten Commandments, plus some now-highly-uncomfortable Regulations on matters such as the "proper" administration of slavery and indentured servitude (for example, it's OK to beat slaves senseless, as long as you don't actually kill them, *Exodus* 21:20), on the proper treatment of witches (they must be put to death, *Exodus*: 22:18), and on proper respect for parents (anyone who curses –curses! – his mother or father must be put to death, *Exodus* 21:17). Collectively, this body of social legislation, from Exodus 20:1 to 23:31, looks less like the divinely delivered distillation of moral excellence it purports to be, and more like a clumsy attempt, by a profoundly poor and primitive people, to maintain social cohesion against competing human societies, to maintain a minimum of social order within the preferred group, and to achieve both aims by instilling stark terror, both metaphysical (the Jealous God) and temporal (prompt execution), into the hearts of the people to be controlled. This Covenant with God is sealed by His promising, in return for our coerced faith, Divine intervention in and support for the gradual takeover of all neighboring nations and the subsequent geographical expulsion of the "alien" peoples that constitute them (*Exodus* 23: 20-31). (Whatever happened, one wonders, to the Tenth Commandment, only just laid down, the one that precludes coveting thy neighbor's house and other belongings?)

Contradictions aside, this body of legislation is curious for a number of reasons; first, for the positive law that it contains. Some requirements now appear just silly, such as the practice of regularly sacrificing goats and young bulls as mandatory gestures of solidarity with Jehovah. Other laws are decidedly darker, as with "Thou shalt not suffer a witch to live" (*Exodus* 22:18). A law requiring such harsh treatment for non-existent things seems a needless and foolish luxury, at best, and a palpable cruelty if, at worst, the category was intended to include those women – who claim to hear spirit voices and who engage in opaque practices – whom we moderns would now identify as the innocent victims of schizophrenia, a morally neutral brain disorder. The New International Version of the Bible attempts to finesse this embarrassing probability by offering the alternative translation, "Do not allow a *sorceress* to live." Unfortunately, with sorceresses also being nonexistent, this leaves the original puzzle about Divine Laws for empty categories untouched, and it prompts the further question, "A sorce*rer* is OK?)

This legislative corpus is further curious for the laws that it does *not* contain. For example, there is neither Commandment nor Regulation concerning the proper care and treatment of *children.* It is hard to imagine a more fundamental need for any society, or a more compelling moral imperative for any adult, than the protection and rearing of the children of one's community. (Even baboon troops are faithful at doing that.) And yet this ancient legislative corpus, allegedly divine in its provenance, is simply silent on the matter.

Withal, and despite their primitive character, such ancient bodies of extra-cortical cognitive scaffolding surely helped to sustain a much more cohesive, effective, and productive social order than could ever have been achieved in their absence. I have no desire to minimize *that* contrast. It is enormous. But my principal aim in pointing out some of the more obviously benighted aspects of the Old Testament's social legislation is to highlight a *second* contrast, one of comparable magnitude and importance. Specifically, I ask you to compare the crude and tiny body of extra-cortical social-cognitive scaffolding found in the legal/economic strictures of *Exodus* to the vast and well-tuned body of social-cognitive scaffolding found in the legal and economic systems of a modern country such as England, France, Canada, or the United States.

4.   The Contrast Between Ancient and Modern Scaffolding

A body of behavior-controlling legislation adequate to run an agrarian, bronze-age village is not remotely adequate to run a modern industrial nation with its tens of millions of people and its complex, trillion-dollar, high-tech economy. Our legislation must address practices and facilitate activities of which ancient peoples had little or no conception. The regulation of the activities of large corporations, of labor unions, of the stock market, of the nation's banks and interest rates, of agricultural and environmental policy, of pharmaceutical testing and prescription policy, of school curriculums and scientific research policy, of hospitals and penitentiary-systems, of intellectual property and its industrial applications, of court procedures at the civic, state, and national levels, of traffic behavior on our streets and highways, of licensing for electrical contractors, airline pilots, pharmacists, and a thousand other novel professions – these are all matters whose regulation is essential to the health and well-being of modern society, but whose existence went unanticipated by ancient peoples.

The point is not just that we moderns have accumulated more things to regulate than the ancients, although that is certainly true. The important point is that most of these novel phenomena were *created*, partly or wholly, by the initiation of new practices governed by new regulations. There would be no corporations, stock markets, banks, universities, or supreme courts but for the various sorts of carefully regulated human practices that make them possible. The extra-cortical cognitive scaffolding to which Clark has so aptly drawn our attention is now a glittering skyscraper of monumental proportions. It makes the ancient but cognate scaffolding of *Exodus* look like a plaster hut by comparison. We have constituted ourselves into a Leviathan that even Hobbes could not have anticipated.

This contrast, I assert, represents substantial moral progress on the part of the human race. Of the matters addressed by ancient legislation, we have simply put some aside entirely, and we regulate the others far more consistently, systematically, sensitively, and wisely than did the ancients. This much is unsurprising, perhaps. We have the advantage of more than two millennia of additional social experience, and we now have the luxury of well-tuned social machinery, with long institutional memories, devoted to the case-by-case administration of our more deeply informed discursive legislation.

This, however, is but a small part of the progress to which we can rightly lay claim. More important still is the expanding universe of new *kinds* of social practices, practices brought into existence by the continued development of new sorts of cognitive scaffolding and new topics of discursive legislation. A primitive villager in the Levant could aspire to many things, perhaps, but he or she could not aspire to be a securities investigator, a labor lawyer, a real estate agent, a software engineer, a congressional lobbyist, a child psychologist, a macro-economist, a newspaper columnist, a law professor, or a researcher into the genetic basis of various diseases. All of these regulated activities, and a thousand others here unmentioned, constitute new contributions to the well-being of mankind, and new dimensions of activity in which people can display excellence, mediocrity, or failure. The high-dimensional web of mutual dependence that now embraces each of us delivers a panoply of goods and services, provides many layers of personal protection to each of us, and affords endless opportunities for self-realization, most of a kind that never existed before.

It may be objected that, even where it is realized, the progress here celebrated is more a matter of our having upgraded the quality and the vitality of the social ocean in which all of us swim, than it is a matter of our having upgraded the personal moral virtues of the average individual human beings who happen to swim in it. With this claim, regrettably, I must largely agree. While the procedural and legislative virtues that constitute a modern nation like Canada or the United States no doubt "rub off" to some degree on its individual people – if only by way of the high standards of the examples it continually sets – the moral character of an average modern North American is probably little superior to the moral character of an average inhabitant of the ancient Levant. The bulk of our moral progress, no doubt, lies in our collective institutions rather than in our individual hearts and minds.

A relevant parallel here concerns our *scientific* progress, which has also transformed our world. Here also, the bulk of our progress resides primarily in our collective institutions of research, education, and technology. Some of that accumulated wisdom clearly "rubs off" on the minds of individual humans, if only because the professions they assume often require some expertise in some smallish area of scientific or technological skill. But on the whole, the scientific understanding of an average modern North American is probably little superior to the overall scientific understanding of one of Moses' contemporaries.

Little superior, but still *some*what superior. And small increments are precious because they can yield large differences in the collective quality of life, especially when those marginally improved individual social and intellectual virtues are exercised in an institutional environment that is itself the repository of much accumulated wisdom. This is as true, and as important, in the moral sphere as it is in the scientific sphere. As we remarked in our opening paragraph, the interplay between the personal and the extra-personal levels extends the reach and elevates the quality of the individual's original nondiscursive cognitive activities. Plainly, I assert, there has been real progress here, at both levels of cognition, and in both the scientific and the moral domains. And the dynamic of that progress is much the same in both domains: we *learn* from our unfolding *experience* of a world that is partly *constructed* by our own activities.

5.   On the Requirements for Future Moral Progress

You see, once more, where I am going: if we can come this far, why not go farther still? Specifically, if the introduction of extra-cortical cognitive scaffolding gives humans a "leg up" in some cognitive domains, and if the articulation and improvement of that scaffolding, over time and accumulated experience, leads to further improvements in the quality of our cognition in that domain, then why should we not aspire to make *further* improvements in the character and content of our current extra-cortical scaffolding, so as to make yet further advances in the quality of the cognition at issue?

We may look, once more, at the history of our *scientific* progress for possible insights on how this might unfold in the moral domain. What sorts of things distinguish modern science from the science of the Egyptians and the Babylonians? Most obviously, we have acquired, in sequence, such things as systematic geometry, the algebra of arithmetic unknowns, modern analytic geometry, the infinitesimal calculus, and modern computational theory. Equally obviously, we have escaped the ancient conceptual frameworks of geocentrism, of earth, air, fire, and water, and of "folk physics" generally. Our extra-personal scaffolding now deploys a new framework of concepts, more penetrating than the old, and more reflective of the world's real makeup.

The social domain shows *some* of the same sorts of advances. We do use modern mathematics to serve the making of economic policy (think of the Federal Reserve Board and its macroeconomic models), and to sustain the nation's monetary activities on a minute-minute basis (think of the e-network and the computational facilities that underly your use of a credit card at the supermarket checkout counter). As well, our conceptions of proper social behavior have certainly changed. (For example, *Exodus* prohibits the charging of interest on loans, but modern industrial society would collapse without that crucial practice.) On the whole, however, our self-conception and our social technologies show little of the truly radical change evident in our modern scientific conception of the purely natural world.

That is because, I suggest, the neurobiological, cognitive, and social sciences have yet to achieve the major conceptual advances achieved in physics, chemistry, and biology. Bluntly, the cognitive scaffolding that sustains our social lives is still laboring under the burden of a comparatively primitive conceptual framework. "Folk *physics*" may be gone from our enveloping institutions, but "folk *psychology*" is still very much with us, at least in our social institutions.

My point here is not to trash folk psychology: it performs yeoman service for us, and will continue to do so for some time to come. My point is rather that a still deeper conception of the springs and wheels of human nature might perform all of those same services, and many new ones besides, even better than does our current conception.

The geocentric astronomy of Aristotle, Hipparchus, and Ptolemy – to cite a relevant parallel – allowed us to predict the motions of the planets with some precision, and it allowed us to navigate all of the

Earth's oceans without getting lost by more than a few hundred kilometers. But in other respects, it was a conceptual and technological straightjacket that simply had to be shed if we were to understand the heavens in general. And when it finally was displaced, it opened the door for such novelties as geosynchronous communication satellites, and hand-held GPS (Global Positioning System) devices that will fix your current position on the Earth's surface to within a meter. That technology, and a hundred others, are now an integral part of our personal and institutional activities: they have been absorbed by, and are transforming, the extra-personal cognitive scaffolding that structures our lives.

Similarly, I suggest, will the continuing development of sciences such as cognitive neuroscience, social psychology, neuropathology, neuropharmacology, and vector algebra (the mathematics of neural nets) eventually become absorbed into the extra-personal, social-level scaffolding that already structures our interpersonal lives. And by being absorbed, it will change that scaffolding, and with it, our moral practices and our moral conceptions. It will afford the opportunity to hone entirely new nondiscursive cognitive skills, as we learn to navigate a social environment containing novel structures and novel modes of interaction. It will permit a deeper insight into the intricate dance that is each person's unfolding consciousness, and thus make possible a deeper level of mutual understanding, care, and protection. It will reconfigure our court practices, our correctional practices, our educational practices, and perhaps even our recreational and romantic practices.

Clark's scepticism here notwithstanding, the moral domain evidently offers as much prospect for radical progress as does any other domain of cognitive activity. And such progress will be achieved not because – in a runaway spirit of mad-dog reductionism – we *turn our backs* on the social-level cognitive machinery. On the contrary. The current office-*holder* may be tossed out on its ear, but the high-level *office* will remain. It will then be occupied, however, by a system of concepts and an accompanying vocabulary grounded in a more deeply informed, and technologically more powerful, theory of Human Nature. It will then do all of the old jobs better – those that are worth doing, anyway – and endless new jobs to boot. Accordingly, now is hardly the time to become faint of heart or feeble of vision. The relevant sciences are pregnant with promise, and their effects on social practice are already being felt. The virtues of extra-personal cognitive scaffolding remain obvious, to be sure. But it is equally obvious that new and better scaffolding might sustain a new and even better moral order. The science alone won't build it. But we can.

CANADIAN JOURNAL OF PHILOSOPHY
Supplementary Volume 26

Making Moral Space:
A Reply to Churchland

ANDY CLARK

Like those famous nations divided by a single tongue, my paper (this volume) and Professor P.M. Churchland's deep and engaging reply offer different spins on a common heritage. The common heritage is, of course, a connectionist vision of the inner neural economy – a vision which depicts that economy in terms of supra-sentential state spaces, vector-to-vector transformations, and the kinds of skillful pattern-recognition routine we share with the bulk of terrestrial intelligent life-forms. That which divides us is, as ever, much harder to isolate and name. Clearly, it has something to do with the role of moral talk and exchange, and something to do with the conception of morality itself (and, correlatively, with the conception of moral progress). Most of this Reply will be devoted to clarifying the nature of the disputed territory. First, though (as a prophylactic against misunderstanding), I shall rehearse some points of agreement concerning moral talk and progress.

Professor Churchland and I agree that words, talk, moral labels, and the whole collective infrastructure of moral texts, rules, traditions, tools and practices *matter*. We agree, indeed, that it is this species-specific overlay that gives human thought and reason (in science, morals, and elsewhere) much of its distinctive power and character. Thus, Churchland recognizes and emphasizes "the genuine novelty represented by the evolutionary emergence of language and the cultural emergence of discursive rules," and depicts this novelty as something that "extends the reach and elevates the quality of the original nondiscursive cognition." Furthermore, we agree that words, texts and technologies are, taken alone, cognitively and morally inert, so that "even when that external machinery does get deployed, it is the original and more basic form of cognition that does the deploying. Rules are useless unless the capacity for reliable perception of their categories is already in place, and such perception depends utterly on the inarticulable processes of vector coding and prototype activation." We agree also that even our best moral rules, maxims and guidelines (even God's own moral rules, maxims and guidelines were God forced to formulate them as sentences in some Earthly tongue) are not to be viewed as displaying the full, rich content of our own (or God's) achieved moral expertise. Instead, the rules, maxims and guidelines play a kind of facilitating role. They act as reference points for collaborative moral reasoning and discussion, and they sow the seeds for deeper and more penetrating moral thought (for example, by providing summary labels which can support the discovery of deeper, more abstract, otherwise cognitively invisible, moral concepts – as per the discussion of *Pan troglodytes* in my text). And we agree, finally (though here I suspect I was not clear in the text) that there can be, and indeed has been, genuine moral progress. I concur wholeheartedly with Professor Churchland's forceful description of the many moral mistakes and attitudes enshrined in the Bible and believe, as he does, that many contemporary moral norms represent substantial advances over that primitive foray into moral space.

Where, then, do we disagree? We disagree, I suggest, on two (related) counts.

First, we disagree on the precise *role* of all that external scaffolding and moral infrastructure. As Professor Churchland has it, the role of the scaffolding is largely to offload, preserve, stockpile and share our collective moral wisdom and experience. And moral wisdom itself is conceived as a kind of know-how concerning the successful navigation of social space, a type of know-how we thus share with many other social animals including "baboon troops, wolf packs, dolphin schools, chimpanzee groups, lion prides." What we find in such cases, Churchland suggests, is "the same complex ebb and flow of thoughtful sharing, mutual defense, fair competition, familial sacrifice, staunch alliance, minor deception, major treachery, and the occasional outright ostracism that we see displayed in human societies." What we do *not* find, he notes, is the peculiar kind of discursive language-use or highly articulated non-biological infrastructure that characterizes human societies.

As a result, in the case of other social animals "their social cognition is conducted entirely within the more primitive and nondiscursive form of cognition." The specific social spaces we might navigate are, Churchland allows, deeply transformed by these extra layers of infrastructure. But the discursive infrastructures, Churchland insists, "do not bring moral reasoning into existence for the first time, and they do not provide a conceptual model remotely adequate to the phenomenon of moral cognition in single individuals and nonhuman animals." Moral understanding, it seems, is a more primitive thing.

Here, then, is the first point of real disagreement. For on my account, our practices of moral talk and exchange, and our collective efforts to create the kinds of abstract, shared conceptions (of 'charity,' 'rights,' 'equality,' 'opportunity,' etc.) that such discussions require are part of what *constitutes* our practices as genuinely moral in the first place. I do not dispute, in any way, Professor Churchland's depiction of non-linguistic animals as navigating social spaces. But I do dispute the apparent direct assimilation of such skilled navigation to moral activity. There is, I maintain, a sufficiently profound difference between our human moral projects and the project of successful social navigation to justify treating the latter, but not the former, as distinctively *moral* modes of thought and reason. Such modes are marked, for example, by the requirement to provide reasons for our actions, and to be able to address the important question of the acceptability, or otherwise, of our own underlying needs, desires and goals. They are marked also, I argued, by an essential commitment to collaborative moral endeavor: to finding routes through moral space that accommodate multiple perspectives and points of view. Practices of public moral discussion and exchange create, I tried to argue, these kinds of moral sensitivity in much the same way as the creation of financial institutions creates the space to trade in stocks, shares, options and futures, then options on futures, and so on. In each case, the presence of the infrastructure is partly constitutive of the very possibility of the target phenomenon.

In weak support of this rather strong thesis (the thesis, if you like, of the discursive construction of moral space). I offered a couple of more detailed – but admittedly non-moral – exemplars. One involved the ability of label-exploiting chimps (*Pan troglodytes*) to grasp kinds of abstraction beyond the ken of their unaugmented cousins. The other involved the role of numerals in enabling our communal exploration of mathematical space. The idea here, which I should have made more explicit, was that, despite the clear overlap in base-line neural skills, only the activity of the numeral-enhanced humans counts as genuinely mathematical. The very concept of a number, I would argue, is available to our species only courtesy of it's experiences with the artifactual domain of numeral construction and manipulation. What other animals do by way of counting is not properly conceived as mathematics in the absence of that overlay, just as their skills at social navigation, in the absence of a similar overlay of discursive concepts, do not count as moral skills.

The second point of disagreement follows rather directly from the first. While we both agree on the possibility of moral progress, we harbor subtly different visions of in what such progress might consist. For Professor Churchland, progress consists in greater collective success at the negotiation of increasingly complex social spaces. I claim, by contrast (at least I *think* it is by contrast – see below) that moral progress consists primarily in increased collective sensitivity to the needs, reasons and desires of others. Our communal explorations of moral space serve to sculpt and tweak these needs and desires while simultaneously attempting to accommodate as wide a variety as possible. Now in practice, I concede (hence my hesitation above) that it will be hard indeed to distinguish Churchland's vision from mine. For the typical upshot of all this mutual consideration of needs, reasons and arguments should, one hopes, be a smoother, gentler social swirl. But the emphasis (on the exchange of reasons versus the navigation of social space) strikes me as important. For we make *moral* progress, I want to claim, only by swimming better in a sea of other's needs and reasons, not by simply swimming better in a social sea.

This difference in the conception of the moral domain explains, I think, some of my continued resistance to Professor Churchland's radical visionary stance concerning the future of folk-psychology. While agreeing that future human brains may well come to deploy new and better modes of thought and reason (for example, by learning, courtesy of games such as SIMCITY, better ways to think about complex, decentralized, self-organizing phenomena), I find myself unable to conceive of the future morality that by-passes the communal exchange of discursive representations. And I lack a conception of in what a post-sentential exchange of reasons and justifications might consist (even using a diagram to make a point often depends on some accompanying sentential gloss). I am happy to concede, however, that my failures of imagination are just that, and no more (they are not (precisely!) arguments). So I now record an open verdict on the possible forms of future moral exchange and debate, while still insisting that there must *be* such exchange and debate on pain of failing to re-constitute any genuinely moral realm. Here to stay, I claim, must be some form of interpersonal discursive representation capable of providing rough summary abstractions of the rich contents encoded in high dimensional state spaces. Such abstractions, I argue, play vital roles both in learning and in collaborative thought. In the case at hand, such representations do not simply oil the wheels of moral debate, they actively constitute the thinking as moral.

More generally, Philosophers of Cognitive Science (with the notable exception of Dan Dennett; see, e.g., Dennett 1996) tend to underestimate just how *very* special we humans are. This downplaying is doubtless the result of an otherwise laudable desire to keep things natural and to emphasize the deep and real continuities between human cognition and that of other animals. But we *are* different, and the difference is cognitively deep (even if rooted in only some small neural difference). To appreciate the difference we must abandon our staunchly brain-and-individual-oriented stance and attend equally to the potent cognitive transformations effected by the matrix of words and technologies in which we live and think.

Common ground thus marked, and disputed territory highlighted, what is to be done? Here, I confess, I am at something of a loss. For all I have done, on reflection, is to present a personal, biased picture of in what moral cognition might consist, and to accompany this picture with a couple of (notably non-moral) illustrations. The picture is one in which the moral realm comes into view, and moral cognition is partially constituted, only by the joint action of neural resources we share with other animals and the distinctively human infrastructure of linguaform moral debate and reason. Our status as moral agents depends crucially, if I am right, on the many additional layers of cognitive circuitry we have slowly woven into the worlds within which we now think, reason, act, build and legislate. But Professor Churchland's vision, so wonderfully expressed and powerfully argued in his contribution, stands out as equally clear and compelling. The moral realm, as he depicts it, is one already explored by many social animals and is not at all the peculiar province of the language-and-culture enhanced ('mindware upgraded'; see Clark in press) human species. Who (if either) is right? And how can we tell? My closing thought is that this is, in all likelihood, not exactly an empirical question. The answer depends upon some hard decisions concerning which aspects of current moral practice should be foregrounded in our best philosophical and scientific treatments of morality. And *that*, I venture to suggest, may be a moral, rather than a properly scientific, question.

References

Churchland, P.M. This volume. "Rules, Know-How, and the Future of Moral Cognition."

Clark, A. This volume. "Word and Action: Reconciling Rules and Know-How in Moral Cognition."

Clark, A. In press. *Mindware: An Introduction to the Philosophy of Cognitive Science.* Oxford University Press.

Dennett, D. 1996. *Kinds of Minds.* New York: Basic Books.

Notes on Contributors

LOUISE ANTONY is Professor of Philosophy at the Ohio State University. She has teaching and research interests in philosophy of mind, philosophy of language, epistemology, and feminist theory. She is co-editor, with Charlotte Witt, of *A Mind of One's Own: Feminist Essays on Reason and Objectivity* (Westview Press, 1993), and of numerous essays, including "Natures and Norms," (forthcoming in *Ethics*) and "Multiple Realizability, Projectibility, and the Reality of Mental Properties," (forthcoming in *Philosophical Topics*).

SUSAN BABBITT teaches philosophy and development studies at Queen's University in Kingston, Ontario. She is the author of *Impossible Dreams: Rationality, Integrity and Moral Imagination* (Westview, 1996) and *Artless Integrity: Moral Imagination, Agency and Stories* (Rowman and Littlefield, 2000) She is coeditor (with Sue Campbell) of *Racism and Philosophy* (Cornell, 1999) and has written articles in moral psychology, epistemology and ethics. She is currently involved in two research projects on women and development in Cuba.

RICHMOND CAMPBELL is Professor of Philosophy at Dalhousie University, Halifax, Nova Scotia, and an editor of the *Canadian Journal of Philosophy*. He is the author of *Illusions of Paradox: A Feminist Philosophy Naturalized* (Rowman & Littlefield 1998) and coeditor of *Paradoxes of Cooperation and Rationality: Prisoner's Dilemma and Newcomb's Problem* (UBC Press 1985). His publications include articles in logic, philosophy of science, philosophy of mind, moral epistemology, and feminist theory.

ANDY CLARK is Professor of Philosophy and Cognitive Science at the University of Sussex, UK. He has written extensively on artificial neural networks, robotics and artificial life. His latest book is *Being There: Putting Brain, Body and World Together Again* (MIT Press, 1997).

PAUL CHURCHLAND teaches at University of California at San Diego. He is the author of many influential books and articles in philosophy of science, philosophy of mind, artificial intelligence and cognitive neurobiology, epistemology, and perception, including *The Engine of Reason, The Seat of the Soul: A Philosophical Journey into the Brain, A Neurocomputational Perspective: The Nature of Mind and the Structure of Science,* and *Matter and Consciousness.*

LORRAINE CODE is Distinguished Research Professor in Philosophy at York University in Toronto, cross-appointed to the Graduate Programs in Social & Political Thought, and Women's Studies. In addition to numerous articles and four coedited volumes, she is the author of *Epistemic Responsibility* (1987), *What Can She Know? Feminist Theory and the Construction of Knowledge* (1991), and *Rhetorical Spaces: Essays on (Gendered) Locations* (1995); and General Editor of an *Encyclopedia of Feminist Theories* (Routledge 2000). Her editorial contribution to *Rereading the Canon: Feminist Interpretations of Hans-Georg Gadamer,* is due to be published by Penn State University Press in 2002. As a Canada Council Killam Research Fellow (1999-2001), she is writing a book with the working title "Responsible Knowing, Ecological Imagining, and the Politics of Epistemic Location."

DAVID COPP is Professor of Philosophy and a Senior Research Fellow of the Social Philosophy and Policy Center at Bowling Green State University. He taught previously at the University of California, Davis, the University of Illinois at Chicago, and Simon Fraser University. He is author of *Morality, Normativity, and Society* (Oxford University Press, 1995), and of many articles in moral and political philosophy. He is an Associate Editor of *Ethics.*

BRUCE HUNTER teaches philosophy at the University of Alberta and is an editor of the *Canadian Journal of Philosophy*. He is co-editor (with Phil Hanson) of *Return of the A Priori* (University of Calgary Press, 1992) and has written articles in epistemology, early modern philosophy, and political philosophy.

MICHAEL STINGL is Associate Professor of Philosophy at the University of Lethbridge. In addition to writing on biology and ethics, he has published papers on euthanasia, social justice and the Canadian health system, and the history of twentieth century ethics. He is currently writing on a book on evolution and ethics with John Collier and editing a volume on euthanasia.

MARGARET URBAN WALKER is Professor of Philosophy at Fordham University. She is author of *Moral Understandings: A Feminist Study of Ethics* (Routledge, 1998) and is currently working on a book on "moral repair," responses to wrongdoing that attempt to restore the bases of trust and hope on which moral relations depend.

CATHERINE WILSON is Professor of Philosophy at the University of British Columbia. She is currently interested in understanding how normative idealizations function and also fail to function in a world of empirical inequalities and differential endowments, and in meta-ethical questions pertaining to the nature of social norms. She is the author of two books and numerous papers on relations between seventeenth-century science and metaphysics and is the editor of the 1999 *Canadian Journal of Philosophy* supplementary volume, *Civilization and Oppression*.